CONTENTS

Section V Adolescent Problems, Stress, Health, and Coping

Study Guide

for use with

Adolescence

Ninth Edition

Boston   Burr Ri
Bangkok   Bo
Milan   Montre

McGraw-Hill Higher Education

A Division of The McGraw-Hill Companies

Study Guide for use with
ADOLESCENCE, NINTH EDITION
JOHN W. SANTROCK

Published by McGraw-Hill Higher Education, an imprint of The McGraw-Hill Companies, Inc., 1221 Avenue of the Americas, New York, NY 10020. Copyright © The McGraw-Hill Companies, Inc., 2003, 2001, 1998. All rights reserved.

This book is printed on acid-free paper.

1 2 3 4 5 6 7 8 9 0 QPD QPD 0 3 2 1

ISBN 0-07-249201-5

www.mhhe.com

PREFACE

HOW TO USE THE STUDY GUIDE

You are about to undertake the challenging and exciting task of learning about biological, cognitive, and sociocultural influences on adolescents. This *Study Guide* will assist you as you read *Adolescence* by John W. Santrock. It will help you learn and test your understanding of key terms and key persons as well as facts and theories covered in the text. Do remember, however, that its use should **supplement** rather than **substitute for** a careful and thorough reading of the text. Each chapter of this *Study Guide* contains several features designed to help you master the content of the chapter in *Adolescence:*

- Learning Goals with Key Terms in Boldface

- Key Terms

- Key People

- "Dr. Detail's" Mastery Exercises

- Section Reviews

- Cognitive Challenge

- Adolescence in Research

- Comprehensive Review

- Adolescence in Books

- Adolescence in Movies and Videos

- Answer Key

Each chapter of the *Study Guide* presents a detailed set of learning goals in which key terms designated by the author appear in boldface. These objectives have been organized by major chapter headings, and subheadings, and numbered accordingly. For example, the first section after the Preview and Images of Adolescents in each chapter is numbered 1.0, and the associated goals are numbered 1.1, 1.2, and so forth. These goals cover the bulk of the material in the chapter. The learning goals indicate as specifically as possible what you should be able to do after you have read and mastered the material in a chapter.

It is recommended that you make extensive use of the learning goals. For example, it is a good idea to review the key terms before and after you read each section, or subsection, of a chapter. In addition, you should review the learning goals as you do the section reviews, in that there is substantial overlap. Consistent and extensive review of the learning goals will help you better learn and remember the chapter content, and that in turn, will help you do your best on the examinations.

Key Terms

Devise your own definitions for these key terms based on your understanding of the text's definitions or on how you use the key terms in completing a sentence. This is important because you will not know whether you really understand a term until you can define it and use it in your own way.

Key People

This feature asks you to match the key person involved in adolescent research (related to the chapter's content) to the idea or concept with which they are associated. Some of these people will be featured in the margins of the main text with quotations about their theories and research. In all cases, the individual's research will have been discussed in the chapter.

Dr. Detail's Mastery Exercises

Most chapters will have a section titled "Dr. Detail's." These mastery exercises can cover almost anything relevant to the chapter. Some might cover percentages, whereas others might present "not so key" people in the chapter. Still others may be crossword puzzles or theory mastery exercises. The intent of this section is to give you a review of material that might not be the "primary focus" of the chapter, but might still appear on a test.

Section Review

All sections have their own Section Review consisting of a variety of exercises that help you review and study particularly important concepts and material in the chapter. The activities include matching, classifying, completing tables, defining terms, and providing short-answers to many questions.

Cognitive Challenge

Each chapter has one or more exercises that ask you to think about specific concepts and principles and apply them to your own life and respond from your personal experience and opinion. For these activities there are generally no answers provided, because they will be unique to each student. Nonetheless, these responses are an important guide as to how well you can work with the information you are learning in class and from your text.

Adolescence in Research

Some research articles discussed in the chapter have been chosen; and you are asked to analyze the research hypothesis, methods, and conclusions and suggest the relevance of the findings for adolescent development.

Comprehensive Review

Each chapter contains a selection of multiple-choice questions that cover the main content of the chapter. These questions can be either factual or conceptual in nature. They help prepare you to take a multiple-choice exam as well as reviewing the entire chapters' content one last time.

Adolescence in Books and Movies

After the comprehensive review you will find suggestions for books and movies that explore or depict some facet of the chapter material.

Answer Key

At the end of each Study Guide chapter is the Answer Key. Keep in mind that the answers given for short-answer questions are merely a guide, as individual responses will vary. If you have any questions about whether your answer is accurate after referring to the answer given, always refer to the text for confirmation and clarification.

Some Final Thoughts ...

This *Study Guide* contains activities that will enhance your ability to learn, retrieve, and remember knowledge about *Adolescence*. However, effective studying involves more than the specific things you do to learn the material; it includes developing good general study habits, time management, and strategies that can help to lead to active learning. The learning activities in the *Study Guide* are designed to encourage you to be an active learner. Research has shown that study activities do not really help you unless you use them in a very active way (e.g., working through the section review, studying on your own, and checking the material you could not remember). Likewise, practice makes perfect. You will, therefore, note that many issues are addressed more than once in the guide. This should allow for easier mastery of difficult materials. If you agree with this, I hope that all of the activities in this *Study Guide* will be useful both as ready-made suggestions for study and as models for activities that you invent on your own to help you achieve your own course goals.

To also help you in developing effective study strategies, the publishers have included in this guide a brief section on "Being an Excellent Student." Read this section, written by Anita Rosenfield of DeVry Institute of Technology, Southern California, for more in-depth tips and suggestions on how to succeed in this and other courses.

Enjoy the class!

Dan Houlihan

Being an Excellent Student

by Anita Rosenfield

DeVry Institute of Technology, Southern California

Most students who are in college want to be good students, and most students have some particular goal in mind, which is probably why they chose the particular college or university they are attending. As you chose your college or university, and perhaps even an area of major interest or concentration, you had certain goals in mind, which likely included doing well in school, earning good grades, and graduating.

Unfortunately, many students do not do as well in college as they had hoped and expected. Let's examine some of the reasons for this disappointing outcome to see how to avoid them and to learn, instead, how to be a good student and guide your behavior to improve your chances of achieving your goals.

A common definition of education is that it is "how people learn stuff." For most of our history, educators have focused on the "stuff." Teachers were required to be masters of their respective academic fields. Even today, some states have requirements that speak only to the need to be qualified in the subject matter one teaches, not in the teaching methods themselves.

In the 1960s, we became more interested in the "people" part of the definition, which was evidenced by moving to strategies like open classrooms and free universities. The idea was that, given the opportunity to do so, people will naturally learn. Although these experiments were dismal failures, they taught us something.

The key to the definition of education is the word *how*. Today, thanks to a wealth of research on the principles that guide the phenomenon of learning, and on the nature of learning and memory, we know much more about how learning occurs, and how we can make it better. By using these principles, we can become better students.

Formulating the Plan

Anything worth having is worth planning for. Whether you hope to learn to teach, to fly, to write for profit, or to change diapers correctly, you have in mind a goal. An everyday question from the first days in elementary school is, "What do you want to be when you grow up?" The answer to this question is one way of formulating a goal. Now that you are a college student, many people will expect you to know what you want to do for a profession or career. Yet you may not have the foggiest notion, or you might have an idea that is still slightly foggy. That is OK. What is clear, however, is that you want to succeed in your college courses. This is a relatively long-range goal, and as such can serve a purpose in keeping you on track.

But our day-to-day behavior is often hard to connect to our long-range goals. We need short-term goals to keep us organized and to be sure that the flow of our activities is in the direction we want to be going. To accomplish our long-range goals, we need to focus on three types of short-term goals. First, we need goals for the day; second, we need goals for the week; and third, we need goals for the semester or term. Let's look at each of these separately.

Goals for Today

It is helpful to keep a daily checklist, diary, or schedule as a reminder of what must be done each day. Check off the things as you accomplish them. A pocket calendar is particularly helpful for this task.

Goals for the Week

Students who are successful in college also schedule their time weekly. Sometime during the course of registration, you made up a schedule showing your classes for the whole week. If you have a job, you must allow time for that, too. Also, many college or university students have family obligations that need to be considered as well. Finally, everyone needs some time for relaxing, eating, sleeping, and playing (even in graduate school we were advised that we needed to find some time to have fun in order to keep our balance). With all these things in mind, it is no wonder many students find little time to study.

But good students do all these things, too, yet they study. Do they have more time? No, we all have the same amount of time. But successful students schedule their time carefully. So, make up a weekly schedule and block off time for all these necessary events: classes, work, relaxation, eating, sleeping, playing, family, and studying. Students who actually schedule their time and keep to their schedules are amazed at how much time they find they have!

As you make up your weekly schedule, you may find your study time in a large block. If this is true, please remember to take a short break every twenty to thirty minutes. This is called distributed practice and is far more efficient than studying for hours on end. After the first twenty or thirty minutes, most of us become much less efficient anyway. When you take that break, reward yourself somehow; then get back to your studying. Something I always tell my students is never to try to read a whole chapter in one sitting. In fact, when I am preparing for a new class or have changed texts in a class I have been teaching, I take that advice myself!

Goals for the Semester

At the beginning of each semester, we find ourselves immersed in many new courses. Often, you will be confronted by several new professors with whom you have never worked before. It is difficult to sort out the expectations and demands of these several courses. However, it is important to organize the information that will be needed for completing all of the course requirements in order to be successful in the courses.

If you can, obtain a large wall calendar and mark on it all the dates of tests, exams, and term paper due dates, being sure to write on the calendar the course for which each date applies. Now, estimate how long it will take you to make final preparations for those exams, and mark those dates as warning or alert dates. Look over the dates on which papers are due, and see if they are bunched together. If your college is typical, they will probably be close. You can help yourself to avoid the last-minute all-nighters if you simply determine a spread of due dates for yourself, and mark those on the calendar too. As you do this step, please be sure to avoid any days that have personal significance for you, such as birthdays, anniversaries, and so on. This calendar gives you an overview of major dates in your semester.

If you have followed this carefully, you now have a large semester calendar plastered on your wall, a weekly schedule of major life events, classes, and study times taped over your desk, and a daily checklist of must-do items in your pocket or purse. **So, your scheduling is on its way. Let's look now at other important strategies.**

Attending Classes

Many students believe that, since they are in college, they can decide whether to go to class at all. This is true. Some students also believe that attendance in class is not important to their grade. This is not true! Some colleges or universities have attendance requirements, so that if students miss a given number of classes it will either lower their grade a full letter grade, or the instructor may drop the student from the course; some instructors have in-class activities that count toward students' grades, so if students are not in class, they do not get credit for participating. Even without such strategies, students who do not attend class sessions almost always do more poorly on the tests and exams. Perhaps they were absent when a crucial item was discussed, or when the instructor lectured over the material this examination requires. Remember, that more often than not, instructors will include information in their lectures that is not in your textbook, and that information (whether from class lecture, videos shown in class, guest lectures, and so on) is fair game for tests. Moreover, if you are not there, the instructor cannot get to know you, and therefore cannot give you the benefit of the doubt on your answers. It should come as no surprise that in study after research study, the data clearly show that those students who attend class regularly receive the highest grades and actually learn more, too! So, the first rule of being an effective student is to attend classes. Besides, how else can you get your money's worth?

But okay, now that you've determined you will go to every class, what will you do?

Benefiting from Lectures

Sometimes students think that if they come to class and "pay attention," they will remember what the instructor talked about; they think that if they take notes, they will miss much of what the instructor says. But sitting and paying attention is difficult. For one thing, most people can think much faster than they can speak. While the instructor lectures at 80 words per minute, the student thinks at about 350 words per minute! If the student is using this extra "thinking capacity" to focus on what the instructor is saying, it is fine. This rarely lasts more than five minutes at a time, however. Most of the time, this extra "thinking capacity" is used in daydreaming!

Daydreaming can be helpful in resolving our emotional problems, planning the course of our lives, and avoiding work. Often, it is motivated by the desire to avoid work. For whatever motive, however, daydreaming is not compatible with attending a lecture. Human beings simply cannot attend to more than one stimulus at one time. And you have to admit, your daydreams can be ever so much more interesting than your professor's lectures.

Benefitting from lecture notes is best achieved by taking notes. Use plenty of paper, and leave blank lines at regular intervals, or leave wide side margins. You will use these spaces later (they are not wasted!). If the instructor permits it, be brave and interrupt with questions if you do not understand what is being said. One thing I try to stress to my students is that I may know what I am talking about, but it may be unclear to them--and if it's unclear to one student, it may well be unclear to other students. So, for the sake of the other students who didn't understand what I was talking about, each student should take on the responsibility of asking me to clarify what I said, or to expand in a way that will help them understand. Remember that lectures have a way of progressing and building on earlier information. It is important to understand each point, or later points will be lost. (But please, DO NOT ask the person sitting next to you what the professor said—it disrupts the class, disturbs your neighbor, and you are likely NOT to get an accurate response!)

When you take notes, write out the major points, and try to just make simple notes on the supporting minor points. If you miss something, and you cannot ask a question about it, approach the instructor immediately afterward, when it is likely to still be fresh in both your minds. DO NOT try to write down every word, and DO try to use abbreviations or symbols, or, you could do what I did--learn shorthand! (Or, make up your own.)

Often my students will ask if they may tape record my lectures. Personally, I have no objection to having students do this. In fact, I did this my first term back in college but found it was terribly tedious trying to transcribe the lecture. The students for whom this may be particularly helpful are those who have visual, auditory, or motor impairments. However, do not ever tape record a lecture without first asking for and obtaining the professor's permission.

Within one or two hours after the lecture, on the same day, go back over your notes, and do two things. First, fill in the rest of the minor points. This often amounts to completing the sentence or other element. Second, write brief summaries and any questions that you now have in the blank spaces (lines or margins) you left earlier (clever of you to leave those spaces!). These few minutes spent reviewing and organizing your notes will pay off in greatly improved memory. The questions you have you can ask in class, or during the instructor's office hours, and reap two benefits. First, you will get the answers. Second, you will demonstrate that you are a serious student, and that will impress your instructor.

One other thing about going to class, while this is not always true, I have found that typically my best students sit in front. And most students seem to have a need to have "their seat," while a few students have a need to move around, sitting in one seat one day and a different seat the next. It wasn't until my graduate school days that I realized why I needed "my seat"--as a student, we are being overwhelmed with new information, a stressful experience; we need some structure we can count on to reduce that stress. So, if you are one of those who likes to wander, be considerate of your classmates' needs for stress reduction.

By the way, to get the most out of the lectures, do complete the assigned reading BEFORE the class begins so you are familiar with the material. This will help you keep up with what the instructor is talking about, will reduce the amount of information you do not understand, but may also bring up important questions for you to ask in class if the instructor does not talk about them.

Reading
For Learning

We all know how to read. You are proving it by reading these words. Hopefully, you are also realizing some ideas as a result of reading. If you are only reading words, please WAKE UP! STOP DAYDREAMING!

We can read a variety of things: newspapers, movie reviews, novels, magazines, and textbooks. Textbooks are unlike all the others and must be read with a strategy all their own.

There are many reading and studying strategies, and all of them work to an extent. Perhaps you learned one or more in the course of going to high school. Perhaps you even took a how-to-study course when you entered college. If so, you probably learned one or two of these systems. If you have one you like, that works for you, keep it. If you are interested in learning a new one, read on.

The PQ4R
Method

One of the most successful and most widely used methods of studying written material was the SQ3R method, first developed at The Ohio State University. Researchers had noted that students who were more successful were more active readers. More recently, this method has been updated to the PQ4R Method, which adds an additional step. This method teaches you the same skills that have made many thousands of students successful. If you use this method when you read and study, you will be more successful, too. I have outlined the steps below and the text describes this method in Chapter 13.

The P stands for PREVIEW. After you have read the overview or chapter outline and the list of learning objectives, you should survey the chapter in the text. This is also called skimming. Look at the headings and subheadings, and get the gist of the major points in this chapter. Check off each point in the outline of this Study Guide as you pass it in the pages of the text.

The Q stands for QUESTION. Reading is greatly enhanced if you are searching for the answers to questions. For this text, the Student Study Guide provides learning objectives that can serve as questions. For other texts, make up questions for yourself, based on the chapter overview or on your own survey of the chapter. Be sure that you have at least one question for each major unit in the chapter; you will be less efficient at studying those units for which you do not have questions.

The first of the four Rs is for READ. As you read, look for the answers to the questions you posed, or to the study or learning objectives furnished for you. When you find material that answers these questions, put a mark (X) or a "post-it" note in the margin next to that material. This will help now, since you are actively involved, and later, when you review. It is a good idea to wait to underline or highlight lines of text until after you have read the entire chapter at least once, so you will know what is and what is not most important. (In fact, although some "authorities" suggest you underline or highlight no more than 10% of what you are reading, I find that when most of us begin to underline or highlight, we wind up doing it to most of the chapter—I suggest not doing it at all because it becomes too passive, which counteracts your attempts to read "actively.")

The second R stands for REFLECT. As you are reading, stop every so often and reflect on the material to increase its meaningfulness. This includes analyzing the material, thinking about how to apply it to your own life, interpreting the information, and connecting it with information you already have in your long-term memory.

The third R is for RECITE. One of the oldest classroom techniques in the world (Aristotle used it) is recitation. In the classroom version, the teacher asks the questions and the students answer them. Unless you can get your teacher to study with you regularly, you'll have to play both roles. Periodically stop in your reading and say aloud (if possible) what the author is telling you. Try to put it in your own words, but be sure to use technical terms as you learn them. If you are not in a situation where you can recite out loud, do it in writing. Just thinking it is not enough. When should you pause to recite? A good rule of thumb is that each time you come to the end of a major subheading, you should recite. One professor encourages his students to recite at least one sentence at the end of each paragraph, and two or three or more sentences at the end of each subunit (when you come to a new heading).

People who do not use recitation usually forget half of what they read in one hour and another half of the half they remembered by the end of the day. People who use recitation often remember from 75 to 90 percent of what they studied. This technique pays off. By the way, if anyone questions why you are talking to yourself, tell them that a psychologist recommended it.

The fourth R is for REVIEW. You should review a chapter soon after you have studied it (using the PQ and first 3Rs). You should review it again the day or evening before a test. It is not usually helpful to cram the night before a test, and particularly not the day of the test! That type of studying does not produce good memory and is likely to make you more anxious during the test itself.

Taking Tests

One of the things students fear most is failure. Failure signifies that things are not going well, and alerts us to the possibility that we may not achieve our goals. Unfortunately, many students see tests and exams as opportunities to fail. They prepare by becoming anxious and fearful, and trying to cram as much as possible right before the exam. These students rarely do well on the exam. They often fail, thus accomplishing just what they feared.

Taking tests requires strategy and planning. First, it is helpful to know what type of tests you will have. Your instructor probably told you during the first class meeting, or it may be in the class syllabus or course outline. If you do not know, ask.

If you are going to be taking essay exams, the best way to prepare is by writing essays. Before you do this, it is a good idea to find out what types of questions the instructor asks, and what is expected in a response. Again, it is helpful to ask the instructor for this material. Perhaps you can even see some examples of essay questions from previous years—some instructors at some colleges have copies of their exams on file in the department office or in the library. By finding out what is expected, you can formulate a model against which you can evaluate your answers.

Now, using the learning objectives or some essay questions you wrote, actually sit down and write out the answers. I have prepared at least two essay questions for each chapter in this text. HINT: If you usually feel more anxious during a test, it may help you to practice writing your essays in the room in which the test will be given. Simply find a time when the room is vacant, and make yourself at home.

If your instructor gives multiple-choice tests, then you should practice taking multiple-choice tests. For each chapter, either use questions provided in the Student Study Guide or make up your own. You may find it helpful to work out an arrangement to pool questions with other students, thereby reducing the amount of work you have to do, and developing a network of friends. Or, you may ask your professor if he or she would entertain the idea of having students write some of the exam questions—some of my professors did that in my undergraduate classes, and it is something I sometimes have my students do.

Whichever way you do it, the important thing is to prepare for tests and exams. Preparation is about 95 percent of the secret to getting a good grade. (Yes, there is some actual luck or chance involved in test scores, as even your instructor will admit!) Preparation is not only a good study and review technique, but also helps to reduce anxiety.

Dealing With Test Anxiety

Anxiety can be a helpful response when it occurs at low levels. In 1908, Yerkes and Dodson showed that the amount of anxiety that could benefit performance was a function of the difficulty and complexity of the task. As the difficulty of the task rose, anxiety became less helpful and more likely to interfere with performance.

If you have ever been so anxious in a test situation that you were unable to do well, even though you knew the information, you have test anxiety. If you get your exams back, and are surprised that you marked wrong answers when you knew the correct answers, or if you can only remember the correct answers after you leave the examination room, you too may have test anxiety.

Strategy Number One: Effective Study

Use study habits that promote learning and make the best use of time. Strategies, such as scheduling your time and using the PQ4R system, reduce anxiety by increasing confidence. As you come to realize that you know the material, your confidence rises and anxiety retreats.

Strategy Number Two:
Relaxation

Each of us develops a unique pattern of relaxation. Some people relax by going to a specific place, either in person or mentally. Others relax by playing music, by being with friends, by using autogenic relaxation phrases, or by meditating. Whatever you do, be aware of it, and try to practice relaxation techniques. If you are good at relaxing, try thinking about those situations that make you anxious, and relax while you think of them. To do this, allow yourself to think only briefly (fifteen to thirty seconds at a time) of the situation that makes you anxious, and then relax again. After a number of such pairings, you will find that thinking about that situation no longer makes you anxious. At this point, you may be surprised to find that the situation itself also no longer produces anxiety. You may find that it is helpful to think about these anxiety-provoking situations in a sequence from those that produce very little anxiety to those that are more anxiety-evoking. Such a list, from low to high anxiety, might look something like this:

1. Your instructor announces that there will be a test in four weeks.
2. Your instructor reminds you of the test next week.
3. As you study, you see on the course outline the word *test*, and remember next week's test.
4. One of your friends asks you if you want to study together for the test, which is the day after tomorrow.
5. You choose not to go out with your friends because of the test tomorrow.
6. As you get up in the morning, you remember that today is the day of the test.
7. You are walking down the hall toward the classroom; thinking about what questions might be on the test.
8. The instructor enters the classroom, carrying a sheaf of papers in hand.
9. The instructor distributes the papers, and you see the word *test* or *exam* at the top.
10. After reading the first five questions, you have not been able to think of the answer to any of them.

If you work at it gradually and consistently, pairing these types of thoughts (briefly) with relaxation and remembering to let go and relax after each one, this will dispel test anxiety and make test taking a more productive and successful experience.

Strategy Number Three:
Thinking Clearly

Most students who have test anxiety think in unclear and unproductive ways. They say to themselves things like: "I can't get these answers correct . . . I don't know this stuff . . . I don't know anything at all . . . I'm going to fail this test . . . I'm probably going to flunk out of school . . . I'm just a dumb nerd." These thoughts share two unfortunate characteristics: they are negative and they are absolute. They should be replaced.

When we tell ourselves negative and absolute thoughts, we find it impossible to focus on the test material. The result is that we miss questions even when we know the answers. Our thinking prevents us from doing well.

A good strategy for replacing these negative and absolute thoughts is to practice thinking positive and honest thoughts, such as: "I may not know all the answers, but I know some of them . . . I don't know the answer to that right now, so I will go on to the next one and come back to that . . . I don't have to get them all right . . . I studied hard and carefully, and I can get some of them correct . . . I am a serious student, and have some abilities . . . I am prepared for this test, and know many of the answers . . . This test is important, but it is not going to determine the course of my entire life and if I don't do well, it doesn't mean I'm a horrible person or a dummy."

By thinking clearly, honestly, and positively, we quiet the flood of anxiety and focus on the task at hand. Students who use this technique invariably do better on the tests. It takes practice to think clearly, but it is worth the effort. After a while, you will find that it becomes natural and does not take any noticeable effort. And as anxiety is reduced, more energy is available for studying and for doing well on examinations. The eventual outcome is more enjoyment with learning, better learning, more success in college, and the achievement of your goals.

Strategy Number Four:
Guided Imagery

Something I often do with my students before a test is to have them relax (see strategy Two), close their eyes, and visualize themselves walking into a tall building. They go into the elevator in the building and take it to the top floor, which is fifty-six stories up. They walk out of the elevator, and go to the stairwell, then climb to the top of the building. There is no railing on the top of the building. I direct them to walk over to the very edge of the building and put their toes at the very edge, then look down. I ask them to think about how they are feeling as they are looking down onto the street from the top of this building. I then tell them to back up, have the realization that they can fly—just spread out their arms and they can fly. Then they are directed back to the edge of the building, knowing that they can fly. They put their toes on the edge, look down, and then spread their arms and fly, eventually flying down to land safely on the ground below. Next I have them visualize themselves in the classroom; on the desk before them is their test. They look at the test and see themselves reading the questions saying, "I know that answer. Yes, I remember learning that." They visualize themselves being successful, answering all the questions correctly, and feeling good about themselves. Then I have them visualize getting their tests back, with a big "A" on the test.

Some students are much better able to visualize than others. You can try combining strategy two with this strategy to help you improve your visualization, since it can be an effective success strategy.

Strategy Number Five:
Do the Easy Ones First

One technique I learned while studying for the GRE (Graduate Record Exam) was to read each question and answer the ones I knew, then go back to the harder ones. Two things to watch out for on this: first, be sure you get the answers in the right place—sometimes when we skip a question or two, we wind up marking the wrong space, so check that your answer to question 10 is in space 10; second, you may find you're stumped by the first several questions—don't let that throw you, just keep going because there is bound to be one you jump on and say, "Yes! I know that one." Answer the easy ones first, then go back to the others after you've built up your confidence seeing you DO know "stuff." Then, always go back over the whole test to be sure you answered every question (the exception here is if you have a professor who takes more than one point off for wrong answers—in that case, it's better not to answer than to answer wrong, but I don't know anyone who does that).

Strategy Number Six:
State Dependent Learning

Research has found that we remember information best when we are in the same "state" we were in when we first learned the information. So, for example, you might remember a certain song when prompted by a specific stimulus (seeing someone who reminds you of your "first true love"); or, we will remember things we learned when we were particularly happy if we are again in that mood. This goes for physical contexts as well—so that we have an advantage if we take an exam in the same room where we learned the information in the first place. But it also goes to physical context in terms of our bodies—if you drink coffee or caffeine-laden sodas when you study, try to do the same before your exam. On the other hand, if you don't consume caffeine when you study, by all means, DO NOT suddenly have a cup of coffee before your exam. Because of the power of this phenomenon, you may want to create a particular mental context for yourself when you study so that you can put yourself into the same mental context when you take your exams.

Strategy Number Seven:
Take a Break

If you find yourself getting stressed out during the test, take a break. Put your pencil down, breath deeply, you may even want to put your head down on the desk (please, do not fall asleep!). Use the relaxation techniques or the guided imagery strategy; visualize yourself looking at the test and suddenly realizing that you DO know the answers to at least most of the questions. Then go back to taking the test.

Remember, that with all of these test-taking strategies, if you don't do the first one, none of the others will help! Passing the course requires that you actively study the material.

Memory
Techniques

No matter how much you read, it won't help you if you don't remember *what* you read. The most critical factor in remembering is being able to apply what you have learned. Of course, some things such as people's names, or certain dates, or statistical information are not easily applied to your life, so you'll have to use other techniques. But first, let's talk about the "easy way."

Apply It
To Your Life

If you can take the material you are learning and use it in your everyday life, you will remember it without any problem. Connect it with what you already know, either from life experience or other courses you have taken. Sometimes what you are learning fits nicely with what you already knew; sometimes it will contradict what you learned before. This is an opportunity to look at how the new information fits in with the old—were there new research findings? Or, is it merely a difference of opinion? Make these associations—don't keep the information for any class neatly compartmentalized— if you do, you'll have a hard time trying to find it when you need it.

Teach It
to Someone Else!

When we start teaching something to someone else, we find we HAVE TO learn it, and by trying to explain the material to another person, we examine it and think about it differently. So, take the material you are learning in this class (or any class) and teach it to someone else. When they ask you questions, you can look them up and find the answers, or think them out together, or ask someone else. As you explain these concepts to someone else (your children, your friends, or even your dog), you will suddenly see them in a totally different light.

Mnemonic
Techniques

Some things are just really difficult to apply to your own life. Dates, names, places, statistics, and such may not have a great deal of meaning for you. In that event, use the tricks that memory specialists use—mnemonics. There are many different types. For example, one famous mnemonic is an acronym for remembering the Great Lakes: HOMES = Huron, Ontario, Michigan, Erie, and Superior; or the colors of the rainbow is a man's name: ROY G. BIV = Red, Orange, Yellow, Green, Blue, Indigo, and Violet (if not for this "man," I'd never remember indigo!) You can make up your own acronyms by taking the first initial of any term, person, etc. It's easiest, though, if it's something that makes sense to you.

Another mnemonic technique is called the ***method of loci***, and I've been told it's one that medical students use to remember body parts. You list the things you need to remember, then visualize yourself walking around a familiar place (like your living room), putting one item on a particular piece of furniture. Then, when you need to remember that item, you go through your "living room" to see where it is.

One other mnemonic technique is the story method. Take the information you need to remember and put it into a story.

Be an
"Information Dropper"

This is similar to the suggestion to teach, but less formal. Ask your friends to "indulge" you by listening to what you learned in your Life Span Development class (or any other class). Then *tell* them what you are learning. You may, in fact, find that you have managed to help one of your friends by sharing this information!

Rote
Memory

If you can remember back to grade school when you learned to multiply, somehow the only way that seemed to happen was by repeating the multiplication tables over and over and over again. Personally, I think this is about the worst way to learn most anything, but for some things (like multiplication tables) it works. The Flashcards that are included in each chapter of this Study Guide are a way to help you learn through repeating the material you don't know until you are able to answer the questions posed without looking at the reverse side of the cards. Hopefully you will then go further and apply the information to other areas of your life.

Most Important

Remember this: professors don't actually "teach" their students, rather, they facilitate learning so students end up teaching themselves. Although we try really hard to motivate our students, keep them interested, and present information in a way that helps students to understand, the ultimate responsibility for learning rests with the student. Some students have learned *despite* their professors, others don't learn even with the very best of professors. So keep your goals in mind, study hard, ask questions, and aim for success!

Further Resources

Online Learning Center

http://www.mhhe.com/santrocka9

An expansive resource for students, this site includes:

- Self-assessment quizzes for each chapter
- Study tools, including crossword puzzles
- Links to relevant websites
- Adolescent Development Image Gallery
- Interactive scenarios

McGraw-Hill Developmental Psychology Supersite

http://www.mhhe.com/developmental

This website provides valuable resources to help you, such as Interactive exercises, simulations and links to some of the best developmental psychology sites on the web.

For those of you with "Print Disabilities" including blindness, visual impairment, learning disabilities or other physical disabilities, please check out the **Recording for the Blind and Dyslexic website** at **www.rfbd.org/** or call customer service at **(800) 221-4792**. This educational library has 77,000 taped titles including textbooks and reference and professional materials for people who cannot read standard print because of a disability.

We Want to Hear from You!

Help us to improve the quality of future supplements.

Take a moment to visit our website

and share your thoughts

by completing our supplements evaluation form.

Your feedback will greatly help us in the future.

The form is located at:

http://www.com/developmental

APA Style

For information on APA writing style and guidelines, please refer your students to the American Psychological Association's Website at http://www.apa.org, or link to this site by visiting Santrock's *Adolescence* On-Line Learning Center at http://www.mhhe.com/santrocka8

Using the Internet in Teaching Adolescence

There are numerous possibilities or ways to use the Internet with Adolescence courses. In fact, the shear vastness of available information is often overwhelming for both instructors and students alike. Most of you have some idea about how to search for information available on the Internet, but you need to have the critical thinking skills necessary to discern whether the information you are locating is valid and useful. The following five criteria may be helpful in assisting you with analyzing the appropriateness of information available on the Internet.

1. **Accuracy**

2. **Authority**

3. **Objectivity**

4. **Currency**

5. **Coverage**

You can often struggle with search strategies or become easily frustrated if you cannot locate the type of information you want. There are several excellent tutorials available online which can assist in this process, and most libraries have resources designed to help students create more sophisticated searching methodologies. The following sites may provide some assistance.

Tutorial for Beginning Users:

http://www.lib.berkeley.edu/TeachingLib/Guides/Internet/FindInfo.html

Created by the library staff at Berkeley this is an excellent place for both instructors and students to learn more about using the Internet. The tutorial is divided into two sections with the first providing information about how to access the Internet and use Netscape. The second part of the tutorial discusses how to search for information and includes a comparative chart of the best five search engines, explanations of meta-search tools, and convenient handouts, which can be used for class exercises. Also available in the handouts section are PowerPoint slides and instructor's notes.

Guide to Meta-search Engines:

http://www.indiana.edu/~librcsd/search/meta.html

This is a useful description of 13 meta-search engines with links to each and can aid both instructors and students in searching for Internet resources.

Section I
The Nature of Adolescent Development

Chapter 1   Introduction

Learning Goals with Key Terms and Key People in Boldface

1.0   WHAT IS THE HISTORICAL PERSPECTIVE ON ADOLESCENCE?

A.   Early History

1.1   Compare and contrast Plato's and Aristotle's views of adolescence?

1.2   In which ways are the views regarding adolescence expressed by Plato and **Jean-Jacques Rousseau** similar?

B.   The Twentieth Century

1.3   What was the driving force behind the changing views of adolescence that emerged between 1890 and 1920?

1.4   What factors led historians to label **G. Stanley Hall** the "father of the scientific study of adolescence"?

1.5   What was Hall's **storm-and-stress view** concept of adolescence?

1.6   In what ways were Hall's views similar to those of Charles Darwin?

1.7   Why was **Margaret Mead**'s sociocultural view of adolescence considered pathbreaking in the early 1900s?

1.8   What factors have led to a debate over the accuracy of Mead's findings?

1.9   What is the **inventionist view** of adolescence?

1.10   Why do historians call the period of 1890 to 1920 the "age of adolescence?"

1.11   How are schools, work, and economics important dimensions of the inventionist view?

1.12   Why do some historians suggest that changing laws, in effect, created adolescence?

1.13   What factors combined in the 1960s and 1970s to challenge the position of prominence achieved by adolescents in the 1950s?

1.14   Is life different for an adolescent in 1920 as opposed to 1970?

1.15   What females and individuals from ethnic minorities have contributed to the study of adolescents?

2.0   WHAT IS MEANT BY STEREOTYPING ADOLESCENTS, AND HOW CAN THIS BE CHANGED TO A POSITIVE VIEW?

A.   Stereotyping Adolescents

2.1   What is a **stereotype**, and what are the contemporary stereotypes of adolescence?

2.2   What is the purpose served by a **stereotype**?

2.3   What did Joseph Adelson mean by the **adolescent generalization gap**?

1

B.   A Positive View of Adolescence

2.4   In what way did research by **Daniel Offer** and his colleagues challenge existing stereotypes of adolescence?

2.5   Do adolescents deserve the negative portrayal they get in the media today? Support your answer with information from the book and your own experience.

3.0   WHAT ARE ADOLESCENTS LIKE TODAY?

A.   Current Status

3.1   Why is today both the best of times and the worst of times for adolescents?

3.2   How would you compare the current status of adolescents and public attitudes toward them with that of adolescents of several decades ago?

3.3   What differences in development among adolescents render them a heterogeneous group?

3.4   How do **contexts** of development influence adolescent development?

3.5   What are the **sociocultural contexts** of development?

3.6   What factors lead to a lack of homogeneity in adolescence?

3.7   In what ways have today's families changed from those in decades past, and how have these changes affected adolescents?

B.   Social Policy and Adolescents' Development

3.8   What is a **social policy**, and why do we need one that is concerned with adolescent development?

3.9   According to **Marian Wright Edelman** how are today's politicians falling short in practicing what they preach, i.e., "family values?"

3.10   What is **generational inequity** and how does it relate to social policy issues?

3.11   In what ways are future generations more likely to be challenged by generational inequality?

3.12   Why should the well being of adolescents be one of America's foremost concerns?

3.13   Why is it important to not diminish the role of youth in future generations?

3.14   In what ways might young adults benefit from the existence of social security?

4.0   WHAT IS THE NATURE OF DEVELOPMENT?

A.   What Is Development?

4.1   What do we mean when we speak of an individual's **development**?

B.   Processes and Periods

4.2   What are the three major processes that shape adolescent development?

4.3   Differentiate between **cognitive processes** and **socioemotional processes** and their roles in adolescent development?

4.4   What are the three major developmental periods and their subperiods from conception to death?

4.5   What are the four (4) periods of childhood development?

4.6   What factors reflect the role of biological processes in the adolescent's development?

4.7   Why would it be inappropriate to suggest that a child enters **adolescence** as a blank slate?

4.8   What is **adolescence** and what are its two periods?

4.9   Why do developmentalists no longer believe that change ends with adolescence?

4.10   How do cultural and gender differences impact when children enter adolescence?

5.0 WHAT ARE TRANSITIONS AND ISSUES IN ADOLESCENT DEVELOPMENT?

A. Developmental Transitions

5.1   Do adolescents enter **adulthood** at the same time?

5.2   What are the three (3) periods of adult development?

5.3   What is meant by the saying, "Adolescence begins in biology and ends in culture?"

5.4   What are some biological changes associated with adolescence?

5.5   What transitional period was Kenniston referring to when he proposed the term youth?

5.6   Contrast youth and emerging adulthood.

B. Developmental Issues

5.7   What are the three major issues of adolescent development?

5.8   What is the **nature-nurture issue** and how is it relevant to the concept of **maturation** and experience?

5.9   Differentiate between **continuity of development** and **discontinuity of development**?

5.10   Contrast the views of **nature** proponents with those of **nurture** proponents?

5.11   What are the main issues in **early-later experience** debate?

5.12   What recent changes in the choices being made by young women are reflective of the role **nurture** plays?

5.13   How do beliefs about significant developmental experiences differ in various cultures?

5.14   Why do developmentalists usually refrain from taking extreme positions on developmental issues?

6.0 WHAT MATTERS IN UNDERSTANDING ADOLESCENCE? WHAT CAREERS ARE AVAILABLE IN ADOLESCENT DEVELOPMENT?

A. Understanding Adolescence: What Matters?

6.1   What seven things matter in understanding adolescence?

6.2   What are **biological processes** and why do they matter?

6.3   What are **cognitive processes** and why do they matter?

6.4   What **contexts** are significant in adolescent development?

6.5   What aspects of social and personality development matter?

6.6   What problems and disorders can restrict optimal adolescent development?

6.7   Why does science matter in understanding adolescent development?

6.8   What does it mean to be a critical thinker?

6.9   Why is the ability to think critically an important milestone in adolescence?

B. Careers in Adolescent Development

6.10   What opportunities are available for those who want to pursue a career related to adolescent development?

6.11   How might one's level of education affect their career choices or opportunities in the fields related to adolescent development?

Exercises

KEY TERMS
COMPLETION EXERCISE

Each key term is presented in the form of an incomplete sentence. Complete each sentence by either defining the term or giving an example. Compare your definitions with those given at the end of study guide chapter.

1.   The **storm-and-stress view** of adolescence suggests that

   _____

   _____

2.   According to the **inventionist view,** adolescence began

   _____

   _____

3.   If I were to invoke a common **stereotype**, I would view adolescents

   _____

   _____

4.   Evidence that an **adolescent generalization gap** exists is

   _____

   _____

5.   Examples of **contexts** are

   _____

   _____

6.   In the United States, **social policy** has resulted in

   _____

   _____

7.   In the United States, the biggest threat of **generational inequity** stems from

   _____

   _____

8. **Development** is the

_____

_____

9. **Biological processes** affect a person by

_____

_____

10. The best evidence of changing **cognitive processes** in adolescents is

_____

_____

11. Confirmation of **socioemotional processes** in adolescents is

_____

_____

12. The **prenatal period** is from

_____

_____

13. A child in its **infancy** is often seen

_____

_____

14. **Early childhood** is marked by

_____

_____

15. During **middle and late childhood,** children

_____

_____

16. The change from childhood to **adolescence** involves

_____

_____

17. **Early adolescence** is characterized by

18. The activities that make up **late adolescence** are

19. You can tell that Susan is in **early adulthood** because

20. **Middle adulthood** is marked by

21. A person in **late adulthood** might

22. According to Kenniston, **youth** is

23. The **nature-nurture issue** refers to

24. The **continuity–discontinuity issue** suggests

25. Theorists debating the **early-later experience issue** suggest

KEY PEOPLE
IN THE STUDY OF ADOLESCENCE

Match the name with the concept, issue, or topic related to adolescence with which they are associated.

_____	1. G. Stanley Hall	A.	Studied teenagers in Samoa
_____	2. Margaret Mead	B.	Coined the term "youth"
_____	3. Leta Hollingworth	C.	The father of the scientific study of adolescence
_____	4. Daniel Offer	D.	His work challenged the negative stereotypes of adolescents
_____	5. Marian Wright Edelman	E.	First used the term "gifted" and challenged the theory of male superiority
_____	6. Bernice Neugarten	F.	Argued that adolescents need more opportunities to develop the capacity for initiative
_____	7. Kenneth & Mamie Clark	G.	A child's rights advocate, who champions improvements in social policies affecting young people and their families
_____	8. Kenneth Kenniston	H.	Believes that many segments of society, not just adolescents, are affected by inequities in our social and economic policies
_____	9. George Sanchez	I.	Conducted research on the self-esteem of African-American children
_____	10. Reed Larson	J.	Documented cultural bias in intelligence tests

"DR. DETAIL'S"
MATCHING EXERCISE

Match the correct percentage with the appropriate statement or question.

_____	1. From 1910 to 1930, the number of 10- to 15- year olds gainfully employed dropped by this.	A.	More than 70%
_____	2. Between 1900 and 1930 the number of high school graduates increased by this.	B.	More than 20%
_____	3. Daniel Offer and his colleagues studied the self-images of adolescents around the world and found that _____ had a healthy self-image.	C.	75%
_____	4. What percentage of adolescents today are giving birth?	D.	600%
_____	5. College students who said being an adult means accepting responsibility for the consequences of one's actions:	E.	73%

HISTORICAL PERSPECTIVE/A POSITIVE VIEW OF ADOLESCENCE
SECTION REVIEW

1. Why were the views proposed by Jean-Jacques Rousseau regarding adolescence considered more enlightened than those proposed by Plato and Aristotle?

_____

_____

2.   Compare and contrast Hall's storm-and-stress perspective of adolescence with Margaret Mead's sociocultural view.

_____

_____

3.   Why were Hall's views regarding adolescence strongly influenced by Darwin?

_____

_____

4.   Why were Margaret Mead's Samoan findings met with criticism?

_____

_____

5.   Describe the factors that led to the period between 1890 and 1920 being known as the "age of adolescence."

_____

_____

6.   What accounted for the prominence adolescents gained in society from 1920 to 1950, and what factors would challenge this distinction?

_____

_____

7.   How did Daniel Offer and his colleagues challenge the negative views of adolescents, and what empirical support did they find?

_____

_____

KEY PEOPLE IN SECTION

(Describe the contributions of this individual to the study and understanding of adolescence.)

Plato—

_____

_____

Aristotle—

_____

_____

Jean-Jacques Rousseau—

_____

_____

G. Stanley Hall—

_____

_____

Charles Darwin—

_____

_____

Margaret Mead—

_____

_____

Leta Hollingworth—

_____

_____

Kenneth and Mamie Clark—

_____

_____

George Sanchez—

_____

_____

Joseph Adelson—

_____

_____

Daniel Offer—

_____

_____

TODAY'S ADOLESCENTS
SECTION REVIEW

1. List three facts of contemporary life that makes today "the best of times" for adolescents.

   _____

   _____

2. List three facts of contemporary life that makes today "the worst of times" for adolescents.

   _____

   _____

3. What are four examples that suggest that today's adolescents are growing up in a less stable environment than that of adolescents several decades ago?

   _____

   _____

4. Why are contexts important in understanding adolescent development?

   _____

   _____

5. Why should the well being of adolescents be one of the major concerns for makers of social policy?

   _____

   _____

6. Why does Marian Wright Edelman believe that we must reexamine our nation's policies for families?

   _____

   _____

7. What would be the risk associated with ignoring a problem like generation inequity?

   _____

   _____

KEY PEOPLE
IN SECTION

(Describe the contributions of this individual to the study and understanding of adolescence.)

Peter Benson—

   _____

   _____

Marian Wright Edelman—

_____

_____

Bernice Neugarten—

_____

_____

Reed Larson—

_____

_____

THE NATURE OF DEVELOPMENT/TRANSITIONS
SECTION REVIEW

1.   Complete the table by giving the name and a brief description of the eight periods of development corresponding to the given ages.

Age	Name	Description
Conception to birth		
Birth to 18–25 months		
2 to 5–6 years		
6 to 10–11 years		
10–13 to 18–22 years		
Late teens to early 20s and 30s		
35–45 to 55–65 years		
60–70 years until death		

2.   Explain why biological, cognitive, and socioemotional processes are unavoidably interwoven.

_____

_____

3.   Is there a specific age at which an adolescent becomes an adult?

        _____

        _____

4.   Explain the nature/nurture issue in your own words, using any facet of adolescent physical, cognitive, or emotional development as an example.

        _____

        _____

5.   How does the continuity-discontinuity issue apply to today's youth?

        _____

        _____

6.   Why is the early-later experience issue still such a hotly debated topic?

        _____

        _____

KEY PEOPLE IN SECTION

(Describe the contributions of this individual to the study and understanding of adolescence.)

Kenneth Kenniston—

        _____

        _____

Jerome Kagan—

        _____

        _____

UNDERSTANDING ADOLESCENCE
SECTION REVIEW

1. In what ways do changes in adolescent thinking and cognitive skill affect their lives?

    _____

    _____

2. What does it mean to be a critical thinker?

    _____

    _____

3. List ten characteristics and cognitive processes of critical thinkers.

    _____

    _____

KEY PEOPLE
IN SECTION

(Describe the contributions of this individual to the study and understanding of adolescence.)

Luis Vargas—

    _____

    _____

EXPLORATIONS
IN ADOLESCENCE

1. Have you ever been the target of a stereotype (race, gender, ethnicity, religion, social class, etc.)? Consider what type of stereotype it may have been, and then consider how it may have changed your thinking. How have you been affected by this: positively, or negatively?

    _____

    _____

2. In recent years, adolescents have appeared featured on the covers of prominent magazines and featured in many documentaries? The tone of these discussions is becoming increasingly negative. How might this impact today's children who are just starting to enter adolescence?

    _____

    _____

3.	Is the modern emphasis on education and career training adversely affecting the formation of the family?

_____

_____

COGNITIVE CHALLENGE

1.	Imagine you could time-travel. How would your life, as an adolescent, have been different in each of these different time periods?
	a.	1890–1920

	_____

	_____

	b.	1920–1950

	_____

	_____

	c.	1960–1980

	_____

	_____

2.	Choose any ethnic group other than your own. Imagine how your experiences would have been different in the following domains. Write the ethic group or culture that you have chosen here:

	_____

	_____

	a.	relationship with your parents

	_____

	_____

	b.	relationship with your peers

	_____

	_____

	c.	high school experience

	_____

	_____

d.   your physical health and development

_____

_____

e.   your moral and spiritual development

_____

_____

f.   your intellectual development

_____

_____

g.   your dating behavior and romantic relationships

_____

_____

h.   the neighborhood in which you lived

_____

_____

i.   your family's socioeconomic status

_____

_____

j.   how you would be different today as a result of **these variations in experience**

_____

_____

3.   Referring to the list of areas in number 2, pick the five areas that you think were the most influential in making you who you are today. Discuss the impact of your experiences in these areas on your adult development.

_____

_____

ADOLESCENCE
IN RESEARCH

Concerning Daniel Offer's 1988 study of the negative stereotyping of adolescents, state the hypothesis, the research methods (if known), the research conclusions, and the implications and applications for adolescent development.

_____

_____

☒ COMPREHENSIVE REVIEW

1. That these times are the best of times for today's adolescents is indicated by the observation that
    a.   crack cocaine is more addictive and deadly than marijuana.
    b.   individuals have longer life expectancies than ever before.
    c.   most families include a father who is the breadwinner, a mother, and children.
    d.   television transmits powerful messages about sex and violence.

2. According to Plato, the distinguishing feature of the adolescent period was the development of
    a.   reason.
    b.   self-determination.
    c.   virtues and morals.
    d.   conformity to societal standards.

3. According to Aristotle, this is the most important aspect of adolescence.
    a.   emotional stability
    b.   virtues and morals
    c.   the ability to choose
    d.   reasoning

4. G. Stanley Hall described adolescence as a period of
    a.   emotional stability.
    b.   passivity and conformity.
    c.   considerable turmoil.
    d.   gradual socioemotional development.

5. The _____ century marked the beginning of the scientific exploration of adolescence.
    a.   nineteenth
    b.   fifteenth
    c.   fourth
    d.   twentieth

6.   G. Stanley Hall was strongly influenced by the views of
       a.   Rousseau.
       b.   Mead.
       c.   Darwin.
       d.   Freud.

7.   Margaret Mead proposed that adolescents develop easily into adulthood if their environments are appropriately designed, after observing adolescents in
       a.   Samoa.
       b.   the Philippines.
       c.   the Trobriand Islands.
       d.   Mangia.

8.   The current view of Margaret Mead's research on Samoan adolescents is that
       a.   it was unbiased and error-free.
       b.   it supports the inventionist view rather than G. Stanley Hall's view of adolescence.
       c.   it exemplifies the adolescent generalization gap.
       d.   their lives are more stressful than Mead observed.

9.   Because they believe it was during this time frame that the concept of adolescence was form, historians now call this period the "age of adolescence."
       a.   1910 to 1940
       b.   1890 to 1920
       c.   1920 to 1950
       d.   1960 to 1980

10.   Which of the following factors did NOT contribute to the invention of the concept of adolescence?
       a.   Child-saving legislation
       b.   Increased adolescent employment during the Great Depression
       c.   The separation of work and the home
       d.   The creation of a system of compulsory education

11.   As compulsory laws regarding youth were enacted in the early twentieth century, employment of adolescents _____ and school attendance _____ .
       a.   decreased; increased
       b.   decreased; decreased
       c.   increased; decreased
       d.   increased; increased

12.   You are reading a book about how children and adolescents have historically been treated by their parents. The book describes how a mother tries to imitate her daughter's dance steps. The historical passage probably referred to the
       a.   1890s.
       b.   1920s.
       c.   1940s.
       d.   1960s.

13. What event led to the increase in adolescent rebellion and protest?
    a. The discovery of marijuana
    b. The bombing of Pearl Harbor
    c. The Vietnam War
    d. The Great Depression

14. Which of the following is most likely to be true concerning perceptions of adolescents of the mid 1970s to the 1980s?
    a. They are less interested in physical fitness.
    b. They are more achievement-oriented.
    c. They engage in more radical protests than in the 1970s.
    d. They are less sexually permissive.

15. If you categorized all adolescents as rebellious, lazy, smart alecks, you would be using a(n)
    a. context.
    b. inventionist view.
    c. stereotype.
    d. generation gap view.

16. When you were an adolescent, your parents accused your generation of being lazy and having no respect for authority. Based on the research concerning parents' and adolescents' attitudes, you might have told your parents:
    a. "I guess we just have an insurmountable generation gap."
    b. "What you call a generation gap, I would call a generalization gap."
    c. "Although the majority of adolescents have a generation gap, I don't."
    d. "Only the parents of deviant adolescents have a generalization gap."

17. The research by Daniel Offer and his colleagues in 1988, which examined the self-images of adolescents around the world, had what effect on the belief that adolescents are highly stressed?
    a. It supported that belief.
    b. It challenged its accuracy.
    c. It showed depression to be a larger problem than stress.
    d. It was inconclusive and therefore had no impact.

18. Sociocultural context refers to
    a. the setting in which development occurs.
    b. studies that allow comparisons between different cultures.
    c. the most important influences on development according to G. Stanley Hall.
    d. a term associated with inferiority and deficits in the cultural group in questions.

19. The first individual to use the term "gifted" as a way to describe youth who scored high on intelligence tests was
    a. Leta Hollingworth.
    b. George Sanchez.
    c. Kenneth Clark.
    d. Daniel Offer.

20. The first to document cultural bias in intelligence tests for children and adolescents was
    a. Leta Hollingworth.
    b. George Sanchez.
    c. Kenneth Clark.
    d. Daniel Offer.

21. A national government's actions that influence the welfare of its citizens defines the concept of
    a. family values.
    b. generational inequity.
    c. the inventionist viewpoint.
    d. social policy.

22. According to Marian Wright Edelman, president of the Children's Defense Fund, the most important function of our society should be
    a. eliminating violence.
    b. restructuring our educational system.
    c. parenting and nurturing the next generation.
    d. developing a healthy knowledge of the body and sexuality.

23. The concern that older members of the society benefit disproportionately more than younger members of the society in terms of national allocations of resources is the concept of
    a. generational inequity.
    b. social policy.
    c. the adolescent generalization gap.
    d. the storm-and-stress view.

24. Which of the following is NOT a major process contributing to the scientific study of development?
    a. Cognitive
    b. Biological
    c. Socioemotional
    d. Personal

25. The pattern of change that begins at conception and continues throughout one's life span is represented as
    a. context.
    b. adolescence.
    c. development.
    d. continuity.

26. According to G. Stanley Hall, the dominant process of adolescent development would be
    a. biological.
    b. cognitive.
    c. sexual.
    d. socioemotional.

27. Alterations in an individual's thinking and intelligence suggest a change in
    a. cognitive processes.
    b. biological processes.
    c. context.
    d. socioemotional processes.

28.   First grade typically marks the end of which period?
     a.   Prenatal period
     b.   Infancy
     c.   Toddlerhood
     d.   Early childhood

29.   Developmentalists subdivide the period of development before adolescence into _____ periods.
     a.   two
     b.   six
     c.   four
     d.   eight

30.   If Kenneth Kenniston were correct, a youth would be expected to
     a.   live in several different places.
     b.   be confused about sexual orientation.
     c.   avoid dating.
     d.   be unable to secure full-time employment.

31.   The most widely recognized marker of entry into adulthood is
     a.   the first sexual experience.
     b.   the decision to get married.
     c.   taking a job that is more or less permanent and fulltime.
     d.   learning to drive a car.

32.   On the issue of maturation and experience, most developmentalists
     a.   agree with the position of G. Stanley Hall.
     b.   agree with the position of Margaret Mead.
     c.   agree with the inventionist viewpoint.
     d.   recognize the importance of their interaction.

33.   Many developmentalists believe that humans progress through a number of defined stages in the course of their lives. John Santrock, the author of *Adolescence*, would say that these developmentalists see human development
     a.   as discontinuous.
     b.   as unstable.
     c.   as dominated by environment.
     d.   much as G. Stanley Hall did.

34.   Which of the following examples is the best example of discontinuity in development?
     a.   A seedling growing into an oak
     b.   A worm growing into a night crawler
     c.   A caterpillar becoming a butterfly
     d.   A leaf falling from a tree

35.   Most developmentalists avoid taking extreme positions on major developmental issues because
     a.   differences between male and female adolescents are growing larger.
     b.   heredity is nearly always a stronger force than environment
     c.   adolescents are beginning their sexual encounters at earlier ages.
     d.   simplistic explanations deny the complexity of human development.

36. The fact that many previously well-established differences between adolescent males and females are diminishing as females pursue careers in male-dominated areas and seek greater autonomy supports the _____ perspective.
    a. social policy
    b. nature
    c. nurture
    d. context

37. Which of the following is NOT an important context in the lives of adolescents?
    a. Music
    b. Family
    c. School
    d. Peers

ADOLESCENCE ON THE SCREEN

- *Cider House Rules* is about an orphaned boy whose identity search leads him back to what his foster father wanted for him.

- *The Talented Mr. Ripley* depicts a highly educated and charming sociopath.

- *Girl Interrupted* concerns an adolescent's 1960s hospitalization in a private psychiatric facility.

- *October Sky* tells the story of budding rocket scientists in the 1950s in rural West Virginia.

- *Good Will Hunting* portrays the life and friends of a boy who grew up in foster homes and has learned to be self-sufficient, working as a janitor and living in a lower socioeconomic class neighborhood.

- *Tumbleweeds* follows a displaced single mother and her teenage daughter as they move from place to place and live on a shoestring while the mother looks for a man who will give them a better life.

- *Liberty House* depicts the changing sociopolitical climate of the 1950s, including integration, interracial dating, and changing family structure and influence.

- *Of Hopscotch and Little Girls* A powerful documentary film that explores the plight of girls growing up to be women in different cultures.

- *Daughters of the Dust* explores life and development on a barrier island off the coast of South Carolina. The Gullah subculture, an isolated African-American group, is the focus.

- *The Heart Is a Lonely Hunter* shows the plight of adolescence in pre-WWII America.

ADOLESCENCE
IN BOOKS

■   *You and Your Adolescent (Second Edition)*, by Laurence Steinberg (Harper Perennial: NY, 1997), provides a broad, developmental overview of adolescence, with parental advice mixed in.

■   *The Rise and Fall of the American Teenager*, by Thomas Hine (Avon: NY, 1999), traces the evolution of American adolescence as a social invention shaped by the needs of the twentieth century.

■   *Preparing for Adolescence*, by James C. Dobson (Gospel Light/Regal Books: CA, 1999), examines the preparation of children to handle the stresses of growing up today. Issues such as self-confidence, handling group pressure, and feelings of inferiority are discussed.

■   *Adolescence Isn't Terminal*, by Kevin Leman (Tyndale House Publishing: IL, 2002), examines contemporary topics such as peer pressure, dating, and risky adolescent behaviors.

Answer Key

KEY TERMS

1. **storm-and-stress view** G. Stanley Hall's concept that adolescence is a turbulent time charge with conflict and mood swings.

2. **inventionist view** The view that adolescence is a sociohistorical creation. Especially important in this view are the sociohistorical circumstances at the beginning of the twentieth century, a time when legislation was enacted that ensured the dependency of youth and made their move into the economic sphere more manageable.

3. **stereotype** A broad category that reflects our impressions and beliefs about people. All stereotypes refer to an image of what the typical member of a particular group is like.

4. **adolescent generalization gap** Adelson's concept of widespread generalizations about adolescents based on information about a limited, highly visible group of adolescents.

5. **contexts** Settings in which development occurs. These settings are influenced by historical, economic, social, and cultural factors.

6. **social policy** A national government's course of action designed to influence the welfare of its citizens.

7. **generational inequity** The unfair treatment of younger members of an aging society in which older adults pile up advantage by receiving inequitably large allocations of resources, such as Social Security and Medicare.

8. **development** The pattern of change that begins at conception and continues through the life cycle. Most development involves growth, although it also includes decay (as in death and dying).

9. **biological processes** Changes in an individual's physical nature and appearance.

10. **cognitive processes** Changes in an individual's thinking and intelligence.

11. **socioemotional processes** Changes in an individual's relationships with other people, emotions, personality, and social contexts.

12. **prenatal period** The time from conception to birth.

13. **infancy** The developmental period that extends from birth to 18 or 24 months.

14. **early childhood** The developmental period extending from the end of infancy to about 5 or 6 years of age; sometimes called the preschool years.

15.   **middle and late childhood** The developmental period extending from about 6 to about 10 or 11 years of age; sometimes called the elementary school years.

16.   **adolescence** The developmental period of transition from childhood to early adulthood; it involves biological, cognitive, and socioemotional changes.

17.   **early adolescence** The developmental period that corresponds roughly to the middle school or junior high school years and includes most pubertal change.

18.   **late adolescence** Approximately the latter half of the second decade of life. Career interests, dating, and identity exploration are often more pronounced in late adolescence than in early adolescence.

19.   **early adulthood The developmental period beginning in the late teens or early twenties and lasting into the thirties.**

20.   **middle adulthood** The developmental period that is entered at about 35 to 45 years and exited at about 55 to 65 years of age.

21.   **late adulthood** The developmental period that lasts from about 60 to 70 years of age until death.

22.   **youth** Kenniston's term for the transitional period between adolescence and adulthood that is a time of economic and personal temporariness.

23.   **nature-nurture issue** *Nature* refers to an organism's biological inheritance, *nurture* to environmental experiences. "Nature" proponents claim that biological inheritance is the most important influence on development; "nurture" proponents claim that environmental experiences are the most important.

24.   **continuity-discontinuity issue** Continuity is the gradual, cumulative change from conception to death. Discontinuity is development progressing through distinct stages in the life span.

25.   **early-later experience issue** This issue focuses on the degree to which early experiences (especially early in childhood) or later experiences are the key determinants of development.

KEY PEOPLE
IN THE STUDY OF ADOLESCENCE

1.	C	2.	A	3.	E	4.	D	5.	G
6.	H	7.	I	8.	B	9.	J	10.	F

"DR. DETAIL'S"
MATCHING EXERCISE

1.	C	2.	D	3.	E	4.	B	5.	A

HISTORICAL PERSPECTIVE/A POSITIVE VIEW OF ADOLESCENCE
SECTION REVIEW

1. Rousseau restored the belief that being a child or an adolescent is not the same as being an adult.

2. Hall believed that adolescence is a turbulent time charged with conflict and mood swings. Mead believed that when a culture proves a smooth, gradual transition from childhood to adulthood, little storm and stress occurs.

3. Hall believed that all development is controlled by genetically determined physiological factors and that environment plays a minimal role in development. This view was based on the scientific and biological dimensions of Darwin's views.

4. Theorists currently state that Somoan adolescence is more stressful than Mead had suggested, and that delinquency does occur. Her work has been criticized as biased and error-prone.

5. It is believed that during this time period the concept of adolescence was invented. Adolescence was the end result of changes in the law that changed the way adolescents lived.

6. During the roaring '20's, adolescence took a turn for the better. The depression and war would soon challenge this new status; however, those who survived the war years received new distinction and responsibilities in its aftermath. This would again change in the 1960s as a result of unsettledness associated with the Vietnam War.

7. In measuring the self-images of adolescents around the world, Offer and his colleagues found a healthy self-image in 73 percent of the adolescents studied.

KEY PEOPLE
IN SECTION

Plato—suggested that reasoning is not a characteristic of children, but rather makes its first appearance in adolescence.

Aristotle—argued that the most important aspect of adolescence is the ability to choose and that this self-determination becomes the hallmark of maturity.

Jean-Jacques Rousseau—credited with restoring the belief that being a child or an adolescent is not the same as being an adult.

G. Stanley Hall—credited as being the father of the scientific study of adolescence. Proposed the storm-and-stress view regarding adolescent mood swings.

Charles Darwin—famous evolutionary theorist. His scientific and biological views were applied by Hall to the study of adolescence.

Margaret Mead—studied adolescents on the South Sea island of Samoa. She concluded that the basic nature of adolescence is not biological, but rather sociocultural.

Leta Hollingworth—conducted important research on adolescent development, mental retardation, and gifted children. She was the first individual to use the term *gifted* to describe youth who scored exceptionally high on intelligence tests.

Kenneth and Mamie Clark—conducted research on the self-esteem of African-American children.

George Sanchez—documented cultural bias in intelligence tests for children and adolescents.

Joseph Adelson—called the widespread stereotyping of adolescents so widespread as to represent an "adolescent generation gap."

Daniel Offer—found evidence contradicting the negative view of adolescence. Offer found 73 percent of adolescents around the world had healthy self-images.

TODAY'S ADOLESCENTS
SECTION REVIEW

1. computers; longer life expectancies; television, satellites, and air travel

2. crack cocaine; television images of violence and sex; contradictory messages about sex

3. high divorce rates; high adolescent pregnancy rates; increased geographic mobility of families; adolescent drug use

4. Without a reference to historic, economic, social, and cultural factors, there would be no basis by which to judge the behavior of adolescents today.

5. The future of youth is the future of society. If adolescents don't reach their full potential they will be able to contribute less to society.

6. Edelman doesn't believe that policies currently don't reflect the words of politicians. She believes that we have better health care, safer schools and neighborhoods, better parent education, and improved family support programs.

7. Not addressing generation inequity could result in alienation, distrust, and ill will between the generations.

KEY PEOPLE
IN SECTION

Peter Benson—his Search Institute has determined through research that a number of assets (e.g., family support) serve as a buffer to prevent adolescents from developing problems while making the transition to adulthood.

Marian Wright Edelman—president of the Children's Defense Fund and a tireless advocate of children's rights.

Bernice Neugarten—believed in developing a spirit of support for improving the range of options of all people in society.

Reed Larson—argued that adolescents need more opportunities (e.g., sports and art) to develop the capacity for initiative.

THE NATURE OF DEVELOPMENT/TRANSITIONS
SECTION REVIEW

1.

Age	Name	Description
Conception to birth	Prenatal	Growth from a single cell to a complete organism
Birth to 18–25 months	Infancy	Dependency on adults; early psychological development
2 to 5–6 years	Early childhood	Children learn to care for self, develop school readiness, and play with peers
6 to 10–11 years	Middle and late childhood	Master reading, writing, and arithmetic, exposure to culture; self-control increases; achievement becomes a theme.
10–13 to 18–22 years	Adolescence	Biological, cognitive, and emotional changes; career interests, dating, and identity options explored in late adolescence.
Late teens to early 20s and 30s	Early adulthood	Establishing personal and economic independence; career development; starting a family
35–45 to 55–65 years	Middle adulthood	Transmitting values to the next generation; enhanced concerns about one's body; reflection on meaning of life
60–70 years to death	Late adulthood	Adjusting to decreasing strength and health, retirement and reduced income; adapting to changing social roles; increased freedom; parenthood

2. Socioemotional processes shape cognitive processes, cognitive processes advance or restrict socioemotional processes, and biological processes influence cognitive processes.

3. Is there a specific age at which an adolescent becomes an adult? Early adulthood usually begins in the late teens or early twenties and lasts through the thirties.

4. For instance, nature influences physical differences between boys and girls; but nurture accounts for changing gender roles.

5. It helps to refine the process of maturation and growth and makes it a more understandable process.

6. Some believe that unless infants experience warm, nurturant caregiving in the first year of life, their development will never be optimal. Others argue that children and adolescents are malleable throughout development and that later sensitive caregiving is just as important as earlier sensitive caregiving.

KEY PEOPLE
IN SECTION

Kenneth Kenniston—proposed that a transition occurs between being an adolescent and being an adult, which can last two to eight years or even longer.

Jerome Kagan—pointed out that even children who show the qualities of an inhibited temperament, which is linked to heredity, have the capacity to change their behavior.

UNDERSTANDING ADOLESCENCE
SECTION REVIEW

1. Helps them to solve social as well as academic problems encountered in life.

2. What does it mean to be a critical thinker? It means that you can ask yourself how you know something. Critical thinkers are open-minded and intellectually curious.

3. Critical thinkers think reflectively, productively, and evaluate evidence. They are open-minded, intellectually curious, and look for multiple determinants of behavior. They analyze, infer, connect, synthesize, criticize, evaluate, think, and rethink.

KEY PEOPLE
IN SECTION

Luis Vargas—one of his special interests is the treatment of Latino youth for delinquency and substance abuse.

EXPLORATIONS
IN ADOLESCENCE

No answers given—personal reflection

COGNITIVE
CHALLENGE

No answers given—personal reflection

ADOLESCENCE
IN RESEARCH

Offer and his colleagues tested the hypothesis that adolescents were deserving of many of the negative stereotypes bestowed on them (e.g., the storm-and-stress portrayal of adolescence). Their cross-cultural study showed no support for this negative view of adolescence. They sampled the self-images of adolescents around the world and found that at least 73 percent of the adolescents studied reported a healthy self-image.

⊠ COMPREHENSIVE REVIEW

1	b	2.	a	3.	c	4.	c	5.	d
6.	c	7.	c	8.	d	9.	b	10.	b
11.	a	12.	b	13.	c	14.	b	15.	c
16.	b	17.	b	18.	a	19.	a	20.	b
21.	d	22.	c	23.	a	24.	d	25.	c
26.	a	27.	a	28.	d	29.	c	30.	a
31.	c	32.	d	33.	a	34.	c	35.	d
36.	c	37.	a							

Chapter 2   The Science of Adolescent Development

Learning Goals with Key Terms and Key People in Boldface

1.0   WHAT ARE THE PSYCHOANALYTIC THEORIES OF ADOLESCENT DEVELOPMENT?

    A.   Theories of Sigmund Freud

        1.1   What are the views of psychoanalytic theorists?

        1.2   How did **Sigmund Freud** develop his ideas about **psychoanalytic theory**?

        1.3   What are the id, ego, and superego?

        1.4   What are defense mechanisms?

        1.5   What is repression?

        1.6   What did **Sigmund Freud** mean by his iceberg analogy?

    B.   Theories of Peter Blos and Anna Freud

        1.7   How did **Peter Blos** and **Anna Freud** help to shape the understanding of adolescence?

        1.8   What are the characteristics of Freud's oral, anal, phallic, genital, and latency stages of psychosexual development?

        1.9   What did Freud mean by the Oedipus complex?

        1.10   Who was the first feminine-based criticism of Freud's theory?

    C.   Theories of Erik Erikson

        1.11   How does **Erik Erikson's** theory differ from that of Freud?

        1.12   How do psychosocial stages differ from psychosexual stages?

        1.13   What are the characteristics of Erikson's eight life span stages—trust versus mistrust, autonomy versus shame and doubt, initiative versus guilt, industry versus inferiority, identity versus identity confusion, intimacy versus isolation, generativity versus stagnation, and integrity versus despair?

        1.14   What are the primary contributions of **psychoanalytic theories** of adolescent development?

        1.15   What are the main criticisms of **psychoanalytic theories**?

2.0   WHAT ARE THE COGNITIVE THEORIES OF ADOLESCENT DEVELOPMENT?

    A.   Piaget's Theory

        2.1   What are the three major theories of cognitive development?

        2.2   What are the characteristics of **Piaget's** stages of cognitive development—the sensorimotor, preoperational, concrete operational, and formal stages?

    B.   Vygotsky's Theory

        2.3   How does the cognitive theory of **Lev Vygotsky** differ from that of **Piaget**?

        2.4   What three claims capture the heart of **Vygotsky's** view?

        2.5   How has **Vygotsky's** view stimulated interest in the view that knowledge is situated and collaborative?

    C.   The Information-Processing Approach

        2.6   What is the main emphasis of the **information processing approach**?

        2.7   What are the primary contributions of the cognitive theories of adolescent development?

        2.8   What are the main criticisms of the cognitive theories?

3.0 **WHAT ARE THE BEHAVIORAL AND SOCIAL COGNITIVE THEORIES OF ADOLESCENT DEVELOPMENT?**

A. **Skinner's Behaviorism**

3.1 What do **behavioral** and **social cognitive** theories emphasize?

3.2 What is the main emphasis of **behaviorism**?

3.3 What role does the mind play in development according to **Skinner**?

B. **Social Cognitive Theory**

3.4 Who are the architects of the contemporary version of **social cognitive theory**?

3.5 What is the essence of Bandura's **social cognitive theory**?

3.6 What are the primary contributions of the **behavioral and social cognitive theories** of adolescent development?

3.7 What are the main criticisms of the **behavioral and social cognitive theories**?

4.0 **WHAT ARE THE ECOLOGICAL, CONTEXTUAL THEORIES OF DEVELOPMENT, AND THE ECLECTIC THEORETICAL ORIENTATION?**

A. **Ecological, Contextual Theory**

4.1 How does Urie Bronfenbrenner's **ecological, contextual theory** explain adolescent development?

4.2 What are the characteristics of the five systems that make up Bronfenbrenner's ecological theory—the **microsystem, mesosystem, exosystem, macrosystem,** and **chronosystem**?

4.3 What are the primary contributions of the **ecological, contextual theory** of adolescent development?

4.4 What are the main criticisms of the **ecological, contextual theory**?

B. **Eclectic Theoretical Orientation**

4.5 What is meant by an eclectic theoretical orientation?

5.0 **WHY IS RESEARCH ON ADOLESCENT DEVELOPMENT IMPORTANT?**

A. **Exploring Research**

5.1 Why is research on adolescent development important?

B. **The Scientific Research Approach**

5.2 What are the steps in the **scientific method**?

5.3 What does the science part of adolescent development seek to do?

C. **Adolescent Development Research**

5.4 What factors reflect the growth of research on adolescent development?

5.5 Why were researchers so neglectful of adolescence until recently?

5.6 When did researchers begin to seriously challenge the early-experience doctrine?

5.7 What are the main outlets for the vast amounts of research being done on adolescence?

5.8 Where do you find professional journals?

5.9 What format do articles in professional journals usually follow?

6.0 **HOW ARE PARTICIPANTS AND MEASURES SELECTED?**

A. **Participants**

6.1 What is a population?

6.2 What is a sample?

6.3 What is a random sample?

6.4 What is meant by generalization of research findings?

B. **Measures**

6.5 What is the difference between observation in a **laboratory** and **naturalistic observation**?

6.6   What is the video-recall technique?

6.7   How are interviews and questionnaires used to study adolescent development?

6.8   What is a limitation in using interviews or questionnaires in research?

6.9   What do **standardized tests** contribute to our understanding of adolescent development?

6.10   What is the most widely used **standardized test** of personality?

6.11   What are the three major types of physiological measures used in assessing adolescent development?

6.12   What are **case studies**?

7.0   WHAT RESEARCH METHODS ARE USED TO STUDY ADOLESCENT DEVELOPMENT?

A.   Correlational Research

7.1   What is the goal of **correlational research**?

7.2   Why does correlation not equal causation?

B.   Experimental Research

7.3   What does **experimental research** allow us to conclude about behavior?

7.4   What is the difference between the **independent variable** and the **dependent variable**?

7.5   What are the functions of the **experimental group** and the **control group**?

7.6   Why is it important to have both **experimental** and **control groups** when conducting research?

7.7   What is the value of **random assignment**?

C.   Multiple Measures, Sources, and Contexts

7.8   What is the advantage of using **multiple measures, sources**, and **contexts** to study adolescent development?

D.   Time Span of Research

7.9   What is the difference between **cross-sectional research** and **longitudinal research**?

7.10   What is the value of **longitudinal research**?

8.0   WHAT ARE CHALLENGES FACED BY RESEARCHERS OF ADOLESCENT DEVELOPMENT?

A.   Research Challenges

8.1   What are the four main challenges faced by researchers in adolescent development?

B.   Ethics

8.2   What ethical considerations guide researchers?

8.3   Why did the American Psychological Association (APA) adopt a code of ethics?

8.4   What are three important research ethics topics noted in the text?

C.   Gender

8.5   What gender considerations do researchers need to take into account?

D.   Ethnicity and Culture

8.6   What do ethnicity and culture have to do with research into adolescent development?

8.7   What is ethnic gloss?

8.8   What research error can ethnic gloss result in?

E.   Being a Wise Consumer of Information about Adolescent Development

8.9   What six rules should you follow in order to be a wise consumer of information about adolescent development?

8.10   What is nomothetic research?

8.11   What is meant by idiographic needs?

Exercises

KEY TERMS
COMPLETION EXERCISE

Each key term is presented in the form of an incomplete sentence. Complete each sentence by either defining the term or giving an example. Compare you definitions with those given at the end of the study guide chapter.

1.   A **theory** can be helpful to

     _____

     _____

2.   According to **psychoanalytic theory**, the personality is

     _____

     _____

3.   **Erikson's theory** addresses development from

     _____

     _____

4.   The four stages in **Piaget's theory** are

     _____

     _____

5.   **Vygotsky's theory** is a sociocultural cognitive theory that emphasizes

     _____

     _____

6.   According to the **information-processing approach,**

     _____

     _____

7.   **Behavioral and social cognitive theories** emphasize

     _____

     _____

8.   **Ecological, contextual theory** consists of

_____

_____

9.   A therapist applying an **eclectic theoretical orientation** might try

_____

_____

10.   The **scientific method** is a

_____

_____

11.   A **laboratory** is often used in conducting

_____

_____

12.   A **naturalistic observation** is done

_____

_____

13.   **Standardized tests** are useful in

_____

_____

14.   You might use a **case study** when you are

_____

_____

15.   In **correlational research,** the goal is to

_____

_____

16.   The goal of **experimental research** is to

_____

_____

17.   In research, the **independent variable** is

_____

_____

18.   In research, the **dependent variable** is

_____

_____

19.   In a research study, the **experimental group** is

_____

_____

20.   In research, a **control group** is

_____

_____

21.   In experimental research, **random assignment** is used to

_____

_____

22.   **Cross-sectional research** involves

_____

_____

23.   **Longitudinal research** involves

_____

_____

KEY PEOPLE
IN THE STUDY OF ADOLESCENCE

Match the name with the concept, issue, or topic related to adolescence with which they are associated.

_____	1. Sigmund Freud	A. Associated with social cognitive theory
_____	2. Peter Blos	B. Eight psychosocial stages
_____	3. Anna Freud	C. Four cognitive stages
_____	4. Karen Horney	D. Five systems in which adolescents develop
_____	5. Nancy Chodorow	E. Associated with behaviorism
_____	6. Erik Erikson	F. Proposed a sociocultural cognitive theory that emphasized developmental analysis, the role of language, and social relations.
_____	7. Jean Piaget	G. Five psychosexual stages
_____	8. B. F. Skinner	H. Believed that regression is a normal aspect of puberty
_____	9. Albert Bandura	I. Believed that women define themselves in terms of relationships
_____	10. Lev Vygotsky	J. Believed that defense mechanisms are the key to understanding adolescent adjustment
_____	11. Urie Bronfenbrenner	K. Believes that thinking is information processing
_____	12. Robert Siegler	L. Associated with the first feminist-based criticism of Freud's theory

"DR. DETAIL'S"
MATCHING EXERCISE

Match the stage with the correct developmental information associated with that stage across each of the following theories.

Freud's Psychosexual Stages

_____	1. Genital stage	A. Between 1 ½ and 3 yrs. Pleasure involves the anus and the process of eliminating.
_____	2. Oral stage	B. Occurs between age 6 and puberty. The child focuses on intellectual development while repressing sexual interest.
_____	3. Phallic stage	C. Goes from puberty onward. The source of sexual pleasure now becomes someone outside of the family.
_____	4. Latency stage	D. First 18 months of life. Pleasure centers around the mouth.
_____	5. Anal stage	E. Occurs between ages 3 and 6. Pleasure focuses on the genitals.

Erikson's Eight Life-Span Stages

_____ 1. Autonomy vs. Shame and Doubt	A. Experienced during late adulthood, when people look back and evaluate what they have done with their lives.
_____ 2. Identity vs. Identity Confusion	B. Experienced during middle adulthood. This stage marks what a person has done to help the next generation.
_____ 3. Trust vs. Mistrust	C. Experienced during early adulthood. Individuals face the developmental task of forming intimate relationships with others.
_____ 4. Integrity vs. Despair	D. Experienced during the adolescent years. A time when the individual needs to find out who they are.
_____ 5. Intimacy vs. Isolation	E. Experienced in the elementary school years. Success in school brings a sense of pride; failure brings about a sense of not being good enough.
_____ 6. Initiative vs. Guilt	F. Experienced in the first year of life. A sense of well-being depends upon whether or not one's needs are being met.
_____ 7. Generativity vs. Stagnation	G. Experienced between ages 1 and 3. Is a stage in which infants begin to discover that their behavior is their own.
_____ 8. Industry vs. Inferiority	H. Experienced during the preschool years. Children are asked to accept responsibility for their bodies, their behavior, their toys, and their pets.

Piaget's Stages of Cognitive Development

_____ 1. Concrete Operational stage	A. Infants construct an understanding of the world by coordinating sensory experiences with physical actions.
_____ 2. Preoperational stage	B. Children begin to represent the world with words, images, and drawings.
_____ 3. Formal Operational stage	C. A child in this stage is likely not to be able to imagine the steps needed to complete an algebraic equation.
_____ 4. Sensorimotor stage	D. The child begins to think in more abstract and logical terms.

Vygotsky's Three Claims

_____ 1. Claim one	A. Cognitive skills are mediated by words, language, and forms of discourse, which serve as tools for facilitating and transforming mental activity.
_____ 2. Claim two	B. Cognitive skills have their origins in social relations and are embedded in a sociocultural backdrop.
_____ 3. Claim three	C. Children's and adolescent's cognitive skills can be understood only when they are developmentally analyzed and interpreted.

Bronfenbrenner's Ecological, Contextual Theory

_____ 1. Chronosystem	A. Includes the person's family, peers, school, and neighborhood.
_____ 2. Microsystem	B. The relation of family experiences to school experiences, school experiences to work experiences, and family experiences to peer experiences.
_____ 3. Macrosystem	C. Experiences in another social setting influence what the individual experiences in an immediate context.
_____ 4. Mesosystem	D. Involves the culture in which a person lives.
_____ 5. Exosystem	E. Involves the patterning of environmental events and transactions over the life course and sociohistorical circumstances.

THEORIES OF ADOLESCENT DEVELOPMENT
SECTION REVIEW

1. According to Freud the personality has three structures, explain the role of each of these structures.

   _____

   _____

2. How did Freud come to conceptualize the personality to be like an iceberg?

   _____

   _____

3. Explain the role that ego defense mechanisms have in protecting the personality.

   _____

   _____

4. Compare the views of Anna Freud with those of Peter Blos.

   _____

   _____

5. Discuss some of the criticisms of Freud's views.

   _____

   _____

6. For each of the Freudian stages, state the age and focus of development and pleasure.

Stage	Age	Focus of Development/Pleasure
Oral		
Anal		
Phallic		
Latency		
Genital		

7.   For each of the Erikson stages, provide the age range and focus of psychosocial development.

Stage	Age	Focus of Development
Trust vs. mistrust		
Autonomy vs. shame and doubt		
Initiative vs. guilt		
Industry vs. inferiority		
Identity vs. identity confusion		
Intimacy vs. isolation		
Generativity vs. stagnation		
Integrity vs. despair		

8.   In what ways did Erikson's theory extend the theory presented by Freud?

_____

_____

KEY PEOPLE
IN SECTION

(Describe the contributions of this individual to the study and understanding of adolescence.)

Sigmund Freud—

_____

_____

Peter Blos—

_____

_____

Anna Freud—

_____

_____

Karen Horney—

_____

_____

Nancy Chodorow—

_____

_____

Erik Erikson—

_____

_____

COGNITIVE THEORIES OF ADOLESCENT DEVELOPMENT
SECTION REVIEW

1. Compare and contrast cognitive theories with psychoanalytic theories.

    _____

    _____

2. What two processes underlie Piaget's cognitive construction of the world, and what purpose did they serve?

    _____

    _____

3. What occurs in the Formal Operations Stage that differentiates it from Piaget's other stages?

    _____

    _____

4. For each of Piaget's cognitive stages, state age and manner in which the child/adolescent thinks and understands the world.

Stage	Age	Way of Thinking and Understanding
Sensorimotor		
Preoperational		
Concrete operational		
Formal operational		

5. Why have Vygotsky's views on adolescence become an important addition to the understanding of adolescent cognitive development?

_____

_____

6. What are the primary contributions of cognitive theories to the understanding of adolescent development?

_____

_____

7. What are the main criticisms of the cognitive theories?

_____

_____

KEY PEOPLE
IN SECTION

(Describe the contributions of this individual to the study and understanding of adolescence.)

Jean Piaget—

_____

_____

Lev Vygotsky—

_____

_____

Robert Siegler—

_____

_____

BEHAVIORAL AND SOCIAL COGNITIVE THEORIES
OF ADOLESCENT DEVELOPMENT
SECTION REVIEW

1. In Skinner's view, what is development?

_____

_____

2.   Contrast Skinner's view with that of Albert Bandura?

_____

_____

3.   What role does empirical research play in studying development from both the social cognitive and behavioral perspectives?

_____

_____

4.   What are some of the contributions of the behavioral and social cognitive theories of development?

_____

_____

5.   What are some of the criticisms of the behavioral and social cognitive theories of development?

_____

_____

KEY PEOPLE
IN SECTION

(Describe the contributions of this individual to the study and understanding of adolescence.)

B.F. Skinner—

_____

_____

Albert Bandura—

_____

_____

Walter Mischel—

_____

_____

ECOLOGICAL, CONTEXTUAL THEORIES
OF ADOLESCENT DEVELOPMENT
SECTION REVIEW

1. What are some of the contributions of ecological, contextual theory to the overall understanding of adolescent development?

    _____

    _____

2. What does it mean to say someone follows an eclectic theoretical orientation?

    _____

    _____

3. Describe the five systems in Bronfenbrenner's ecological theory.

System	Description
Microsystem	
Mesosystem	
Exosystem	
Macrosystem	
Chronosystem	

KEY PEOPLE
IN SECTION

(Describe the contributions of this individual to the study and understanding of adolescence.)

Urie Bronfenbrenner—

_____

_____

RESEARCH ON ADOLESCENT DEVELOPMENT
SECTION REVIEW

1. Label each stage of the scientific method and describe what would be done in each stage of a scientific study of mentoring.

Number	Name	Description
One		
Two		
Three		
Four		

2. What are some benefits of using the scientific method?

_____

_____

3. What contributed to the growth of research on adolescent development?

_____

_____

4. Explain the role played by journals in the advancement of scientific theory?

_____

_____

5. Explain which information goes in respective sections of a journal article?

Section	Description
Abstract	
Introduction	
Method	
Results	
Discussion	
References	

RESEARCH PARTICIPANTS AND MEASURES
SECTION REVIEW

1.   How should participants for a research study be selected?

     _____

     _____

2.   What are the two ways that observations can be made for research studies?

     _____

     _____

3.   What are the three types of physiological measures often used in researching adolescents?

     _____

     _____

4.   When is it appropriate to use case studies in conducting research?

     _____

     _____

RESEARCH METHODS USED IN ADOLESCENT DEVELOPMENT
SECTION REVIEW

1.   What is the goal of correlational research?

     _____

     _____

2.   Compare and contrast independent and dependant variables used in research studies.

     _____

     _____

3.   Why is it important to randomly assign participants to experimental or control groups when conducting a study?

     _____

     _____

4.   What are some strengths and limitations of cross-sectional research studies?

     _____

     _____

5.   What are some positives and drawbacks of longitudinal research studies?

_____

_____

CHALLENGES TO ADOLESCENT RESEARCH
SECTION REVIEW

1.   Explain the importance of informed consent, confidentiality, and debriefing in conducting ethical research?

_____

_____

2.   How might gender be a bias that influences the choice of theory, questions, hypotheses, participants, and research design?

_____

_____

3.   What is ethnic gloss, and what are its implications regarding adolescent research?

_____

_____

4.   Why must we always be cautious when reading about adolescent research in the popular media?

_____

_____

5.   Using your own words, list six guidelines to follow when evaluating information about adolescents that you read about in newspapers, magazines, or research journals or hear about on television.

   a.   _____

        _____

   b.   _____

        _____

   c.   _____

        _____

   d.   _____

e. _____

_____

f. _____

_____

EXPLORATIONS IN ADOLESCENCE

Find an article in a research journal (such as Developmental Psychology, Child Development, Journal of Research on Adolescence, Journal of Early Adolescence, or Journal of Youth and Adolescence) about any topic in the text. Then look for an article on the same subject in either a newspaper or are a magazine. Compare how the research article on the topic differs from the newspaper or magazine article. What are the differences between the nature, type, and quality of information presented?

COGNITIVE CHALLENGE

In the chapter, we were given a brief look at the lives of Jean Piaget and Erik Erikson. From that look at their lives, we are given a glimpse at what factors might have led them to formulate the theories they did. In looking back at your life (childhood, adolescence, college experience), what kind of theory could you formulate and what factors would contribute to this.

ADOLESCENCE IN RESEARCH

Concerning Albert Bandura's and Walter Mischel's research on social cognitive theory, state the hypothesis, the research methods (if known), the research conclusions, and the implications and applications for adolescent development.

_____

_____

⊠ COMPREHENSIVE REVIEW

1. Sigmund Freud developed his ideas about psychoanalytic theory
   a. while being held in a Nazi detention camp.
   b. while reviewing the published theories of Erik Erikson.
   c. from work he did with mental patients.
   d. while studying to become a medical doctor.

2.   Which of the following is NOT one of Freud's three structures of the personality?
   a.   Ego
   b.   Repression
   c.   Superego
   d.   Id

3.   Developing a study schedule is a function of the
   a.   id.
   b.   ego.
   c.   superego.
   d.   ego-ideal.

4.   Feeling guilty over adolescent sexual exploration is a result of
   a.   ego.
   b.   libido.
   c.   superego.
   d.   id.

5.   Which of the following is an example of an ego defense mechanism?
   a.   Autonomy
   b.   Latency
   c.   Oedipus complex
   d.   Repression

6.   Unconsciously hating your younger brother might be an example of
   a.   ego-centrism.
   b.   repression.
   c.   the Oedipus complex.
   d.   id-ideals.

7.   According to Peter Blos and Anna Freud,
   a.   it is permissible to make generalizations about the role of defense mechanisms in adolescent development on the basis of small or clinical samples of subjects.
   b.   research on adolescent defense mechanisms should be nonsexist.
   c.   defense mechanisms are a normal aspect of adolescent development.
   d.   Sigmund Freud's original analysis of the role of defense mechanisms in adolescent development has been confirmed many times.

8.   Louella believes all boys have "cooties." She devotes herself to athletics and caring for various pets. A psychoanalyst would say Louella is
   a.   behaving normally for someone in the latency stage.
   b.   being overly controlled by her superego.
   c.   experiencing unconscious conflicts between her ego and id.
   d.   fixated at the phallic stage of development.

9. Bobby tells his mom, "When I grow up I'm going to marry you." Freud might consider this an example of
    a. repression.
    b. the Oedipus complex.
    c. latency.
    d. the id.

10. Horney and Chodorow criticized Freud for
    a. his conceptualization of the Oedipus complex.
    b. male-bias reflected in his theories.
    c. discussing children sexuality too extensively in his theories.
    d. ignoring sexuality in the elderly.

11. The decision to get married might indicate that Johnny is in which of Freud's psychosexual stages?
    a. Latency
    b. Oral
    c. Genital
    d. Phallic

12. An infant left to cry in her crib for long periods of time might, according to Erikson, develops
    a. autonomy.
    b. guilt.
    c. initiative.
    d. mistrust.

13. Susan changed her major three times in college, and now that she has graduated, she still cannot decide what type of job she wants. Erik Erickson would describe Susan as going through a period of
    a. shame and doubt.
    b. identity confusion.
    c. despair.
    d. generativity and stagnation.

14. In the futuristic film *2001:A Space Odyssey*, a computer named HAL performs many humanlike activities in outer space. Psychologists might justifiably argue that while HAL could memorize and pay attention, he could never have arguments with his family nor be a "social" machine. These criticisms could also be leveled against the _____ view of adolescents.
    a. information-processing
    b. Piagetian
    c. social learning
    d. psychoanalytic

15. Dotty often finds herself daydreaming about boy's and wondering what her life will be like when she gets married. According to Piaget, Dotty is likely in which stage?
    a. Sensorimotor stage
    b. Preoperational stage
    c. Concrete operational stage
    d. Formal operational stage

16. The information processing approach emphasizes
    a. the quality of thinking among adolescent of different ages.
    b. overcoming age related problems or "crises."
    c. age appropriate expressions of sexual energy.
    d. perception, memory, reasoning ability, and problem solving.

17. Because of the need to translate their writings, the important works of these two scholars remained unknown to American scholars for many years.
    a. Sigmund and Anna Freud
    b. Bandura and Skinner
    c. Horney and Chodorow
    d. Piaget and Vygotsky

18. Sam is shy when around his friends, teachers, and family. Skinner would suggest that this behavior is
    a. modeled after his father's behavior.
    b. learned.
    c. repressed.
    d. ecological.

19. One of the strong points of behavior theory is its
    a. belief that cognitive processes are irrelevant for understanding development.
    b. emphasis on the relationship between environmental stimuli and adolescent behavior.
    c. emphasis on reducing adolescent behavior to fine-grained elements.
    d. emphasis on the role of information processing as a mediator between behavior and environment.

20. Cindy receives a job promotion that requires her to travel often. Because of this, she has less time to spend with her adolescent son and it impacts their relationship. According to Bronfenbrenner, this is an example of a(n)
    a. microsystem.
    b. mesosystem.
    c. chronosystem.
    d. exosystem.

21. From B. F. Skinner's point of view, the best way to explain adolescent behavior is to
    a. pay attention to the external consequences of that behavior.
    b. pay attention to the self-produced consequences of that behavior.
    c. focus on adolescent cognitive interpretation of her environmental experiences.
    d. identify the biological processes that determine adolescent maturation.

22. The frequent finding that adults who abuse their children and adolescents typically come from families in which they themselves were abused supports which theory of development?
    a. Freudian psychoanalytic theory
    b. Information processing theory
    c. Ecological theory
    d. Social cognitive theory

23. A researcher who takes the best aspect from many theories in constructing a research model could be said to be applying
    a. ecological theory.
    b. information-processing theory.
    c. eclectic theory.
    d. social cognitive theory.

24. A major strength of ecological theory is its framework for explaining
    a. environmental influences on development.
    b. biological influences on development.
    c. cognitive development.
    d. affective processes in development.

25. Many developmentalists have chosen to subscribe to an eclectic viewpoint because
    a. they cannot afford to subscribe to all the other viewpoints; the annual dues are too high.
    b. none of the current theories is at all correct.
    c. they believe that not enough data have been collected so far to even begin proposing a definitive theory.
    d. each of the major theories has both valid points and flaws.

26. Which of the following is true about theories that endeavor to explain adolescent development?
    a. If theorists keep working at it they will eventually come up with one theory that explains development.
    b. Cognitive, psychoanalytic, and humanistic theories have nothing in common and can never be reconciled.
    c. The theories proposed should be thought of as complementary rather than competitive.
    d. One theory from biology, one theory from cognitive psychology, and one theory from social psychology are all that is needed to explain development.

27. One difficulty of doing research on adolescents in a laboratory setting is that
    a. an unnatural behavior may occur.
    b. random assignment is impossible.
    c. extraneous factors are difficult to control.
    d. the experimenter's judgments are of unknown reliability.

28. An investigator interested in gender differences in helping behavior spends three hours a day in the mall watching who opens doors for shoppers burdened with packages. Which of the following methods of data collection is being used?
    a. Naturalistic observation
    b. Experimental
    c. Correlational
    d. Case studies

29. Which of the following is NOT a component in the scientific method?
    a. Conceptualizing the problem
    b. Drawing conclusions
    c. Collecting information
    d. Publishing results in a journal

30. Which of the following is NOT a section typically found in a research article published in a journal?
    a. Discussion
    b. Statistical design
    c. Results
    d. Method

31. A psychologist treats Bill's irrational fear of balloons. The assessment of Bill's problem and his treatment is an example of a(n)
    a. hypothesis.
    b. correlational research.
    c. case study.
    d. context.

32. The experimental factor that is manipulated in an experiment is referred to as a(n) _____ .
    a. independent variable
    b. dependent variable
    c. control group
    d. method

33. The factor that is measured as the result of an experiment is referred to as a(n) _____ .
    a. independent variable
    b. dependent variable
    c. control group
    d. method

34. _____ is the assignment of participants to experimental and control groups by chance.
    a. Naturalistic observation
    b. Longitudinal research
    c. Random assignment
    d. Experimental research

35. In conducting her research on adolescent self-esteem, professor Radcliff gathered information from 14-year-old students in 20 different states. This is an example of
    a. case study research.
    b. longitudinal research.
    c. cross-sectional research.
    d. correlational research.

36. When Clint was in pre-school, he was part of a large study on temperament. The same researchers would again observe Clint's behavior in the fifth grade, the tenth grade, and when he turned 30 years old. Clint was likely a subject in which type of study?
    a. Case study research
    b. Longitudinal research
    c. Cross-sectional research
    d. Correlational Research

37.   Which of the following is NOT an important topic in research ethics?
    a.   Informed consent
    b.   Naturalistic observation
    c.   Confidentiality
    d.   Debriefing

38.   Stating that your research study contained 10 "Latino" subjects, is an example of
    a.   informed consent.
    b.   random assignment.
    c.   debriefing.
    d.   ethnic gloss.

ADOLESCENCE ON THE SCREEN

■   *Good Will Hunting* concerns an adolescent named Will (played by Matt Damon) in treatment for attachment problems brought on by his being abandoned by his biological parents and abused by his foster parents. Will's therapist Sean (played by Robin Williams) uses a psychodynamic treatment model.

■   *Ordinary People* portrays a surviving son's guilt and suicidal depression over what he feels was his role in his brother's death. He pulls through with the help of hospitalization and a psychodynamic therapist whom he trusts.

■   *American Flyers* portrays a youngest son's difficulty in following in the steps of a highly successful, but dying older brother.

ADOLESCENCE IN BOOKS

Two recent biographies about Erikson and Freud demonstrate how individual life events—as well as historical events, time, and place—influenced their theories.

■   *Freud: A Life for Our Time*, by Peter Gay (W.W. Norton: NY, 1998), is a balanced and comprehensive biography of Sigmund Freud that places his theories in the context of the times.

■   *Identity's Architect: A Biography of Erik H. Erikson*, by Lawrence J. Friedman (Simon & Schuster: NY, 1999), traces the origins of Erikson's concern with identity and identity crises to his early life experiences.

■   *Self-efficacy in Changing Societies*, by Albert Bandura (Cambridge University Press: NY, 1997), takes a look at changing views of self in adolescents across time.

Answer Key

KEY TERMS

1. **theory** An interrelated, coherent set of ideas that helps to explain and make predictions.

2. **psychoanalytic theory** Describes development as primarily unconscious – that is, beyond awareness – and is heavily colored by emotion.

3. **Erikson's theory** Eight stages of development that unfold as we go through the life span. Each stage consists of a unique developmental task that confronts individuals with a crisis that must be faced.

4. **Piaget's theory** States that individuals actively construct their understanding of the world and go through four stages of cognitive development.

5. **Vygotsky's theory** A socioculturally cognitive theory that emphasizes developmental analysis, the role of language, and social relations.

6. **information-processing approach** Emphasizes that individuals manipulate information, monitor it, and strategize about it. Central to this approach are the processes of memory and thinking.

7. **behavioral and social cognitive theories** Emphasis is placed on the importance of studying environmental experiences and observable behavior. Social cognitive theorists emphasize person/cognitive factors in development.

8. **ecological, contextual theory** Bronfenbrenner's view of development, involving five environmental systems—microsystem, exosystem, ecosystem, macrosystem, and chronosystem. These emphasize the role of social contexts in development.

9. **eclectic theoretical orientation** Not following any one theoretical approach, but rather selecting from each theory whatever is considered the best in it.

10. **scientific method** An approach that can be used to discover accurate information. It includes the following steps: conceptualize the problem, collect data, draw conclusions, and revise research conclusions and theory.

11. **laboratory** A controlled setting from which many of the complex factors of the real world have been removed.

12. **naturalistic observation** Observation made in the "real world" outside of the laboratory.

13. **standardized tests** Commercially prepared tests that assess performance in different domains. A standardized test often allows an adolescent's performance to be compared to that of other adolescents of the same age.

14.   **case study** An in-depth look at an individual.

15.   **correlation research** Describes the strength of the relationship between two or more events or characteristics.

16.   **experimental research** Allows researchers to appropriately determine the causes of behavior.

17.   **independent variable** The manipulated, influential, experimental factor.

18.   **dependent variable** The factor that is measured in an experiment.

19.   **experimental group** A group whose experience is manipulated in an experiment.

20.   **control group** A comparison group in an experiment that is treated like the experimental group except for the manipulated factor.

21.   **random assignment** The assignment of participants to experimental and control groups by chance.

22.   **cross-sectional research** Research that studies all people at one time.

23.   **longitudinal research** Involves studying the same individuals over a period of time, usually several years or more.

KEY PEOPLE
IN THE STUDY OF ADOLESCENCE

1.	G	2.	H	3.	J	4.	L	5.	I
6.	B	7.	C	8.	E	9.	A	10.	F
11.	D	12.	K						

"DR. DETAIL'S"
MATCHING EXERCISE

Freud's Psychosexual Stages

| 1. | C | 2. | D | 3. | E | 4. | B | 5. | A |

Erikson's Eight Life-Span Stages

| 1. | G | 2. | D | 3. | F | 4. | A | 5. | C |
| 6. | H | 7. | B | 8. | E | | | | |

Piaget's Stages of Cognitive Development

| 1. | C | 2. | B | 3. | D | 4. | A |

Vygotsky's Three Claims

1. C   **2.** A   **3.** B

Bronfenbrenner's Ecological, Contextual Theory

1. E   **2.** A   **3.** D   **4.** B   **5.** C

THEORIES OF ADOLESCENT DEVELOPMENT
SECTION REVIEW

1.   *Id*—consists of instincts, which are an individual's reservoir of psychic energy. *Ego*—the structure of the personality that deals with the demands of reality. *Superego*—the moral branch of the personality.

2.   Freud felt that most of our personality exists below our level of awareness. Just as an iceberg has it's greatest mass below the surface of the water and out of sight.

3.   Ego defense mechanisms are unconscious methods the ego uses to distort reality and protect itself from anxiety.

4.   Blos stated that regression during adolescence is actually not defensive at all, but rather an integral, normal, inevitable, and universal part of puberty. Anna Freud developed the idea that defense mechanisms are the key to understanding adolescent adjustment.

5.   Most contemporary psychoanalytic theorists place less emphasis on sexual instincts and more emphasis on cultural experiences as determinants of an individual's development. Most theorists today also feel that conscious thought makes up more of the iceberg than Freud envisioned. Lastly, Freud's theories have been viewed as too focused on males.

6.

Stage	Age	Focus of Development/pleasure
Oral	0–1 1/2 years	Pleasure focused on the mouth; sucking reduces tension.
Anal	1 1/2–3 years	Pleasure involves the anus; eliminative functions reduce tension.
Phallic	3–6 years	Pleasure focuses on the genitals; child discovers self-manipulation is enjoyable.
Latency	6 years–puberty	Child represses interest in sexuality and develops social and intellectual skills
Genital	Adolescence–adulthood	Sexual pleasure is focused on those outside of the family.

7.

Stage	Age	Focus of Development
Trust vs. mistrust	Infancy	Feeling of physical comfort and minimal amount of fear and apprehension.
Autonomy vs. shame and doubt	1–3 years	Begin to assert independence or autonomy in behavior.
Initiative vs. guilt	3–5 years	Engage in active, purposeful behavior to cope with challenges of the world.
Industry vs. inferiority	6 years–puberty	Direct energy toward mastering knowledge and intellectual skills.
Identity vs. identity confusion	10–20 years	Finding out who they are, what they are about, and where they are going in life.
Intimacy vs. isolation	20s and 30s	Forming intimate relationships.
Generativity vs. stagnation	40s and 50s	Assist younger generation in developing and leading useful lives.
Integrity vs. despair	60s to death	Look back and evaluate life's accomplishments.

8. For Freud, the primary motivation for human behavior was sexual in nature, for Erikson it was social and reflected a desire to affiliate with other people.

KEY PEOPLE
IN SECTION

Sigmund Freud—A medical doctor who specialized in neurology, he developed his ideas about psychoanalytic theory from work with mental patients.

Peter Blos—A British psychoanalyst who felt that regression during adolescence is actually not defensive at all, but rather a normal part of puberty.

Anna Freud—Sigmund's daughter Anna developed the idea that defense mechanisms are the key to understanding adolescent adjustment.

Karen Horney—Developed a model of women with positive feminine qualities and self-evaluation. She was a critic of Sigmund Freud's male-oriented theories.

Nancy Chodorow—Another Freud critic. She noted that many more women than men define themselves in terms of their relationships with others.

Erik Erikson—Developed the theory that people develop in psychosocial stages. Erikson emphasized developmental changes throughout the human life span.

COGNITIVE THEORIES OF ADOLESCENT DEVELOPMENT
SECTION REVIEW

1. Whereas psychoanalytic theories stress the importance of adolescents' unconscious thoughts, cognitive theories emphasize their conscious thoughts.

2. Organization and adaptation. We organize our experiences and adapt our thinking to include new ideas.

3. In formal operations, hypothetical or abstract thinking is possible. This greatly increases the thinking capacity of the child in this stage.

4.

Stage	Age	Way of Thinking and Understanding
Sensorimotor	Birth–2	Coordinates sensory experiences with physical actions.
Preoperational	2–7	Uses words and images to represent the world.
Concrete operational	7–11	Reason logically about concrete events and classify objects.
Formal operational	11–adulthood	Reasons in abstract, idealistic, and logical ways.

5. Vygotsky's theory has stimulated considerable interest in the view that knowledge is situated and collaborative. That is to say that within our communities we are immersed in an environment rich with knowledge.

6. They present a positive view of development. They emphasize the individual's active construction of understanding. They underscore the importance of examining developmental changes in children's thinking. The information-processing approach offers detailed descriptions of cognitive processes.

7. There is skepticism about the pureness of Piaget's stages. The cognitive theories do not give adequate attention to individual variations in cognitive development. The information processing does not give an adequate description of developmental changes in cognition. Psychoanalytic theorists argue that the cognitive theories do not give enough credit to unconscious thought.

KEY PEOPLE
IN SECTION

Jean Piaget—He proposed that individuals actively construct their understanding of the world and go through four stages of cognitive development.

Lev Vygotsky—He proposed a sociocultural cognitive theory that emphasizes developmental analysis, the role of language, and social relations.

Robert Siegler—He is a leading expert on children's information processing, and believes that thinking is information processing.

BEHAVIORAL AND SOCIAL COGNITIVE THEORIES OF ADOLESCENT DEVELOPMENT SECTION REVIEW

1. For Skinner, development is behavior.

2. Bandura believes observational learning is a key aspect of how we learn. This adds a cognitive component that differs from Skinner's views.

3. Like Skinner's behavioral approach, the social cognitive approach emphasizes the importance of empirical research in studying development.

4. An emphasis on the importance of scientific research. A focus on the environmental determinants of behavior. An underscoring of the importance of observational learning. An emphasis on person and cognitive factors.

5. Too little emphasis on cognition. Too much emphasis on environmental determinants. Inadequate attention to developmental changes. Too mechanical and inadequate consideration of the spontaneity and creativity of humans.

KEY PEOPLE IN SECTION

B.F. Skinner—To Skinner, development is behavior. The mind, conscious or unconscious, is not needed to explain behavior and development.

Albert Bandura—Believes that observational learning is a key aspect of how we learn.

Walter Mischel—Along with Bandura, is an architect of the contemporary version of social cognitive theory, which Mischel initially labeled *cognitive social learning theory*.

ECOLOGICAL, CONTEXTUAL THEORIES OF ADOLESCENT DEVELOPMENT SECTION REVIEW

1. A systematic examination of macro and micro dimensions of environmental systems. Attention to connections between environmental settings. Consideration of sociohistorical influences on development.

2. An eclectic theoretical orientation does not follow any one theoretical approach, but rather selects and uses whatever is considered the best in each theory.

3.

System	Description
Microsystem	family, peers, school, neighborhood
Mesosystem	school and parents; parents and friends
Exosystem	lack of facilities for a handicapped person
Macrosystem	ethnic or racial group
Chronosystem	wider range of gender roles for men and women

KEY PEOPLE
IN SECTION

Urie Bronfenbrenner—Proposed a strong environmental view of children's development that is receiving increased attention today, Ecological, Contextual Theory.

RESEARCH ON ADOLESCENT DEVELOPMENT
SECTION REVIEW

1.

Number	Name	Description
One	Conceptualize the problem	Identify the problem; develop hypothesis that mentoring will improve achievement of adolescents from impoverished backgrounds.
Two	Collect information (data)	Conduct the mentoring program for six months and collect data before and after program begins.
Three	Draw conclusions	Analyze the data that shows improvement over period of program; conclude that mentoring helped increase achievement.
Four	Revise research conclusions and theory	Research will increase likelihood that mentoring will be considered an important component to help improve achievement of low-income adolescents.

2.   It is an objective, systematic, and testable approach that can be used to discover accurate information.

3.   The growth of research on adolescent development is reflected in the increasing number of research journals and scholars from different disciplines devoted to advancing scientific knowledge about adolescents.

4.   Journals are the main outlets for the vast amount of research being conducted on adolescence.

5.

Section	Description
Abstract	A brief summary that appears at the beginning of the article.
Introduction	Introduces the problem or issue that is being studied.
Method	Consists of a clear description of the participants evaluated in the study, the measures used, and the procedures that were followed.
Results	Reports the analysis of the data collected. Might be difficult for nonprofessionals to understand.
Discussion	Presents the author's conclusions, inferences, and interpretation of what was found. Statements are usually made about whether the hypotheses presented in the introduction were supported, limitations of the study, and suggestions for future research.
References	Gives a bibliographic listing for every source cited in the article.

RESEARCH PARTICIPANTS AND MEASURES
SECTION REVIEW

1. Because it is often impossible to study an entire population, researchers often choose to study a sample of the targeted population. It is then best that this sample be selected randomly to avoid potential bias to the study.

2. Observations can be made in either laboratory settings or naturalistic settings.

3. a. Hormones in the bloodstream, b. body composition, and c. brain activity.

4. A case study is most relevant when the phenomenon being studied is rare and you want an in-depth look at the individual being studied.

RESEARCH METHODS USED IN ADOLESCENT DEVELOPMENT
SECTION REVIEW

1. The goal is to describe the strength of the relation between two or more events or characteristics.

2. The independent variable is the manipulated, influential factor in an experiment. The dependent variable is measured as the result of an experiment.

3. Random assignment reduces the likelihood that the experiment's results will be due to any preexisting differences between the groups.

4. The cross-sectional study's main advantage is that the researcher does not have to wait for the children to grow older. However, a disadvantage is that this approach provides no information about the stability of the children's and adolescent's feelings or attitudes over time.

5. A positive is that you can evaluate how the individual children and adolescents change as they get older. However, a drawback is that this approach is costly and time consuming.

CHALLENGES TO ADOLESCENT RESEARCH
SECTION REVIEW

1.   Informed consent means that the participants' legal guardians have been told what participation will entail and any risks that might be involved. Confidentiality means that researchers are responsible for keeping all of the data they gather completely confidential, and when possible, completely anonymous. Debriefing consists of informing participants of the purpose and methods used in a study after the study has been completed.

2.   Because most of the early research opportunities in developmental psychology went to men, they tended to study what they were most familiar with, which were males. This means that many hypotheses have not been adequately tested with female participants even to this day.

3.   Ethnic gloss means using an ethnic label in a superficial way that makes an ethnic group look more homogeneous than it really is.

4.   Because the media tend to focus on sensational or dramatic findings. This leads to the potential for inaccuracy.

5.   a.   Be cautious.
        b.   Avoid assuming that individual needs can be determined from group research.
        c.   Don't over generalize about small or clinical samples.
        d.   Be aware that a single study is usually not conclusive about a topic or issue.
        e.   Remember that correlational studies don't prove causal relationships.
        f.   Evaluate the source of the information.

EXPLORATIONS
IN ADOLESCENCE

Individual assignment – various articles and responses could be appropriate.

COGNITIVE
CHALLENGE

Individual reflection—no answers provided.

ADOLESCENCE
IN RESEARCH

The hypothesis was that observational learning is a key aspect of how we learn. The methods varied, but often appeared to be individual case histories. Emphasized a focus on the environmental determinants of behavior, and did show observational learning to play a big role in who we become.

☒ COMPREHENSIVE REVIEW

1.	a	**2.**	b	**3.**	b	**4.**	c	**5.**	d
6.	b	**7.**	c	**8.**	a	**9.**	b	**10.**	b
11.	c	**12.**	d	**13.**	b	**14.**	a	**15.**	d
16.	d	**17.**	d	**18.**	b	**19.**	b	**20.**	d
21.	a	**22.**	d	**23.**	c	**24.**	a	**25.**	d
26.	c	**27.**	a	**28.**	a	**29.**	d	**30.**	b
31.	c	**32.**	a	**33.**	b	**34.**	c	**35.**	c
36.	b	**37.**	b	**38.**	d						

SECTION II
BIOLOGICAL AND COGNITIVE
DEVELOPMENT

Chapter 3   Puberty, Health, and Biological Foundations

Learning Goals with Key Terms and Key People in Boldface

1.0   UNDERSTANDING PUBERTAL CHANGE

A.   Determinants of Puberty

1.1   What is **puberty**?

1.2   What role does heredity play in puberty?

1.3   What are **hormones**, and what is their role in **puberty**?

1.4   What are the two classes of **hormones**, and how do they affect males and females differently?

1.5   What is testosterone, and what role does it play in male development?

1.6   What is the role of the endocrine system in puberty?

1.7   What are the different endocrine glands, and what are their functions?

1.8   How does the endocrine system work?

1.9   How does the negative feedback system in the endocrine system work?

1.10   What are the two phases of **puberty** that are linked with hormonal changes?

1.11   What role is played **menarche** and **spermarche** with regards to a girl or boy's entry into gonadarche?

B.   Growth Spurt

1.12   What physical changes coincide with the growth spurt?

C.   Sexual Maturation

1.13   What is the order of physical changes during sexual maturation?

D.   Secular Trends in Puberty

1.14   What does the term secular trends refer to?

1.15   What is a likely contributor to the earlier maturation of girls today?

1.16   What are the five pubertal stages of male and female sexual development?

E.   Psychological Dimensions

1.17   What accounts for adolescent preoccupation with their bodies?

1.18   What are some gender differences in adolescents' perception of their bodies?

1.19   How do hormones affect behavior in adolescents?

1.20   What is the typical reaction of young girls to **menarche**?

1.21   What effect does early or late maturation have on a developing boy or girl?

1.22   Are the effects of puberty exaggerated?

F.   Pubertal Timing and Health Care

1.23   What can be done to help off-time maturers who are at risk for health problems?

2.0   KNOWING ABOUT DEVELOPMENTAL CHANGES IN THE BRAIN

A.   Neurons

2.1   What are **neurons**?

2.2   What are the three basic parts of the **neuron**?

2.3   How do **neurons** change in adolescence?

2.4   What are synapses?

2.5   What is meant by synaptic "blooming and pruning?"

2.6   What determines the timing and course of synaptic overproduction and retraction?

B.   Brain Structure

2.7   What are the four lobes of the brain?

2.8   What recent technological advances have allowed for more in-depth study of the adolescent brain?

2.9   What role might the amygdala play in adolescent thought processes?

2.10   What is the significance of increased synaptic density in the brain?

3.0   EVALUATING ADOLESCENT HEALTH

A.   A Critical Juncture in Health

3.1   Why are health related behaviors of adolescents so important?

B.   Nutrition

3.2   What is **basal metabolism** rate?

3.3   Why is the consumption of 'fast-foods' a concern for today's adolescents?

3.4   Why are eating patterns formed in childhood of special interest to medical professionals?

C.   Exercise and Sports

3.5   How extensive is the role of sports in adolescent's lives?

3.6   Are adolescents getting enough exercise?

3.7   Do adolescents in the U.S. exercise less than those in other countries?

3.8   What role does school play in the development of attitudes towards exercise?

3.9   Does it make a difference if children and adolescents are pushed to exercise in school?

3.10   What is the role of exercise in reducing adolescent stress?

3.11   What are some positive side benefits of adolescent involvement in sports?

3.12   What are some potential negative outcomes of youth participation in sports?

D.   Sleep

3.13   Why have adolescent sleep patterns become a recent focus of interest?

3.14   What can be the results of disrupted sleep in adolescence?

E.   Health Services

3.15   What are some reasons that adolescents might not be receiving adequate health care?

F.   Leading Causes of Death

3.16   What are the three leading causes of death in adolescence?

4.0   EXPLAINING HEREDITY AND ENVIRONMENTS

A.   The Nature of Genes

4.1   What is the nature of genes?

4.2   What is the difference between a **genotype** and **phenotype**?

4.3   What physical traits are included in **phenotypes**?

4.4   Would measured introversion-extroversion be predictable from knowledge of the specific genes?

B.   Methods

4.5   What are the research methods of **behavior genetics**?

4.6   How is the influence of heredity on behavior studied?

4.7 What is a **twin study**?

4.8 How do **twin studies** examine the difference between identical twins and fraternal twins?

4.9 What are some issues that develop as a result of **twin studies**?

4.10 What is an **adoption study**?

4.11 What is the basis of the enthusiasm regarding the study of molecular genetics?

4.12 What is a genome?

4.13 What is the importance of the Human Genome Project?

C. **Exploring Heredity and Environment**

4.14 According to behavior geneticist Sandra Scarr, what three ways are heredity and environment correlated?

4.15 What distinguishes Scarr's concepts of **passive genotype-environment correlations, evocative genotype-environment correlations,** and **active (niche-picking) genotype-environment correlations**?

4.16 What is the difference between **shared environmental influences** and **nonshared environmental influences**?

4.17 What are the most reasonable conclusions we can make about the interaction of heredity and environment?

4.18 Why are the views of Judith Harris both intriguing and controversial?

Exercises

KEY TERMS
COMPLETION EXERCISE

Each key term is presented in the form of an incomplete sentence. Complete each sentence by either defining the term or giving an example. Compare your definitions with those given at the end of the study guide chapter.

1.   One of the early signs of **puberty** is

2.   **Hormones** play a major role in

3.   Testosterone is an **androgen** that

4.   Estradiol is an **estrogen** that

5.   Suzy is probably entering **menarche** because

6.   John is probably entering **spermarche** because

7.   **Neurons** are made up of

8.   **Basal metabolism rate (BMR)** gradually declines

9.   A **genotype** is a

_____

_____

10.   Shirley's **phenotype** can be observed in her appearance by

_____

_____

11.   The study of **behavior genetics** might involve

_____

_____

12.   In a **twin study**, a comparison is made between

_____

_____

13.   In an **adoption study**, researchers seek

_____

_____

14.   **Passive genotype-environment correlations** lead parents to

_____

_____

15.   **Evocative genotype-environment correlations** might explain Tom's happiness because

_____

_____

16.   **Active (niche-picking) genotype-environment correlations** might explain why athletic boys seek out

_____

_____

17.   Examples of **shared environmental influences** are

_____

_____

18.   Examples of **nonshared environmental influences** are

_____

_____

KEY PEOPLE
IN ADOLESCENT DEVELOPMENT

Match the person with the event or concept in adolescent development with which they are associated.

_____ 1. Sandra Scarr

_____ 2. Mary Carskadon

_____ 3. Roberta Simmons and Dale Blyth

A. Studied adolescent sleep patterns. Determined that early school starting times may result in lack of attention and poor performance on tests.

B. Associated with theory of natural selection.

C. Studied the effects of being an early or late maturing male or female.

"DR. DETAIL'S"
PUZZLE EXERCISE

Down
1.   The main class female hormones
2.   Powerful chemical substances secreted by the endocrine glands and carried through the body by the bloodstream
3.   The way an individual's genotype is expressed in observed and measurable characteristics
4.   The nervous system's basic units

Across
1.   A girl's first menstrual period
2.   The main class of male sex hormones
3.   A period of rapid physical maturing involving hormonal and bodily changes
4.   A person's genetic heritage
5.   A boy's first ejaculation of semen

UNDERSTANDING PUBERTAL CHANGE
SECTION REVIEW

1.   How can puberty be distinguished from adolescence?

     _____

     _____

2.   How is the emergence of puberty timed, and what can impact it?

     _____

     _____

3.   Differentiate between the two classes of hormones, and how they specifically impact males and females?

     _____

     _____

4.   What physical changes in boys is testosterone associated with?

     _____

     _____

5.   What is the endocrine system's role in puberty?

     _____

     _____

6.   Contrast the functions of the hypothalamus and pituitary gland.

     _____

     _____

7.   How does the endocrine system work?

     _____

     _____

8.   Describe the role of the negative feedback system in the endocrine system.

     _____

     _____

9.   What are the two phases of puberty linked with hormonal changes?

_____

_____

10.   What is the order of appearance of physical changes in females?

_____

_____

11.   Explain what is meant by secular trends?

_____

_____

12.   Describe each of the five pubertal stages of male and female sexual development.

   a.   Male

   _____

   _____

   b.   Female

   _____

   _____

13.   Explain the gender differences apparent in how adolescents view their bodies.

_____

_____

14.   Are there links between concentrations of hormones and adolescent behavior?

_____

_____

15.   In historical accounts of adolescence, why is menarche often described as a "main event?"

_____

_____

16.   What are some advantages and disadvantages of being an "early" or "late" maturing adolescent?

_____

_____

17.   If puberty and development are unusually late, what steps can be taken to help the adolescent?

_____

_____

KEY PEOPLE
IN SECTION

(Describe the contributions of this individual to the study and understanding of adolescence.)

Roberta Simmons and Dale Blyth—

_____

_____

Anne Petersen—

_____

_____

KNOWING ABOUT DEVELOPMENTAL CHANGES IN THE BRAIN
SECTION REVIEW

1.   What are the three basic parts of the neuron?

_____

_____

2.   How do neurons change in adolescence?

_____

_____

3.   Match the lobe of the brain with its primary function.

     _____ 1. Occipital lobe   A. Involved in bodily sensations
     _____ 2. Parietal lobe   B. Involved in hearing
     _____ 3. Temporal lobe   C. Involved in the control of voluntary muscles, personality, and intelligence
     _____ 4. Frontal lobe   D. Involved in visual functioning

4.   In what ways, has the development of MRIs (magnetic resonance imaging) enhanced the understanding of how the brain works?

_____

_____

EVALUATING ADOLESCENT HEALTH
SECTION REVIEW

1.   Why is adolescence a critical juncture in the adoption of behaviors related to health?

_____

_____

2.   What is basal metabolism rate, and what role does it play in adolescence?

_____

_____

3.   Are American adolescents getting enough exercise?

_____

_____

4.   With regards to eating and exercise, how do U.S. adolescents compare with those from other countries?

_____

_____

5.   What are some positive and negative influences sports can have on adolescent development?

_____

_____

6.   According to Carskadon, what might improve adolescent performance in class and on tests?

7.   What are the three leading causes of death in adolescence?

KEY PEOPLE
IN SECTION

(Describe the contributions of this individual to the study and understanding of adolescence.)

Aristotle—

Mary Carskadon—

EXPLAINING HEREDITY AND ENVIRONMENTS
SECTION REVIEW

1.   Explain the difference between genotypes and phenotypes and how each impacts development.

2.   In the study of adolescence, what has been learned from twin studies and adoption studies?

3.   Why does behavior geneticist, Robert Plomin, believe that shared environment accounts for little of the variation in adolescent's personalities or interests?

4.   What was the cause of the most recent nature-nurture controversy?

_____

_____

KEY PEOPLE
IN SECTION

(Describe the contributions of this individual to the study and understanding of adolescence.)

Sandra Scarr—

_____

_____

Robert Plomin—

_____

_____

Eleanor Maccoby—

_____

_____

Judith Harris—

_____

_____

T. Berry Brazelton—

_____

_____

Jerome Kagan—

_____

_____

EXPLORATIONS
IN ADOLESCENCE

Which of the following most closely resembles you?

Early maturing male   ____
Late maturing male   ____
Early maturing female   ____
Late maturing female   ____

Depending upon which you checked, how might your life (e.g., experiences, opportunities, dating, sports, leadership experiences, etc.) have been effected by when you matured?

_____

_____

_____

_____

_____

_____

_____

COGNITIVE
CHALLENGE

Looking at the following characteristics, first circle whether you believe nature or nurture is more responsible for these characteristics in you. Then briefly explain your reasoning.

Height   (nature | nurture)   _____

_____

Weight   (nature | nurture)   _____

_____

Skin color   (nature | nurture)   _____

_____

Temperament   (nature | nurture)   _____

_____

Intelligence   (nature | nurture)   _____

_____

Humor   (nature | nurture)   _____

_____

Hair color   (nature | nurture)   _____

_____

Athleticism   (nature | nurture)   _____

_____

Age at maturation   (nature | nurture)   _____

_____

Academic ability   (nature | nurture)   _____

_____

ADOLESCENCE IN RESEARCH

Concerning Simmons's and Blyth's 1987 research about early and late maturation, state the hypothesis, the research methods (if known), the research conclusions, and the implications and applications for adolescent development.

_____

_____

⊠ COMPREHENSIVE REVIEW

1.   _____ is a period of rapid physical maturation involving hormonal and bodily changes that take place primarily in early adolescence.
    a.   menarche
    b.   heredity
    c.   adolescence
    d.   puberty

2.   _____ are the main class of male sex hormones.
    a.   estrogens
    b.   androgens
    c.   neurons
    d.   spermarche

3.   _____ are the main class of female sex hormones.
    a.   estrogens
    b.   androgens
    c.   menarche
    d.   spermarche

4. _____ are powerful chemical substances secreted by the endocrine glands and carried through the body by the bloodstream.
   a. neurons
   b. hormones
   c. genotypes
   d. phenotypes

5. Which of the following is NOT monitored by the hypothalamus?
   a. Sex
   b. Eating
   c. Hearing
   d. Drinking

6. Which of the following is most similar in function to how the negative feedback system works?
   a. Refrigerator
   b. Television set
   c. A thermostat-furnace system
   d. A washing machine and dryer unit

7. Sandra Scarr proposed all the following heredity-environment interactions EXCEPT:
   a. passive genotype-environmental interactions.
   b. heritable genotype-environmental interactions.
   c. evocative genotype-environmental interactions.
   d. active genotype-environmental interactions.

8. _____ is the only time during development in which growth is faster than during puberty.
   a. toddlerhood
   b. middle childhood
   c. infancy
   d. young adulthood

9. On average, females enter puberty at an earlier age than males, and that's why
   a. women are typically shorter than men.
   b. fifth- and sixth-grade girls are usually taller than boys.
   c. girls and boys do not get along well during puberty.
   d. boys are more muscular, and girls have more fat.

10. Sue started her menstrual period about two years earlier than Mary, even though both girls are very healthy. A likely explanation for this event is that
   a. Sue is an athlete.
   b. Sue has greater body mass than Mary.
   c. Mary has greater body mass than Sue.
   d. Sue has better genes than Mary.

11. Androgens are to females as _____ are to males.
   a. testosterone
   b. gonadotropins
   c. hormones
   d. estrogens

12.   _____ is important in the pubertal development of females.
   a.   Thyroxin
   b.   Estradiol
   c.   Androgen
   d.   Estrogen

13.   Your son and daughter are fraternal twins, both in the sixth grade. Your son gets angry because people tease him about his sister being taller than he. You can legitimately tell your son that
   a.   although his sister is taller, his sexual maturation is more advanced.
   b.   his sister is probably taller because she doesn't eat as much junk food.
   c.   he needn't worry, because he'll probably catch up with or surpass his sister's height by the end of the eighth grade.
   d.   since his sister was taller than he during childhood, she'll be taller than he during adolescence.

14.   The fact that some adolescent males begin puberty as early as 10 years of age and others as late as 17 years (or even later) is an example of
   a.   environmental influences.
   b.   individual differences.
   c.   biologically caused psychological disturbance.
   d.   behavior genetics in action.

15.   In the Berkeley Longitudinal Study, males who matured early
   a.   perceived themselves as more successful in peer relations.
   b.   perceived themselves more negatively because of additional parental pressure.
   c.   were perceived by peers as unattractive due to the accompanying occurrence of acne.
   d.   perceived themselves more negatively because they were "ahead of the others."

16.   In a college course in human sexuality, Jill was asked to describe her initial reactions to menarche. She described the experience very negatively, emphasizing the discomfort and messiness. Jill probably was
   a.   well prepared for the event.
   b.   unlikely to tell her mother about the event.
   c.   an early maturer.
   d.   on time in her pubertal development.

17.   Johnny is just entering puberty. The first of many changes that he is likely to notice is
   a.   minor voice change
   b.   growth of hair in the armpits
   c.   appearance of straight pubic hair
   d.   increase in penis and testicle size

18.   Jenny is just entering puberty. The first of many changes that she is likely to notice is
   a.   growth of hair in the armpits
   b.   increase in hip width
   c.   increase in breast size
   d.   significant increase in height

19. _____ refers to patterns over time or across generations.
     a.   menarche
     b.   phenotype
     c.   secular trends
     d.   spermarche

20. Which of the following has NOT been mentioned as a possible reason for the earlier onset of puberty in the twentieth century?
     a.   Girlhood obesity
     b.   The deterioration of the ozone
     c.   Improvements in health
     d.   Improvements in nutrition

21. Immediately following the onset of menarche, who are girls most likely to discuss the matter with?
     a.   A best friend
     b.   A trusted teacher
     c.   A sibling
     d.   Her mother

22. Stephanie is a late-maturing female. She has an increased probability of
     a.   being tall and thin.
     b.   being shorter and stockier.
     c.   having no skin problems.
     d.   having to visit the dermatologist.

23. Early-maturing adolescents often date at an earlier age than their later-maturing friends. For females, at least, this early social involvement may be welcomed uneasily by the adolescent, because many adolescent females are
     a.   unprepared for puberty.
     b.   emotionally secure.
     c.   unattractive.
     d.   not interested in heterosexual interactions.

24. Which of the following is NOT one of the three basic parts of a neuron?
     a.   Cell body
     b.   Axon
     c.   Occipital lobe
     d.   Dendrites

25. What role does the myelin sheath play in the functioning of a neuron?
     a.   It carries information away from the cell body to other cells.
     b.   It receives information from other cells.
     c.   It helps to insulate the axon and speeds transmission.
     d.   It provides the neuron with nutrition.

26. Which role does the axon play in the functioning of a neuron?
     a.   It carries information away from the cell body to other cells.
     b.   It receives information from other cells.
     c.   It helps to insulate the axon and speeds transmission.
     d.   It provides the neuron with nutrition.

27.   Which role does the dendrite play in the functioning of a neuron?
    a.   It carries information away from the cell body to other cells.
    b.   It receives information from other neurons.
    c.   It helps to insulate the axon and speeds transmission.
    d.   It provides the neuron with nutrition.

28.   Which of the following lobes of the brain is involved in hearing?
    a.   Temporal
    b.   Frontal
    c.   Parietal
    d.   Occipital

29.   Which of the following lobes of the brain is involved in visual functioning?
    a.   Temporal
    b.   Frontal
    c.   Parietal
    d.   Occipital

30.   Which of the following lobes of the brain is involved in bodily sensations?
    a.   Temporal
    b.   Frontal
    c.   Parietal
    d.   Occipital

31.   Which of the following lobes of the brain is most involved in personality?
    a.   Temporal
    b.   Frontal
    c.   Parietal
    d.   Occipital

32.   Which of the following structures of the brain is most involved in emotion?
    a.   Temporal
    b.   Frontal
    c.   Amygdala
    d.   Occipital

33.   Which of the following is NOT one of the things blamed for the poor physical condition of American adolescents?
    a.   Computers
    b.   Fast food
    c.   Television
    d.   Schools

34.   Which of the following hormones is associated with adolescent sleep patterns?
    a.   Estrogen
    b.   Androgen
    c.   Estradiol
    d.   Melatonin

35. Which of the following is NOT one of the three leading causes of death for adolescents in America?
    a. Homicide
    b. Suicide
    c. Accidents
    d. HIV/AIDS

36. The unique arrangement of chromosomes and genes inherited by each adolescent is referred to as the _____ , whereas the adolescent's observed characteristics are called the _____ .
    a. phenotype; genotype
    b. phenotype; reaction range
    c. genotype; reaction range
    d. genotype; phenotype

37. _____ is the area concerned with the degree and nature of the hereditary basis of behavior.
    a. Genetic psychology
    b. Behavioral psychology
    c. Behavior genetics
    d. Developmental genetics

38. A behavioral geneticist comparing the IQs of monozygotic twins with those of dizygotic twins is applying the
    a. twin-study method.
    b. family-of-twins method.
    c. kinship method.
    d. habitability method.

ADOLESCENCE
ON THE SCREEN

- *My Left Foot* addresses how a boy deals with physical deformity.

- *Trainspotting* depicts the decadent lifestyle of Scottish teenagers bent on self-destruction through heroin addiction.

- *Ordinary People* tells of an adolescent boy's struggle with suicidal tendencies arising out of the guilt he feels for an accident that took his younger brother's life.

- *Antonia's Line*—longitudinal portrayal of the transformation from early adolescence to womanhood, and life's decisions involved.

- *The Body Beautiful*—a generative example of how our various bodily and social identities are built and given meaning concurrently.

- *Daughters of the Dust*—life and development on a barrier island amongst the Gullah subculture, an isolated African-American culture off the coast of South Carolina.

ADOLESCENCE
IN BOOKS

- *The What's Happening to My Body? Book for Boys,* by Lynda Madaras and D. Ssveddra (Newmarket: NY, 1991), is written for parents and focuses on how to help boys cope with pubertal transitions.

- *You're in Charge,* by Niels Lauersen and Eileen Stukane (Fawcett: NY, 1993), is written for teenage girls and describes the changing female body.

Answer Key

KEY TERMS

1. **puberty** A period of rapid physical maturation involving hormonal and bodily changes that occur primarily in early adolescence.

2. **hormones** Powerful chemical substances secreted by the endocrine glands and carried through the body by the bloodstream.

3. **androgen** The main class of male sex hormones.

4. **estrogen** The main class of female sex hormones.

5. **menarche** A girl's first menstruation.

6. **spermarche** A boy's first ejaculation of semen.

7. **neurons** Are the nervous system's basic units.

8. **basal metabolism rate (BMR)** is the minimum amount of energy an individual uses in a resting state.

9. **genotype** A person's genetic heritage; the actual genetic material.

10. **phenotype** The way an individual's genotype is expressed in observed and measurable characteristics.

11. **behavior genetics** The study of the degree and nature of behavior's hereditary basis.

12. **twin study** A study in which the behavioral similarity of identical twins is compared with the behavioral similarity of fraternal twins.

13. **adoption study** A study in which investigators seek to discover whether, in behavior and psychological characteristics, adopted children and adolescents are more like their adoptive parents, who provided a home environment, or their biological parents, who contributed their heredity. Another form of adoption study is to compare adoptive and biological siblings.

14. **passive genotype-environment correlations** Occur when parents who are genetically related to the child provide a rearing environment for the child.

15. **evocative genotype-environment correlations** Occur when the adolescent's genotype elicits certain types of physical and social environments.

16. **active (niche-picking) genotype-environment correlations** Occur when adolescents seek out environments they find compatible and stimulating.

17.   **shared environmental influences** Adolescent's common environmental experiences that are shared with their sibling, such as their parents' personalities and intellectual orientation, the family's social class, and the neighborhood in which they live.

18.   **nonshared environmental influences** The adolescent's own unique experiences, both within a family and outside the family that are not shared by another sibling.

KEY PEOPLE
IN ADOLESCENT DEVELOPMENT

1.   B   **2.**   A   **3.**   C

"DR. DETAIL'S" PUZZLE EXERCISE

Down		*Across*	
1.	estrogens	**1.**	menarche
2.	hormones	**2.**	androgens
3.	phenotype	**3.**	puberty
4.	neurons	**4.**	genotype
		5.	spermarche

UNDERSTANDING PUBERTAL CHANGE
SECTION REVIEW

1.   Puberty ends long before adolescence exits.

2.   It is programmed into the genes, but can be impacted by the environment.

3.   Androgen plays an important role in male pubertal development. Estrogen plays an important role in the pubertal development of females.

4.   Testosterone is associated with the development of external genitals, increase in height, and change in voice.

5.   The endocrine system's role in puberty involves the interaction of the hypothalamus, the pituitary gland, and the gonads.

6.   The hypothalamus monitors eating, drinking, and sex. The pituitary gland controls growth and regulates other glands.

7.   The pituitary gland sends a signal via gonadotropins to the appropriate gland to manufacture the hormone. Then the pituitary gland, through interaction with the hypothalamus, detects when the optimal level of hormones is reached and responds by maintaining gonadotropin secretion.

8.   It works in the body like a thermostat-furnace system.

9.   Andrenarche and gonadarche.

10.   First breasts enlarge or pubic hair appears. Later, hair appears in the armpits, height increases and the hips become wider.

11.   The term refers to patterns over time, especially across generations.

12.   a.   Male—No pubic hair; soft long hair at the base of the penis; hair becomes coarse and curly; pubic hair is now as coarse and curly as that of an adult, but does not cover as much area; the hair is now spread to the thighs, and the penis and scrotum are the size of an adult male.

      b.   Female—The nipple is raised just a little; the breast bud stage; the areola and the breast are both larger than in stage 2; the areola and the nipple make up a mound that sticks up above the shape of the breast; the mature adult stage where the breasts are fully developed.

13.   Girls are less happy with their bodies and have more negative body images, compared to boys, who are pleased to see their muscles develop.

14.   Hormonal factors are thought to account for at least part of the increase in negative and variable emotions that characterize adolescents.

15.   The dramatic changes in the body that occur during adolescence require a considerable change in self-concept, sometimes resulting in an identity crisis.

16.   Early boys—perceived themselves more positively and had more successful peer relations. Early girls—similar outcome as early boys only not as pronounced. Some are cognitively not ready for social activities. Late boys—faced many challenges, but developed a strong sense of identity; perhaps due to adversity. Late girls—develop at a better pace. Tend to grow to be tall and slender, which can be socially appealing.

17.   A physician may recommend hormonal treatment.

KEY PEOPLE
IN SECTION

Roberta Simmons and Dale Blyth—longitudinally studied early and late maturing males and females.

Anne Petersen—associate professor and Senior Vice-President of the W.K. Kellogg Foundation.

KNOWING ABOUT DEVELOPMENTAL CHANGES IN THE BRAIN
SECTION REVIEW

1.   The dendrite, cell body, and axon.

2.   Much of the neuron does not change. However, axons develop throughout adolescence.

3.   1.   D   2.   A   3.   B   4.   C

4.   MRIs have shown the significant changes that the brain goes through between ages 3 and 15.

EVALUATING ADOLESCENT HEALTH
SECTION REVIEW

1.   Because many of the factors linked to poor health habits and early death in the adult years begin during adolescence.

2.   Basal metabolism rate (BMR) is the minimum amount of energy an individual uses in a resting state. BRM declines during adolescence.

3.   Recent studies show they are not getting nearly enough exercise.

4.   U.S. adolescents exercise less than their counterparts in other countries and eat more junk food that is high in fat.

5.   Positives are they eat healthier, are less likely to use drugs, smoke cigarettes or drink alcohol. Negatives are that there is more likelihood of a win-at-all-costs attitude to develop amongst adolescent athletes and their parents.

6.   Carskadon made the suggestion that adolescents might benefit from a later start to the school day.

7.   Accidents, homicide, and suicide are the leading causes of death in adolescence.

KEY PEOPLE
IN SECTION

Aristotle—commented that the quality of life is determined by its activities.

Mary Carskadon—conducted a number of research studies on adolescent sleep patterns.

EXPLAINING HEREDITY AND ENVIRONMENT
SECTION REVIEW

1.   A genotype is a person's genetic heritage, the actual genetic material. A phenotype is the way an individual's genotype is expressed and observed.

2.   Twin and adoption studies are often used to study heredity's influence on behavior.

3.   Plomin has noted that even when living under the same roof, experiences are often very different.

4.   Judith Harris's recent book, *The Nurture Assumption*, dramatically downplays the role that parents play in the development of their child's personality. This caused much new debate on nature versus nurture.

KEY PEOPLE
IN SECTION

Sandra Scarr—describes three ways heredity and environment are correlated: passively, evocatively, and actively.

Robert Plomin—believes that common rearing accounts for little of the difference in adolescent's personality or interests.

Eleanor Maccoby—argued that there are a number of important aspects of family contexts that are shared by all family members.

Judith Harris—her provocative book, *The Nurture Assumption*, ignited the most recent nature-nurture controversy.

T. Berry Brazelton—called *The Nurture Assumption* very disturbing, and suggested that it might encourage parents to withdraw from their children's lives altogether.

Jerome Kagan—concluded that whether children are cooperative or competitive, achievement-oriented or not, they are strongly influenced by their parents for better or worse.

EXPLORATIONS
IN ADOLESCENCE

No answers provided—individual reflection and response.

COGNITIVE
CHALLENGE

No answers provided—individual reflection and response.

ADOLESCENCE
IN RESEARCH

This was a longitudinal study, following more than 450 individuals in Milwaukee, Wisconsin, for 5 years, from sixth to tenth grade. The students were individually interviewed, and their achievement test scores and grade point averages were obtained. The researchers found that early-maturing girls had more problems in school, were more independent, and were more popular with boys than late-maturing girls were.

⊠ COMPREHENSIVE REVIEW

1.	d	**2.**	b	**3.**	a	**4.**	b	**5.**	c
6.	c	**7.**	b	**8.**	c	**9.**	b	**10.**	b
11.	d	**12.**	b	**13.**	c	**14.**	b	**15.**	a
16.	c	**17.**	d	**18.**	c	**19.**	c	**20.**	b
21.	d	**22.**	a	**23.**	a	**24.**	c	**25.**	c
26.	a	**27.**	b	**28.**	a	**29.**	d	**30.**	c
31.	b	**32.**	c	**33.**	a	**34.**	d	**35.**	d
36.	d	**37.**	c	**38.**	a						

Chapter 4   Cognitive Development

Learning Goals with Key Terms and Key People in Boldface

1.0   WHAT IS PIAGET'S THEORY?

A.   Piaget's Theory

1.1   What is the nature of Piaget's theory of cognitive processes?
1.2   What is a **schema**?
1.3   What roles do **assimilation** and **accommodation** play in cognitive development?
1.4   What did Piaget mean by **equilibration**?
1.5   What are names and defining characteristics of Piaget's four stages of cognitive development?
1.6   How does an infant learn about the world in the **sensorimotor stage**?
1.7   What happens in the **preoperational stage**?
1.8   What are the characteristics of the **concrete operational stage**?
1.9   What did Piaget mean by **operations**?
1.10   What are the characteristics of **conservation** and **classification**?
1.11   What are the indicators of the **formal operational stage**?
1.12   What is **hypothetical-deductive reasoning**?
1.13   What has been the significance of Piaget's theory for adolescent education?
1.14   What were Piaget's main contributions to understanding cognitive development?
1.15   What are the major criticisms of Piaget's theory?
1.16   What are the distinctions between **early formal operational thought** and **late** formal operational thought?
1.17   What principles of Piaget's theory of cognitive development can be applied to education?
1.18   What were Piaget's main contributions, and has the theory withstood the test of time?
1.19   Who are the **neo-Piagetians** who expanded and modified Piaget's theory?
1.20   How strong is the evidence for a fifth, postformal stage of cognitive development?

2.0   WHAT IS VYGOTSKY'S THEORY?

A.   Vygotsky's Theory

2.1   What were Vygotsky's main contributions to cognitive developmental theory?
2.2   What did Lev Vygotsky mean by the **zone of proximal development (ZPD)**?
2.3   How do the concepts of **scaffolding**, **cognitive apprenticeship**, **tutoring**, **cooperative learning**, and **reciprocal teaching** contribute to cognitive development and learning?
2.4   Why do we say that Piaget and Vygotsky both were proponents of **constructivism**?
2.5   What is the difference between a cognitive constructivist approach and a social constructivist approach?

3.0   WHAT IS THE INFORMATION-PROCESSING VIEW OF COGNITIVE DEVELOPMENT?

A.   Characteristics

3.1   What, according to Robert Siegler, are the three main characteristics of the information processing approach to cognitive development?
3.2   What are the components of thinking, change mechanisms, and self-modification?

B.   Attention and Memory

3.3   What are **attention** and **memory** and why are they such important adolescent cognitive processes?

3.4   What are the functions of short-term memory and long-term memory?

3.5   Why do many theorists choose to apply the concept of working memory?

3.6   How is long-term memory different from working memory?

C.   Decision Making

3.7   What do we know about adolescent decision-making ability?

3.8   How is adolescent decision making different from that of children?

D.   Critical Thinking

3.9   What does **critical thinking** involve?

3.10   What are the adolescent cognitive changes that allow improved critical thinking?

3.11   How does the **Jasper Project** enhance critical thinking skills?

3.12   What are the two main debates concerning critical thinking and adolescents?

E.   Creative Thinking

3.13   What is **creativity**?

3.14   What is the difference between **convergent thinking** and **divergent thinking**?

3.15   What are seven strategies that can help adolescents become more creative?

3.16   What is **brainstorming** and how does it contribute to creative thinking?

F.   Metacognition and Self-Regulatory Learning

3.17   What is **metacognition**?

3.18   How can adolescents develop better learning strategies?

3.19   What is **self-regulatory learning**?

3.20   What are five characteristics of self-regulatory learners?

3.21   How can teachers or parents help students become self-regulatory learners?

4.0   WHAT IS THE PSYCHOMETRIC/INTELLIGENCE POINT OF VIEW OF COGNITIVE DEVELOPMENT?

A.   The Psychometric/Intelligence View

4.1   What does the psychometric/intelligence view emphasize?

4.2   What did Huxley mean when he used the word intelligence?

4.3   What is the traditional definition of intelligence?

B.   Intelligence Tests

4.4   What was the first valid intelligence test and why was it developed?

4.5   What was Binet's concept of **mental age (MA)**?

4.6   What is an **intelligence quotient (IQ)**?

4.7   What is a **normal distribution**?

4.8   What are the Wechsler scales and what kind of IQ scores do they yield?

4.9   How are the Wechsler and Stanford-Binet scales similar or different?

C.   Theories of Multiple Intelligences

4.10   What was the concept of general intelligence and what are its origins?

4.11   What were Thurstone's seven primary mental abilities?

4.12   What are the components of Sternberg's **triarchic theory of intelligence**?

4.13   According to Howard Gardner, what are the eight types of intelligence?

4.14   How are Gardner's and Sternberg's theories different, and how are they the same?

4.15   What are some of the criticisms of Gardner's theory?

D.   Emotional Intelligence

4.16   What is **emotional intelligence** and who is its major proponent?

4.17   According to Goleman's views, what are the four main areas of **emotional intelligence**?

E.   Controversies and Issues in Intelligence
    4.18   What are the three main controversies surrounding the topic of intelligence?
    4.19   Is nature or nurture more important in determining intelligence?
    4.20   Why is intelligence increasing around the globe?
    4.21   Are there ethnic differences in intelligence?
    4.22   What are the characteristics of **culture-fair tests**?
    4.23   Are intelligence tests culturally biased?
    4.24   What are the appropriate uses of intelligence tests? What uses are inappropriate?

5.0   WHAT IS SOCIAL COGNITION?

A.   Adolescent Egocentrism
    5.1   What is **adolescent egocentrism** and what types of thinking does it include?
    5.2   What does David Elkind believe brings on adolescent egocentrism?
    5.3   What is an **imaginary audience**?
    5.4   What is the **personal fable**?

B.   Perspective Taking
    5.5   According to Robert Selman, what are the five stages of perspective taking?
    5.6   What is meant by perspective taking and according to Selman, what are its five stages?

C.   Implicit Personality Theory
    5.7   What is implicit **personality theory**?
    5.8   Do adolescents conceptualize an individual's personality differently than children do?

D.   Social Cognition in the Rest of the Text
    5.9   What areas of adolescent development have been influenced by the concept of social cognition?

Exercises

KEY TERMS
COMPLETION EXERCISE

Each key term is presented in the form of an incomplete sentence. Complete each sentence by either defining the term or giving an example. Compare your definitions with those given at the end of the study guide chapter.

1.   Piaget's interest in **schema's**

        _____

        _____

2.   **Assimilation** occurs when

        _____

        _____

3.   Suzy demonstrates **accommodation** when she

        _____

        _____

4.   **Equilibration** is a mechanism

        _____

        _____

5.   You can tell that Jill is in the **sensorimotor stage** because

        _____

        _____

6.   John has now entered the **preoperational stage** in that he

        _____

        _____

7.   In the **concrete operational stage**, children can engage in

        _____

        _____

8.   You can tell that Ramone is in the **formal operational stage** because

     _____

     _____

9.   **Hypothetical-deductive reasoning** is used to

     _____

     _____

10.   **Neo-Piagetians** argue that

     _____

     _____

11.   **Postformal thought** is most likely seen in

     _____

     _____

12.   The **zone of proximal development (ZPD)** refers to

     _____

     _____

13.   Alex is good at **critical thinking** because

     _____

     _____

14.   **Creativity** is the ability to

     _____

     _____

15.   An example of **convergent thinking** is

     _____

     _____

16.   An example of **divergent thinking** is

     _____

     _____

17.   Cognitive psychologists define **metacognition** as

_____

_____

18.   **Self-regulatory learning** consists of

_____

_____

19.   The **psychometric/intelligence view** emphasizes

_____

_____

20.   Some experts describe **intelligence** as

_____

_____

21.   **Mental age (MA)** is an individual's

_____

_____

22.   William Stern created the **intelligence quotient (IQ)**, which refers to

_____

_____

23.   A **normal distribution** is

_____

_____

24.   According to the **triarchic theory of intelligence**,

_____

_____

25.   **Emotional intelligence** was proposed as a

_____

_____

26. What are examples of **culture fair tests**?

_____

_____

27. John is going through a stage of **adolescent egocentrism** that is leading him to

_____

_____

28. **Implicit personality theory** suggests that

_____

_____

KEY PEOPLE
IN THE STUDY OF ADOLESCENCE

Match the name with the concept, issue, or topic related to adolescence with which they are associated.

_____ 1. Jean Piaget	A.	Multiple intelligences
_____ 2. Lev Vygotsky	B.	Mental age (MA)
_____ 3. Barbara Rogoff	C.	Four stages of cognitive development
_____ 4. Annamarie Palincsar and Ann Brown	D.	General intelligence
_____ 5. Robert Siegler	E.	Triarchic theory of intelligence
_____ 6. Robbie Case	F.	Zone of proximal development
_____ 7. Daniel Keating	G.	Cognitive apprenticeships
_____ 8. J.P. Guilford	H.	Information processing view
_____ 9. Mihalyi Csikszentmihalyi	I.	Reciprocal teaching
_____ 10. Michael Pressley	J.	Automaticity
_____ 11. Deanna Kuhn	K.	Creativity
_____ 12. Alfred Binet	L.	Metacognition & critical thinking
_____ 13. William Stern	M.	Strategies
_____ 14. David Wechsler	N.	Primary abilities related to intelligence
_____ 15. Charles Spearman	O.	Developed IQ tests with several subscales
_____ 16. L. L. Thurstone	P.	Emotional intelligence
_____ 17. Robert Sternberg	Q.	Imaginary audience & personal fable
_____ 18. Howard Gardner	R.	Perspective taking
_____ 19. Daniel Goleman	S.	Adolescent decision-making
_____ 20. David Elkind	T.	Convergent & divergent thinking
_____ 21. Robert Selman	U.	Intelligence quotient (IQ)

"DR. DETAIL'S"
TERM MATCHING EXERCISE

Match the term with the correct definition.

_____	1.	operations	A. Refers to changing the level of support over the course of a teaching session
_____	2.	conservation	B. An expert stretches and supports the novice's understanding of and use of the culture's skills
_____	3.	classification	C. The retention of information over time
_____	4.	early formal operational thought	D. Emphasis is on the individual's cognitive construction of knowledge and understanding.
_____	5.	late formal operational thought	E. May appear during the middle adolescent years
_____	6.	scaffolding	F. Involves students taking turns leading a small-group discussion
_____	7.	cognitive apprenticeship	G. Mental actions that allow the individual to do mentally what was done before physically
_____	8.	cooperative learning	H. Limited capacity memory where information is retained for 30 seconds unless rehearsed
_____	9.	reciprocal teaching	I. Emphasizes that individuals actively construct knowledge and understanding
_____	10.	constructivism	J. Emphasis is on collaboration with others to produce knowledge and understanding
_____	11.	cognitive constructivist approach	K. Piaget's term for an individual's ability to recognize that the length, number, mass, quantity, area, weight, and volume of objects and substances do not change through transformations that alter their appearance
_____	12.	social constructivist approach	L. Involves students working in small groups to help each other learn
_____	13.	memory	M. Adolescent's have increased ability to think hypothetically
_____	14.	short-term memory	N. Piaget's concept of concrete operational thought, in which children systematically organize objects into hierarchies of classes and subclasses
_____	15.	working memory	O. Knowing about one's own (and others') knowing
_____	16.	long-term memory	P. A sense that adolescents have that they are unique, untouchable, and that no one else can understand them
_____	17.	meta-knowing skills	Q. Mental workbench where information is manipulated and assembled to help make decisions
_____	18.	imaginary audience	R. A relatively permanent memory system
_____	19.	personal fable	S. Adolescents believe they are the main actors in an imagined play, and all others are in the audience

PIAGET'S THEORY
SECTION REVIEW

1. Using any event or experience of your choice, describe how an existing schema was changed as a result of disequilibrium, assimilation, and accommodation.

    _____

    _____

2. Compare and contrast assimilation and accommodation.

    _____

    _____

3. How do children apply the mechanism, equilibration, in everyday life?

    _____

    _____

4. List and discuss the four stages of cognitive development according to Piaget.

    _____

    _____

    _____

    _____

5. Compare and contrast conservation and classification.

    _____

    _____

6. What were Piaget's main contributions to developmental theory?

    _____

    _____

7. How has Piaget's theory withstood the test of time?

    _____

    _____

8. What are some criticisms of Piaget's theory?

    _____

    _____

9.   What information supports the existence of a fifth, postformal stage in Piaget's theory?

_____

_____

KEY PEOPLE
IN SECTION

(Describe the contributions of this individual to the study and understanding of adolescence.)

David Elkind—

_____

_____

Robbie Case—

_____

_____

William Perry—

_____

_____

VYGOTSKY'S THEORY
SECTION REVIEW

1.   Fill in the boxes with the descriptions comparing the views of Piaget and Vygotsky.

Topic	Vygotsky	Piaget
Constructivism		
Stages		
View on education		
Teaching implications		

2.   What did Vygotsky mean by the zone of proximal development?

_____

_____

3. Explain how each of these contemporary cognitive concepts would be utilized in a secondary high school classroom.

   a. Scaffolding

   _____

   _____

   b. cognitive apprenticeship

   _____

   _____

   c. tutoring

   _____

   _____

   d. cooperative learning

   _____

   _____

   e. reciprocal teaching

   _____

   _____

4. Contrast the cognitive constructivist approach and social constructiveness approach.

   _____

   _____

KEY PEOPLE
IN SECTION

(Describe the contributions of this individual to the study and understanding of adolescence.)

Barbara Rogoff—

_____

_____

Ann Brown and Annamarie Palinscar—

_____

_____

THE INFORMATION –PROCESSING VIEW
SECTION REVIEW

1.   Describe the three main characteristics of the information-processing approach.

      _____

      _____

2.   Describe the following types of memory.

      a.   short-term memory

            _____

            _____

      b.   working memory

            _____

            _____

      c.   long-term memory

            _____

            _____

3.   How competent are adolescents at making decisions?

      _____

      _____

4.   What are some cognitive changes that allow for improved critical thinking in adolescence?

      _____

      _____

5.   Compare and contrast convergent and divergent thinking.

      _____

      _____

6.   Outline strategies to help adolescents become more creative.

      _____

      _____

7.   What are critical thinking skills that Sternberg believes adolescents need in everyday living?

_____

_____

8.   What are the characteristics of self-regulatory learners?

_____

_____

KEY PEOPLE
IN SECTION

(Describe the contributions of this individual to the study and understanding of adolescence.)

Robert Siegler—

_____

_____

Robbie Case—

_____

_____

Robert Sternberg—

_____

_____

Alan Baddeley—

_____

_____

Daniel Keating—

_____

_____

Richard Lewis—

_____

_____

Mark Strand—

_____

_____

Deanna Kuhn—

_____

_____

Michael Pressley—

_____

_____

Barry Zimmerman, Sebastian Bonner, and Robert Kovach —

_____

_____

THE PSYCHOMETRIC/INTELLIGENCE VIEW
SECTION REVIEW

1. Work the following IQs using Stern's formula ($IQ=MA/CA \times 100$).
    a.   MA = 10, CA = 8   _____
    b.   MA = 5, CA = 9   _____
    c.   MA = 15, CA = 12   _____

2. How do the Wechsler scales differ from the tests developed by Binet?

    _____

    _____

3. Describe how each of components of Sternberg's triarchic theory of intelligence would be utilized in writing a book report.

    _____

    _____

4. Match the skills indicative of each of Gardner's eight frames of mind to the profession or vocation in which they are most likely to be associated.

    _____ 1. scientists, engineers, accountants   A. verbal skills
    _____ 2. farmers, botanists, landscapers   B. intrapersonal
    _____ 3. teachers, mental health professionals   C. mathematical
    _____ 4. surgeons, dancers, athletes   D. naturalist
    _____ 5. composers, musicians   E. spatial
    _____ 6. theologians, psychologists   F. interpersonal
    _____ 7. authors, journalists, speakers   G. bodily-kinesthetic
    _____ 8. architects, artists, sailors   H. musical

5. According to Goleman, emotional intelligence involves four main areas:

    _____

    _____

6. Summarize the current status of the following debates about intelligence:

    a. Nature and nurture

        _____

        _____

    b. Ethnicity and culture

        _____

        _____

    c. Use and misuse of intelligence tests

        _____

        _____

KEY PEOPLE IN SECTION

(Describe the contributions of this individual to the study and understanding of adolescence.)

Aldous Huxley—

_____

_____

Alfred Binet—

_____

_____

Theophile Simon—

_____

_____

William Stern—

_____

_____

David Wechsler—

_____

_____

Charles Spearman—

_____

_____

L.L. Thurstone—

_____

_____

Robert Sternberg—

_____

_____

Howard Gardner—

_____

_____

Daniel Goleman—

_____

_____

SOCIAL COGNITION
SECTION REVIEW

1. Fill in the blanks with the name, age, and description of each of Selman's Stages of Perspective Taking.

Stage #	Stage name	Ages	Description
0			
1			
2			
3			
4			

2. Do you have a personal fable? What does it consist of? Do you think that it is important to have a personal fable? Why or why not?

_____

_____

3. Can the imaginary audience lead adolescents to make bad decisions?

_____

_____

4. Do adolescents conceptualize an individual's personality differently than children do?

_____

_____

KEY PEOPLE
IN SECTION

(Describe the contributions of this individual to the study and understanding of adolescence.)

David Elkind—

_____

_____

Robert Selman—

_____

_____

EXPLORATIONS
IN ADOLESCENCE

How can the *imaginary audience* and *personal fable* affect you in a positive or negative way?

a.   imaginary audience

_____

_____

b.   personal fable

_____

_____

COGNITIVE
CHALLENGE

If you could go back to high school, and restructure the courses and curriculum there, how could you add more critical opportunities?

_____

_____

ADOLESCENCE
IN RESEARCH

Concerning Selman's 1980 research about adolescent perspective taking, state the hypothesis, the research methods (if known), the research conclusions, and the implications and applications for adolescent development.

_____

_____

⊠ COMPREHENSIVE REVIEW

1.   According to Jean Piaget, the fundamental ways in which adolescents adapt their thinking entails
   a.   conservation and classification.
   b.   social information processing and perspective taking.
   c.   the imaginary audience and the personal fable.
   d.   assimilation and accommodation.

2.   When he learned the value of money, Kenny initially thought that a nickel was worth more than a dime. Recently, as he has begun to buy items, Kenny has come to realize the value of a dime. The process by which Kenny adapted his schema is
      a.   assimilation.
      b.   accommodation.
      c.   equilibration.
      d.   metacognition.

3.   Piaget believed that there is considerable movement between states of cognitive equilibrium and disequalibrium as assimilation and accommodation work in concert to produce cognitive change. He called this
      a.   assimilation.
      b.   accommodation.
      c.   equilibration.
      d.   metacognition.

4.   Which of the following is NOT a stage of cognitive development according to Piaget?
      a.   Sensorimotor
      b.   Preoperational
      c.   Concrete operational
      d.   Informal operational

5.   When children begin representing their worlds in images and words, they are in which stage of cognitive development?
      a.   Sensorimotor
      b.   Preoperational
      c.   Concrete operational
      d.   Informal operational

6.   A child begins to pull toys from her toy box; in so doing, she sorts them into piles of cars, trucks, and animals. She also understands that some toys can be switched from one pile to another or can form new piles based on types having similar colors. This behavior reflects the cognitive ability called
      a.   perspective taking.
      b.   classification.
      c.   organization.
      d.   conservation.

7.   Unlike the concrete operational child, the formal operational adolescent can demonstrate
      a.   assimilation.
      b.   reversible mental operations.
      c.   conservation ability.
      d.   hypothetical-deductive reasoning.

8.   Compared to the early formal operational problem solver, the late formal operational solver
      a.   derives her hypothesis from the problem data.
      b.   looks for a general hypothesis to explain what has happened.
      c.   is satisfied with general statements about cause and effect.
      d.   searches for necessary and sufficient conditions to explain the results.

9. Which of the following statements does not describe one of Jean Piaget's contributions to the field of cognitive development?
   a. Jean Piaget contributed a number of important concepts such as conservation and object permanence.
   b. Jean Piaget demonstrated that culture and education influence cognitive development.
   c. Jean Piaget demonstrated that we adapt to our environment.
   d. Jean Piaget made many insightful and systematic observations of children.

10. Which group of developmentalists believes that cognitive development is more specific in many respects than did Piaget?
    a. Piagetians
    b. Neo-Piagetians
    c. competency-based developmentalists
    d. information-processing developmentalists

11. Perhaps the greatest general criticism is that Piaget's theory tends to underestimate the importance of _____ in cognitive development.
    a. culture and education
    b. arts and entertainment
    c. authority and mystery
    d. sexuality and role playing

12. Which of the following is NOT a criticism of Piaget's theory?
    a. His theory assumes developmental synchrony, but that is often not the case.
    b. Some cognitive abilities emerge earlier than Piaget thought.
    c. Some children can be trained to perform at a higher level.
    d. Piaget's theory focuses too much on childhood sexual development.

13. Which of the following has been proposed as a probable fifth stage in Piaget's stages of development?
    a. Informal thought
    b. Formal thought
    c. Situational thought
    d. Postformal thought

14. Tasks too difficult for an individual that can be mastered with the help of more-skilled individuals defines what
    a. Jean Piaget called hypothetical-deductive reasoning.
    b. Lev Vygotsky called the zone of proximal development.
    c. Kurt Fisher called abstract relations.
    d. Neo-Piagetians called social information.

15. _____ refers to the changing of the level of support over the course of a teaching session.
    a. Intelligence
    b. Metacognition
    c. Scaffolding
    d. Equilibration

16.   Adolescent egocentrism is represented by two types of thinking referred to as
    a.   the imaginary audience and the personal fable.
    b.   the abiding self and the transient self.
    c.   narcissism and the imaginary audience.
    d.   the indestructible self and the transient self.

17.   Your 20-year-old friend confesses to you that she has always thought that somehow she was very different from everyone she knew, in her feelings and her understanding of the world. You might suspect that her sense of herself reflects
    a.   David Elkind's notion of the personal fable.
    b.   an organic pathology, perhaps a temporal lobe tumor.
    c.   a failure to achieve formal operational thought.
    d.   developmental delay of adolescence.

18.   Short-term memory is a limited-capacity memory system in which information is retained
    a.   for as long as 1 minute.
    b.   for as long as 1 hour.
    c.   for as long as 1 day.
    d.   for as long as 30 seconds.

19.   Alfred Binet and Theophile Simon created the first standardized IQ test, which was called
    a.   the Binet-Simon test.
    b.   the Stanford-Binet test.
    c.   the 1905 Scale.
    d.   the IQ Scale.

20.   _____ is credited with developing the concept of mental age (MA)?
    a.   William Stern
    b.   Theophile Simon
    c.   Alfred Binet
    d.   David Wechsler

21.   _____ is credited with developing the formula for calculating IQs ($IQ = MA/CA \times 100$)?
    a.   William Stern
    b.   Theophile Simon
    c.   Alfred Binet
    d.   David Wechsler

22.   Which of the following is NOT one of Howard Gardner's eight types of intelligence?
    a.   Verbal skills
    b.   Musical skills
    c.   Cooking skills
    d.   Naturalist skills

23.   Who is credited with proposing the concept of emotional intelligence?
    a.   Robert Sternberg
    b.   Daniel Goleman
    c.   Howard Gardner
    d.   Robert Selman

24. Which of the following is NOT one of Goleman's four main areas of emotional intelligence?
    a. Developing emotional self-awareness
    b. Reading emotions
    c. Controlling anger
    d. Managing emotions

25. Your adolescent sister says that people with red hair cannot be trusted. Your recognize that she is developing
    a. an inability to take another person's perspective.
    b. a dangerous form of prejudice.
    c. an implicit personality theory.
    d. a personal fable.

26. A Stanford-Binet test used in 1932 that was normed at 100 would yield an average score of _____ if administered to a large group of individuals today.
    a. 90
    b. 100
    c. 120
    d. 130

27. Which of the following is generally considered to be a culture-fair test?
    a. The Stanford-Binet test
    b. The Wechsler test
    c. The Raven Progressive Matrices test
    d. The Kaufman Assessment Battery for Children

28. While taking an IQ test, a series of numbers is read aloud to a student, with the student being asked to repeat them as quickly as possible. Which kind of memory is being assessed?
    a. Long-term
    b. Short-term
    c. Digital
    d. Conceptual

29. Which term includes the ability to learn from and adapt to our everyday lives?
    a. self
    b. intelligence
    c. knowable self
    d. learned personality

30. Alfred Binet developed intelligence tests to
    a. show that intelligence is largely the result of heredity.
    b. identify students who would not profit from typical schooling.
    c. identify students who were gifted, and needed extra challenges in their schooling.
    d. distinguish convergent thinkers from divergent thinkers.

31. One of the main advantages of the Wechsler scales over the Binet test is that the Wechsler scales include measures that are
    a. progressive.
    b. culturally specific.
    c. verbal.
    d. screen for brain damage.

32. The _____ intelligence test is often employed in assessing older adolescents because it is particularly good in identifying specific strengths and weaknesses in mental performance.
    a. Stanford-Binet
    b. WAIS-R
    c. WC-R
    d. Terman Intelligence Scale

33. Which of the following individuals did not propose a theory of intelligence?
    a. L.L. Thurstone
    b. Lewis Terman
    c. Charles Spearman
    d. Howard Gardner

34. The type or aspect of intelligence measured by the Binet and Wechsler tests is most closely matched to the aspect Sternberg calls
    a. componential intelligence.
    b. experiential intelligence.
    c. contextual intelligence.
    d. tacit knowledge.

35. According to Howard Gardner
    a. it is better to administer intelligence tests to individuals than to groups.
    b. intelligence is best defined in terms of eight frames of mind.
    c. individuals have a general intelligence rather than various specific intelligences.
    d. intelligence is best defined in terms of three main components.

36. In addition to the question of whether intelligence is primarily inherited, another important question about intelligence concerns
    a. the arbitrary distinction between aptitude and achievement tests.
    b. cultural and ethnic differences in test scores.
    c. using the computer as a model for information processing.
    d. the emotional and social adjustment of gifted individuals.

37. Intelligence tests explicit designed to minimize the differences between ethnic groups are called
    a. bias liberated.
    b. culture fair.
    c. socially equitable.
    d. psychometrically equivalent.

38. A psychology professor asks his students to think of as many uses as possible for a paper clip. The professor is encouraging
    a. brainstorming.
    b. divergent thinking
    c. convergent thinking.
    d. ideational originality.

ADOLESCENCE
ON THE SCREEN

■   *Phenomenon* explores the problems that come with high levels of intelligence.

■   *Little Man Tate* depicts the education of a young child prodigy.

■   *Searching for Bobby Fischer* depicts parents facing the dilemma of raising a gifted chess prodigy.

ADOLESCENCE
IN BOOKS

■   *Teaching and Learning Through Multiple Intelligences (Second Edition)*, by Linda Campbell, Bruce Campbell, and Dee Dickonson (Allyn & Bacon, 1999), provides applications of Gardner's eight intelligences to classrooms.

■   *How People Learn*, by Committee on Developments in the Science of Learning (National Academy Press, 1999), describes the current state of knowledge about how children and youth think and learn.

■   *Creating Minds*, by Howard Gardner (Basic Books: NY, 1993), proposes that intelligence can be divided into seven basic forms.

Answer Key

KEY TERMS

1. **schema** Piaget's theory of a concept or framework that exists in the individual's mind to organize and interpret information.

2. **assimilation** Occurs when individuals incorporate new information into existing knowledge.

3. **accommodation** Occurs when individuals adjust to new information.

4. **equilibration** A mechanism in Piaget's theory that explains how children or adolescents shift from one stage of thought to the next. The shift occurs as they experience cognitive conflict or a disequilibrium in trying to understand the world. Eventually, the child or adolescent resolves the conflict and reaches a balance or equilibrium.

5. **sensorimotor stage** Piaget's first stage of development, lasting from birth to about 2 years of age. In this stage, infants construct an understanding of the world by coordinating sensory experiences with physical, motoric actions.

6. **preoperational stage** Piaget's second stage, which lasts from about 2 to 7 years of age. In this stage children begin to represent their world with words, images, and drawings.

7. **concrete operational stage** Piaget's third stage, which lasts from about 7 to 11 years of age. In this stage, children can perform operations. Logical reasoning replaces intuitive thought as long as the reasoning can be applied to specific or concrete examples.

8. **formal operational stage** Piaget's fourth and final stage of cognitive development, which he believes emerges between 11 to 15 years of age. It is characterized by abstract, idealistic, and logical thought.

9. **hypothetical-deductive reasoning** Piaget's term for adolescents' ability, in the formal operational stage, to develop hypotheses, or best guesses, about ways to solve problems; they then systematically deduce, or conclude the best path to follow in solving the problem.

10. **neo-Piagetians** They argue that Piaget got some things right, but that his theory needs considerable revisions. In their revision, they give more emphasis to information processing that involves attention, memory, and strategies; they also seek to provide more precise explanations of cognitive changes.

11. **postformal thought** Postformal thought involves understanding that the correct answer to a problem requires reflective thinking and can vary from one situation to another, and that the search for truth is often an ongoing, never-ending process.

12. **zone of proximal development (ZPD)** Vygotsky's concept that refers to the range of tasks that are too difficult for individuals to master alone, but that can be mastered with the guidance or assistance of adults or more skilled peers.

13. **critical thinking** Thinking reflectively, productively, and evaluating the evidence.

14.   **creativity** The ability to think about something in novel and unusual ways and come up with unique solutions to problems.

15.   **convergent thinking** According to Guilford, a pattern of thinking in which individuals produce one correct answer; characteristic of the terms on conventional intelligence tests.

16.   **divergent thinking** According to Guilford, a pattern of thinking in which individuals produce many answers to the same question; more characteristic of creativity than convergent thinking.

17.   **metacognition** Cognition about cognition, or "knowing about knowing."

18.   **self-regulatory learning** Consists of the self-generation and self-monitoring of thoughts, feelings, and behaviors to reach a goal.

19.   **psychometric/intelligence view** Emphasizes the importance of individual differences in intelligence. Many advocates of this view also argue that intelligence should be assessed with intelligence tests.

20.   **intelligence** Mental ability related to verbal and problem-solving skills, and the ability to adapt to and learn from life's everyday experiences. Not everyone agrees on what constitutes intelligence.

21.   **mental age (MA)** Developed by Binet, an individual's level of mental development relative to others.

22.   **intelligent quotient (IQ)** A person's tested mental age divided by chronological age, multiplied by 100.

23.   **normal distribution** A symmetrical distribution of values or scores with a majority of scores falling in the middle of the possible range of scores and few scores appearing toward the extremes of the range; a distribution that yields what is called a "bell-shaped curve."

24.   **triarchic theory of intelligence** Sternberg's view that intelligence comes in three main forms: analytical, experiential, and contextual.

25.   **emotional intelligence** A form of social intelligence that involves the ability to monitor one's own and others' feelings and emotions, to discriminate among them, and to sue this information to guide one's thinking and action.

26.   **culture-fair tests** Tests of intelligence that attempt to be free of cultural bias.

27.   **adolescent egocentrism** The heightened self-consciousness of adolescents, which is reflected in their belief that others are as interested in them as they are in themselves.

28.   **implicit personality theory** The layperson's conception of personality.

KEY PEOPLE
IN THE STUDY OF ADOLESCENCE

1.	C	2.	F	3.	G	4.	I	5.	H
6.	J	7.	S	8.	T	9.	K	10.	M
11.	L	12.	B	13.	U	14.	O	15.	D
16.	N	17.	E	18.	A	19.	P	20.	Q
21.	R								

"DR. DETAIL'S"
TERM MATCHING EXERCISE

1.	G	**2.**	K	**3.**	N	**4.**	M	**5.**	E
6.	A	**7.**	B	**8.**	L	**9.**	F	**10.**	I
11.	D	**12.**	J	**13.**	C	**14.**	H	**15.**	Q
16.	R	**17.**	O	**18.**	S	**19.**	P		

PIAGET'S THEORY
SECTION REVIEW

1. No answer provided—personal reflection. However, the answer should describe the preexisting schema, the disequilibrium that resulted as the result of the new information or experience, indicate the new information that was assimilated, and state how the old schema accommodated the new information.

2. Assimilation occurs when individuals incorporate new information into existing knowledge. Accommodation occurs when individuals adjust to new information.

3. Equilibration is a mechanism in Piaget's theory that explains how children or adolescents shift from one state of thought to the next. The shift occurs as they experience cognitive conflict or disequilibrium in trying to understand the world. Eventually, the child or adolescent resolves the conflict and reaches a balance, or equilibrium of thought.

4. Sensorimotor stage—infants construct an understanding of the world by coordinating sensory experiences with physical, motoric actions.
Preoperational stage—children begin to represent their world with words, images, and drawings.
Concrete operational thought—children can perform operations. Logical reasoning replaces intuitive thought as long as the reasoning can be applied to specific or concrete examples.
Formal operational stage—characterized by abstract, idealistic, and logical thought.

5. Conservation is Piaget's term for an individual's ability to recognize that the length, number, mass, quantities, area, weight, and volume of objects and substances do not change through transformations that alter their appearance.
Classification is Piaget's concept of concrete operational thought, in which children systematically organize objects into hierarchies of classes and subclasses.

6. Piaget was the foundation for much of the current field of cognitive development.

7. Piaget's theory has withstood the test of time quite well. However, it has not gone unchallenged, in particular by those with specific criticisms (neo-Piagetians).

8. Questions have been raised regarding these areas: *Estimates of children's competence*—abilities are probably too fluid to be measured in Piaget's fashion; *Stages*—Piaget's theory assumes developmental synchrony, which is not consistent; *Training children to reason at a higher level*—it would appear that if properly trained, children can skip whole stages; *Culture and education*—these exert more influence on development than Piaget envisioned.

9. Evidence for the fifth, postformal stage has yet to be documented that would clearly show a more advanced stage than formal operational thought.

KEY PEOPLE
IN SECTION

David Elkind—proposed communication and interaction with the environment in applying cognitive development to education.

Robbie Case—Canadian developmental psychologist that believes more precise description of changes within each stage needs to be carried out.

William Perry—said that younger adolescents tend to view the world in terms of polarities (i.e., right/wrong, or good/bad).

VYGOTSKY'S THEORY
SECTION REVIEW

1.

Topic	Vygotsky	Piaget
Constructivism	Social constructivist	Cognitive constructivist
Stages	No general stages of development proposed	Strong emphasis on stages—sensorimotor, preoperational, concrete operational, and formal operational.
View on education	Education plays a central role in helping children learn the tools of the culture	Education merely refines the child's cognitive skills that already have emerged.
Teaching implications	Teacher is facilitator and guide, not director; establishes learning opportunities for children to learn with teacher and more skilled peers	Teacher is facilitator and guide, but not director; teacher provides support for children to explore their world and discover knowledge.

2. Zone of proximal development refers to the range of tasks that are too difficult for an individual to master alone, but can be mastered with the guidance of adults or skilled peers.

3. a. Scaffolding involves direct teaching, with less guidance provided by teacher or more advanced peer as student learns more.
   b. Cognitive apprenticeship involves an adult or expert modeling thinking strategies and allowing students to anticipate or complete the expert's next step or idea.
   c. Tutoring involves a cognitive apprenticeship between an adult or more skilled adolescent. Fellow students are more effective tutors, and peer tutoring also benefits the tutor.
   d. Cooperative learning involves working and learning in small groups.
   e. Reciprocal teaching involves students taking turns leading a small group discussion. The teacher gradually assumes a less active role, letting the student assume more initiative.

4. In a cognitive constructivist approach, emphasis is on the individual's cognitive construction of knowledge and understanding. In a social constructivist approach emphasis is on collaboration with others to produce knowledge and understanding.

KEY PEOPLE
IN SECTION

Barbara Rogoff—felt that cognitive development occurs as new generations collaborate with older generations in varying forms of interpersonal engagement.

Ann Brown and Annamarie Palinscar—used reciprocal teaching to improve students' abilities to enact certain strategies to improve their reading comprehension.

THE INFORMATION-PROCESSING VIEW
SECTION REVIEW

1. Thinking, change mechanisms, and encoding.

2. a. Short-term memory—is a limited-capacity memory system in which information is retained for as long as 30 seconds.
    b. Working memory—is a kind of "mental workbench" where information is manipulated and assembled to help make decisions, solve problems, and comprehend written and spoken language.
    c. Long-term memory—is a relatively permanent memory system that holds huge amounts of information for a long period of time.

3. Compared to children, young adolescents are more likely to generate options that will lead to appropriate decisions.

4. Increased speed and capacity of information processing, which free cognitive resources for other purposes. More breadth of content knowledge in a variety of domains. Increased ability to construct new combinations of knowledge. A greater range and more spontaneous use of strategies or procedures for applying or obtaining knowledge.

5. Convergent thinking produces one correct answer and is characteristic of the kind of thinking required on a conventional intelligence test. Divergent thinking produces many answers to the same question and is more characteristic of creativity.

6. a. Have adolescents engage in brainstorming and come up with as many meaningful ideas as possible.
    b. Provide adolescents with environments that stimulate creativity.
    c. Don't overcontrol.
    d. Encourage internal motivation.
    e. Foster flexible and playful thinking.
    f. Introduce adolescents to creative people.
    g. Talk with adolescents about creative people or have them read about them.

7. Intelligence comes in three forms: analytical, experiental, and contextual.

8. Self regulatory learners (1) set goals for extending their knowledge and sustaining their motivation; (2) are aware of their emotional make-up and have strategies for managing their emotions; (3) periodically monitor their progress toward a goal; (4) fine tune or revise their strategies based on the progress they are making; and (5) evaluate obstacles that may arise and make the necessary adaptations.

KEY PEOPLE IN SECTION

Robert Siegler—Developed views related to information processing.

Robbie Case—Believed adolescents process information differently than children.

Robert Sternberg—Developed the triarchic theory of intelligence.

Alan Baddeley—Proposed the concept of working memory.

Daniel Keating—Researched decision making in adolescents.

Richard Lewis—Poet who visits classrooms in New York City to assist in developing creative thinking skills in children.

Mark Strand—A Poet Laureate who said that his most creative moments come when he loses a sense of time and is absorbed in what he is doing.

Deanna Kuhn—Believes that metacognition should be a stronger focus of efforts to help individuals become better critical thinkers.

Michael Pressley—Felt the key to education is helping students learn a rich repertoire of strategies that result in solutions to problems.

Barry Zimmerman, Sebastian Bonner, and Robert Kovach—Developed a model of turning low-self-regulatory students into students who engaged in adopting specific, positive learning goals.

PSYCHOMETRIC/INTELLIGENCE VIEW
SECTION REVIEW

1. a.   125
    b.   55
    c.   125

2. Wechsler has both verbal and performance subscales, whereas the tests developed by Binet are predominantly verbally loaded.

3. Analytical—Analyze the book's main themes.
    Creative—Generate new ideas about how the book might have been better written.
    Practical—Think about how the book's themes can be applied to real life.

4. | 1. C | 2. D | 3. F | 4. G | 5. H |
    |------|------|------|------|------|
    | 6. B | 7. A | 8. E | | |

5. Developing emotional self-awareness; managing emotions; reading emotions; and, handling relationships.

6. a.   Nature and nurture—Heredity is an important part of intelligence.
    b.   Ethnicity and culture—There are ethnic differences in the average scores on standardized intelligence tests between African American and White American adolescents, but the differences

are believed to be the result of environmental factors such as social, economic, and educational opportunities.

    c.   Use and misuse of intelligence tests—Intelligence tests can lead to stereotypes and expectations about adolescents and should not be used as the main or sole characteristic of competence. Further, intelligence tests do not take into account the many domains of intelligence, such as those described by Sternberg and Gardner.

KEY PEOPLE
IN SECTION

Aldous Huxley—Said that children are remarkable for their curiosity and intelligence.

Alfred Binet—Develop the concept of mental age (MA).

Theophile Simon—Binet's student and collaborator in developing the 1905 test.

William Stern—Created the concept of the intelligence quotient (IQ).

David Wechsler—Developed several IQ tests with multiple subscales.

Charles Spearman—Said that people have both a general intelligence (*g*), and specific types of intelligence (*s*).

L.L. Thurstone—Identified primary mental abilities: verbal comprehension, number ability, word fluency, spatial visualization, associative memory, reasoning, and perceptual speed.

Robert Sternberg—Developed the triarchic theory of intelligence.

Howard Gardner—Identified eight types of intelligence.

Daniel Goleman—Feels that emotional intelligence is more important than IQ when predicting an adolescent's competence.

SOCIAL COGNITION
SECTION REVIEW

1.

Stage #	Stage name	Ages	Description
0	Egocentric	3–6	No distinction between social perspective of self and others
1	Social-informational perspective taking	6–8	Ability to focus on one social perspective rather than coordinating viewpoints
2	Self-reflective perspective taking	8–10	Can form coordinated chain of perspectives but cannot understand simultaneous mutuality
3	Mutual perspective taking	10–12	Understands simultaneous mutuality between two people and can also view the interaction from an additional third person perspective
4	Social and conventional system perspective taking	12–15	Adolescent realizes mutual perspective taking is a necessary social convention

2. No answer provided—personal reflection.

3. Yes. Popular examples suggest that they may lead to acts of violence, amongst other things.

4. Adolescents are more likely to interpret an individual's personality in the way that many personality theorists do, as opposed to children.

KEY PEOPLE
IN SECTION

David Elkind—Believes that adolescent egocentrism can be dissected into two types of social thinking – imaginary audience and personal fable.

Robert Selman—Proposed a developmental theory of perspective taking.

EXPLORATIONS
IN ADOLESCENCE

No answer provided—personal reflection.

COGNITIVE
CHALLENGE

No answer provided—personal reflection.

ADOLESCENCE
IN RESEARCH

The hypothesis, perspective taking involves a series of five stages, ranging from 3 years of age through adolescence. By analyzing children's and adolescent's responses to perspective taking dilemmas, Selman concluded that their perspective taking follows the developmental sequence he proposed.

⊠ COMPREHENSIVE REVIEW

1.	d	2.	b	3.	c	4.	d	5.	b
6.	b	7.	d	8.	d	9.	b	10.	b
11.	a	12.	d	13.	d	14.	b	15.	c
16.	a	17.	a	18.	d	19.	c	20.	c
21.	a	22.	c	23.	b	24.	c	25.	c
26.	c	27.	c	28.	b	29.	b	30.	c
31.	c	32.	b	33.	b	34.	a	35.	b

36. b   37.   b   38.   b

Chapter 5   Families

Learning Goals with Key Terms and Key People in Boldface

1.0   EXPLAIN THE NATURE OF FAMILY PROCESSES

A.   Reciprocal Socialization, Synchrony, and the Family As A System
- 1.1   What is **reciprocal socialization**, and how does it affect adolescent development?
- 1.2   What is meant by parent-adolescent **synchrony**?
- 1.3   What defines a family's social system?

B.   Developmental Construction of Relationships
- 1.4   What is the **developmental construction** of relationships?
- 1.5   Why are close relationships with parents important for adolescent's development?
- 1.6   What are the main variations of the **developmental construction views**?
- 1.7   What is the difference between the **continuity view** and the **discontinuity view**?
- 1.8   What research evidence exists in support of each view?

C.   Maturation of the Adolescent and Maturation of Parents
- 1.9   What parental and adolescent maturation processes affect parent-adolescent interaction?
- 1.10   What are the major changes in adolescence that influence parent-adolescent relationships?
- 1.11   What dimensions of the adolescent's social world contribute to parent-adolescent relationships?
- 1.12   What parental changes contribute to parent-adolescent relationships?
- 1.13   How does the timing of parenthood affect parent-adolescent interaction?

D.   Sociocultural and Historical Changes
- 1.14   What sociocultural and historical changes affect family processes?
- 1.15   What sociocultural changes have made families different than they were 50 years ago?

E.   The Roles of Cognition and Emotion in Family Relationships
- 1.16   What roles do cognition and emotions play in family socialization?
- 1.17   What parental cognitive factors affect their children's social development?
- 1.18   What processes help us understand family relationships?

2.0   DISCUSS PARENT-ADOLESCENT RELATIONSHIPS

A.   Parents as Managers
- 2.1   What do we mean when we say that parents should manage their adolescent's lives?

B.   Parenting Techniques
- 2.2   What are the four main parenting categories according to Baumrind, and which one is most closely associated with socially competent behavior?

2.3   What is the nature of authoritarian, authoritative, neglectful, and indulgent parenting styles?

2.4   Which is the most effective parenting style?

C.   Parent-Adolescent Conflict

2.5   What is the nature and extent of parent-adolescent conflict?

2.6   At what point in adolescence does conflict peak?

2.7   What is the subject of most parental-adolescent conflict?

2.8   What beneficial effects may conflict have on adolescents?

2.9   What is the generation gap?

2.10   How much empirical support is there for the existence of a generation gap?

2.11   What percentage of families is parent-adolescent conflict high?

2.12   What problems are associated with intense, prolonged conflict?

D.   Autonomy and Attachment

2.13   How important are autonomy and attachment in an adolescent's successful adaptation to adulthood?

2.14   What is the difference between autonomy and **emotional autonomy**?

2.15   What is the appropriate time for adolescents to achieve autonomy from their parents?

2.16   What problems do parents have with their adolescent's achieving autonomy?

2.17   Are there gender differences seen with regards to adolescent autonomy?

2.18   What developmental transition signals autonomy?

2.19   Explain the four distinct patterns (dimensions) of adolescent autonomy.

2.20   Why do some adolescents run away from home, and what problems might they be susceptible to as a result?

2.21   What is the best advice to give a parent about their adolescent's need for autonomy?

2.22   Why is it important that adolescents be both autonomous and attached to their parents?

2.23   What is the difference between **secure attachment** and **insecure attachment**?

2.24   Why is secure attachment related social competence and successful adaptation to the world?

2.25   What is the Adult Attachment Interview (AAI)?

2.26   What is the difference between **dismissing/avoidant attachment, preoccupied/ambivalent attachment,** and **unresolved/disorganized attachment**?

3.0   KNOW ABOUT SIBLING RELATIONSHIPS

A.   Sibling Roles

3.1   What is the nature and extent of conflict in many sibling relationships?

3.2   How much does conflict characterize adolescent relationships?

B.   Developmental Changes

3.3   How do sibling relationships change over time?

C.   Birth Order

3.4   How does birth order affect sibling and parent relationships?

3.5   Is an only child likely to be a "spoiled brat"?

3.6   What is the most reasonable conclusion to be gained from research about the effects of birth order on adolescent behavior and achievement?

4.0   DESCRIBE THE EFFECTS OF DIVORCE, STEPFAMILIES, AND WORKING PARENTS

A.   Divorce

4.1   How do adolescents adjust to divorce in their families?

4.2   Should parents stay together for the sake of the children?

4.3   Should parents stay together for the sake of their children and adolescents?

4.4   How much do parenting skills matter in divorced families?

4.5   How much do post-divorce family processes affect adolescent adjustment to divorce?

4.6   What factors contribute to adolescent risk and vulnerability to divorce?

4.7   What role does socioeconomic status play in the lives of adolescents in divorced families?

B.   Stepfamilies

4.8   What adjustment problems are associated with adolescents who live in stepfamilies?

4.9   What is the most difficult time for adolescents to experience their parents' remarriage?

4.10   What is **boundary ambiguity**?

4.11   How do you compare adolescent's relationships with their biological and stepparents?

4.12   What is the difference between complex and simple stepfamilies and in which do adolescents have more problems?

C.   Working Parents

4.13   What is the effect of parental work on the development of children and adolescents?

4.14   What effect do working mothers have on adolescent development?

4.15   What are the special adjustment problems of latchkey adolescents?

4.16   What is the effect of relocation on adolescent development?

4.17   How does parental unemployment affect adolescents?

5.0 UNDERSTAND CULTURE, ETHNICITY, GENDER, AND PARENTING

A.   Culture and Ethnicity

5.1   What roles do culture and ethnicity play in families?

5.2   What is the effect of culture on parental roles and discipline styles and family support systems?

5.3   In what ways do ethnic minority families differ from White American families?

5.4   What are the main differences between White-American families and African-American and Latino families?

B.   Gender and Parenting

5.5   How do gender and gender roles affect families?

5.6   What is the mother's role in the family today?

5.7   What is the father's role in today's family?

5.8   How can mothers and fathers become cooperative and effective parenting partners?

6.0 EVALUATE SOCIAL POLICY AND FAMILIES

6.1   What are the recommendations of the Carnegie Council on Adolescent Development regarding social policies for families with adolescents?

Exercises

KEY TERMS
COMPLETION EXERCISE

Each key term is presented in the form of an incomplete sentence. Complete each sentence by either defining the term or giving an example. Compare your definitions with those given at the end of the study guide chapter.

1.   By using **reciprocal socialization**, Suzy has changed her parents

_____

_____

2.   **Synchrony** can best be explained as

_____

_____

3.   According to the **developmental construction view**

_____

_____

4.   The **continuity view** holds that

_____

_____

5.   The **discontinuity view** holds that

_____

_____

6.   Billy's mom uses **authoritarian parenting** in that

_____

_____

7.   **Authoritative parenting** allows a child to

_____

_____

8.   **Neglectful parenting** can result in

_____

_____

9.   **Indulgent parenting** over time can lead to

_____

_____

10.   **Emotional autonomy** is the capacity to

_____

_____

11.   **Insecure attachment** is a maladaptive pattern that is seen in

_____

_____

12.   **Secure attachment** is very important because

_____

_____

13.   **Dismissing/avoidant attachment** can result in

_____

_____

14.   **Preoccupied/ambivalent attachment** can result in

_____

_____

15.   **Unresolved/disorganized attachment** can lead to

_____

_____

16.   **Boundary ambiguity** can be a problem in stepfamilies because

_____

_____

KEY PEOPLE
IN ADOLESCENT DEVELOPMENT

Match the person with the event or concept in adolescent development with which they are associated.

_____	1. Andrew Collins	A.	Parenting styles
_____	2. Diana Baumrind	B.	Infant attachment research
_____	3. John Bowlby and Mary Ainsworth	C.	Adolescent adjustment to parental divorce
_____	4. Joseph Allen	D.	Adolescent-parental attachment
_____	5. E. Mavis Hetherington	E.	Adolescent cognitive changes
_____	6. Lois Hoffman	F.	Studied effects of maternal employment

"DR. DETAIL'S"
LIBRARY EXERCISE

Go to the library at your institution and look up archival materials that go into some detail as to what family life was in the year 1900. Then, using that information, compare families then with families now. How are they similar, and how are they different?

_____

_____

_____

_____

_____

_____

_____

_____

THE NATURE OF FAMILY PROCESSES
SECTION REVIEW

1. Describe how a child might use the process of reciprocal socialization to his/her advantage.

_____

_____

2. Differentiate between reciprocal socialization and synchrony.

_____

_____

3.   Compare and contrast the continuity and discontinuity views.

_____

_____

4.   In Mark Twain's view, what transforms as adolescents move from childhood to adulthood?

_____

_____

5.   What dimensions of the adolescent's social world contribute to parent-adolescent relationships?

_____

_____

6.   Is parent-child interaction different for families in which parents delay having children until their thirties or forties?

_____

_____

7.   What kinds of effects did the Great Depression have on families?

_____

_____

8.   What role do cognitive processes play in socialization within families?

_____

_____

KEY PEOPLE IN SECTION

(Describe the contributions of this individual to the study and understanding of adolescence.)

Alan Sroufe—

_____

_____

Andrew Collins—

_____

_____

Mark Twain—

_____

_____

Margaret Mead—

_____

_____

PARENT-ADOLESCENT RELATIONSHIPS
SECTION REVIEW

1. Match the terms with the correct definitions or descriptions.

_____	1. autonomy	A.	Parents are uninvolved
_____	2. emotional autonomy	B.	Highly restrictive, punitive parenting style
_____	3. authoritarian parenting style	C.	Adolescents de-emphasize the importance of attachment
_____	4. authoritative parenting style	D.	Adolescents are hypertuned to attachment issues
_____	5. indulgent parenting style	E.	Parenting style associated with social competence
_____	6. neglectful parenting style	F.	Parenting style associated with social incompetence
_____	7. dismissing/avoidant attachment	G.	Relinquishing childlike dependence on parents
_____	8. preoccupied/ambivalent attachment	H.	Adolescent has an unusually high fear
_____	9. unresolved/disorganized attachment	I.	Caregiver (usually mom) is used as a secure base from which to explore the environment
_____	10. secure attachment	J.	Related with independence and self-direction
_____	11. insecure attachment	K.	Infants avoid the caregiver or show ambivalence toward them

2. Why do adolescents run away from their homes?

_____

_____

KEY PEOPLE
IN SECTION

(Describe the contributions of this individual to the study and understanding of adolescence.)

Diana Baumrind—

_____

_____

Judith Smetana—

_____

_____

Reed Larson—

_____

_____

John Bowlby—

_____

_____

Mary Ainsworth—

_____

_____

SIBLING RELATIONSHIPS
SECTION REVIEW

1.   How much of a problem is sibling conflict in adolescence?

_____

_____

2.   What are later-born children like as compared to first-born?

_____

_____

3.   Is the 'only child' always a "spoiled brat?"

_____

_____

THE EFFECTS OF DIVORCE, STEPFAMILIES, AND WORKING PARENTS SECTION REVIEW

1.   What factors affect the adolescent's individual risk and vulnerability in a divorced family?

_____

_____

2.   What role does socioeconomic status play in the lives of adolescents in divorced families?

_____

_____

3.   How much do family processes matter in a divorce?

_____

_____

4.   What are the three common types of stepfamily structures?

_____

_____

5.   Do children in stepfamilies have more adjustment problems than other children?

_____

_____

6.   What are some negative experiences faced by 'latchkey' adolescents?

_____

_____

7.   What effect does unemployment have on families and on adolescents' development?

_____

_____

KEY PEOPLE
IN SECTION

(Describe the contributions of this individual to the study and understanding of adolescence.)

James Bray—

_____

_____

E. Mavis Hetherington—

_____

_____

Lois Hoffman—

_____

_____

Nancy Galambos—

_____

_____

Thomas and Lynette Long—

_____

_____

Joan Lipsitz—

_____

_____

UNDERSTANDING CULTURE, ETHNICITY, GENDER, AND PARENTING
SECTION REVIEW

1.   In what ways do minority families differ from White American families?

_____

_____

2.   What is the mother's role in the family?

_____

_____

3.   What is the father's role in the family?

_____

_____

4.   How actively are today's fathers involved with their children and adolescents?

_____

_____

KEY PEOPLE
IN SECTION

(Describe the contributions of this individual to the study and understanding of adolescence.)

Frank Furstenburg and Kathleen Harris—

_____

_____

SOCIAL POLICY AND FAMILIES
SECTION REVIEW

1.   What must parents do if they wish to see their adolescents develop in a competent manner?

_____

_____

EXPLORATIONS
IN ADOLESCENCE

1.   Compare and contrast the extended family structures in African-American and Mexican-American families. What positive effects do these systems have on adolescent development?

_____

_____

COGNITIVE CHALLENGE

1. Write down your ideas for how an adolescent boy or girl (you choose which one you would like to discuss) and his or her parents could engage in collaborative problem solving to set ground rules for dating.

   _____

   _____

2. Talk to one of your friends or acquaintances whose parents separated when they were teenagers (or use yourself if your parents did so). When, how, and what did their parents tell them about the separation? Could they have done it in a better way? What suggestions would they give to parents of teenagers who are about to separate?

   _____

   _____

ADOLESCENCE IN RESEARCH

Concerning Diana Baumrind's 1991 research analyzing parenting styles and social competence in adolescence, state the hypothesis, the research methods (if known), the research conclusions, and the implications and applications for adolescent development.

   _____

   _____

 COMPREHENSIVE REVIEW

1. The carefully coordinated interaction between the parent and the child or adolescent.
   a. reciprocal socialization
   b. maturation
   c. discontinuity
   d. synchrony

2. Relationships more likely to consist of participants who relate to each other on equal terms.
   a. Sibling-child
   b. Parent-child
   c. Peer-child
   d. Teacher-child

3.   Once remarked that when he was 14 his father was so ignorant he could hardly stand him, but by age 21 he was surprised how much his father had learned in those 7 years?
    a.   Jean Piaget
    b.   Charles Darwin
    c.   Mark Twain
    d.   Sigmund Freud

4.   The time when marital dissatisfaction is greater
    a.   when offspring is a newborn.
    b.   when offspring is an adolescent.
    c.   when offspring is a child.
    d.   when offspring is an adult.

5.   What frequently happens between adolescents and parents?
    a.   They compete for family resources.
    b.   They violate one another's expectations.
    c.   They reject one another's personal space.
    d.   They get along well because they share similar levels of cognitive development.

6.   Marital dissatisfaction is greatest when their offspring are
    a.   adolescents.
    b.   young children.
    c.   older children.
    d.   adults.

7.   Which of the following is NOT one of Baumrind's four types of parenting?
    a.   Indulgent.
    b.   Power assertion.
    c.   Authoritarian.
    d.   Neglectful.

8.   A restrictive, punitive style of parenting.
    a.   Indulgent
    b.   Authoritative
    c.   Authoritarian
    d.   Neglectful

9.   Parents who encourage their adolescents to be independent, but still place limits on what they can do.
    a.   Indulgent
    b.   Authoritative
    c.   Authoritarian
    d.   Neglectful

10.   A style in which the parent is very uninvolved in the life of the adolescent.
    a.   Indulgent
    b.   Authoritative
    c.   Authoritarian
    d.   Neglectful

11. Diane Baumrind describes authoritative parents as
    a. restrictive, punitive, and allowing little verbal guide.
    b. encouraging independence and placing limits on adolescents' actions.
    c. power assertive, rejecting, unresponsive, and parent centered.
    d. undemanding, rejecting, uninvolved, and controlling.

12. Bill's parents have few rules for household conduct or academic expectations. They do not punish Bill when he violates rules, but merely accept his behavior. Bill is likely to develop
    a. social competence because his parents unconditionally accept him.
    b. anxiety about social comparisons and social inferiority feelings.
    c. self-reliance, social responsibility, and autonomy.
    d. little impulse control and disregard for rules.

13. The increased independence that typifies adolescence.
    a. Synchrony
    b. Autonomy
    c. Indulgence
    d. Reciprocal socialization

14. Conflict between adolescents and parents is typically strongest in early adolescence, and may be a healthy aspect of the development of
    a. autonomy.
    b. attachment.
    c. parenting skills.
    d. dating skills.

15. You are depressed because you argue with your 10-year-old daughter almost daily, and these arguments last for several minutes. Experts on adolescents would tell you that
    a. this high level of conflict will lead to later disturbances.
    b. this type of conflict is normal, and you should not worry about it.
    c. if you are arguing this much now, your arguments will increase in later adolescence.
    d. these arguments will prevent your daughter from developing an autonomous identity.

16. The most crucial transition for the development of adolescent autonomy is from
    a. school to work.
    b. high school to college.
    c. middle school to high school.
    d. virginity to sexual activity.

17. What percent of American adolescents currently have one or more siblings?
    a. 50%
    b. 25%
    c. 60%
    d. 80%

18. Adolescents who are securely attached to their parents
     a. cannot adequately develop autonomy.
     b. show less secure attachment to peers.
     c. have more difficulty engaging with peers and separating from parents.
     d. have higher self-esteem than insecurely attached peers.

19. Sibling conflict is often lower in adolescence than in childhood due to changes in
     a. social development.
     b. physical development.
     c. the power relationship.
     d. the way parents deal with conflict.

20. Firstborn children are
     a. more achievement-oriented than those born later.
     b. less achievement-oriented than those born later.
     c. more psychologically well adjusted than those born later.
     d. on the average, less socially responsible than those born later.

21. Which of the following is NOT one of the three common types of stepfamily structures?
     a. Stepfather
     b. Compound
     c. Complex
     d. Stepmother

22. _____ refers to the confusion in stepfamilies regarding the membership of the family and each individual's responsibility.
     a. Family blending
     b. Boundary ambiguity
     c. Stepfamily dynamism
     d. Stepfamily individuation

23. According to James Bray, given time stepfamilies fall into three types based on their relationships. Which of the following is NOT one of those types?
     a. Neo-traditional
     b. Matriarchal
     c. Romantic
     d. New breed

24. After coming home from school, Juan washes the breakfast dishes, does the laundry, and starts dinner before his parents get home at 6 P.M. Juan is a
     a. hurried child.
     b. latchkey child.
     c. neglected child.
     d. stepchild.

25. Ethnic families tend to differ from White American families in that the former
    a. are smaller.
    b. show more extended networks.
    c. encourage more autonomy among girls than boys.
    d. have more employed mothers.

26. It is a mistake to attribute the problems of adolescents to their mothers because
    a. fathers spend more time with children and adolescents than ever before.
    b. mothers and fathers are partners in parenting.
    c. behavior is determined by multiple factors.
    d. peers and siblings have more influence on adolescents than parents.

27. Fathers of adolescents who are older than most other fathers of children that age are
    a. more likely to enforce rules than younger fathers.
    b. warmer and communicate better than younger fathers.
    c. more aloof than younger fathers.
    d. more demanding than younger fathers.

28. African American and Latino adolescents are most likely to differ from White adolescents in that the former are more likely to
    a. live in extended families.
    b. live in rural areas.
    c. attend church.
    d. use drugs.

ADOLESCENCE ON THE SCREEN

- *Ordinary People* concerns parents and their teenage son's struggle to deal with the death of a younger sibling. The surviving son feels guilt and blame, leading him to suicidal depression.

- *Tumbleweeds* is the story of a displaced single mother and her teenage daughter who move from place to place and live on a shoestring, while the mother looks for a man that will give them a better life.

- *Liberty House* depicts the changing sociopolitical climate of the 1950s, including integration, interracial dating, and changing family structure and influence.

ADOLESCENCE IN BOOKS

- *Between Parent & Teenager*, by Haim Ginott (Avon: NY, 1999), continues to be one of the most widely read and recommended books for parents who want to communicate more effectively with their teenagers.

- *Surviving the Breakup: How Children and Parents Cope with Divorce*, by Judith Wallerstein & Joan B. Kelly (Basic Books: NY, 1996), adds more empirical data to back up theories regarding what happens after divorce.

- *Growing Up with Divorce*, by Neil Kalter (Free Press: NY, 1990), provides divorced parents with information to help their children and youth avoid emotional problems.

- *I'm Not Mad, I Just Hate You!*, by R. Cohen-Sandler & M. Silver (Viking: NY, 1999), deals with adolescent mother/daughter conflict.

- *The Shelter of Each Other: Rebuilding Our Families*, by Mary Pipher (Ballantine: NY, 1996), calls for strengthening the family for the benefit of children, parents, and grandparents.

Answer Key

KEY TERMS

1.   **reciprocal socialization** The process by which children and adolescents socialize parents, just as parents socialize them.

2.   **synchrony** The carefully coordinated interaction between the parent and the child or adolescent in which, often unknowingly, they are attuned to each other's behavior.

3.   **developmental construction views** Views sharing the belief that as individuals grow up, they acquire modes of relating to others. There are two main variations of this view. One emphasizes continuity and stability in relationships throughout the life span, the other emphasizes discontinuity and changes in relationships throughout the life span.

4.   **continuity view** A developmental view that emphasizes the role of early parent-child relationships in constructing a basic way of relating to people throughout the life span.

5.   **discontinuity view** A developmental view that emphasizes change and growth in relationships over time.

6.   **authoritarian parenting** This is a restrictive, punitive style in which the parent exhorts the adolescent to follow the parent's directions and to respect work and effort. Firm limits and controls are placed on adolescents, and little verbal exchange is allowed. This style is associated with adolescents' socially incompetent behavior.

7.   **authoritative parenting** This style encourages adolescents to be independent but still places limits and controls on their actions. Extensive verbal give-and-take is allowed, and parents are warm and nurturing toward the adolescent. This style is associated with adolescents' socially competent behavior.

8.   **neglectful parenting** A style in which the parent is very uninvolved in the adolescent's life. It is associated with adolescents' social incompetence, especially a lack of self-control.

9.   **indulgent parenting** A style in which parents are highly involved with their adolescents but place few demands or controls on them. This is associated with adolescents' social incompetence, especially a lack of self-control.

10.   **emotional autonomy** The capacity to relinquish childlike dependencies on parents.

11.   **insecure attachment** In this attachment pattern, infants either avoid the caregiver or show considerable resistance or ambivalence toward the caregiver. This pattern is theorized to be related to difficulties in relationships and problems in later development.

12.   **secure attachment** In this attachment pattern infants use their primary caregiver, usually the mother, as a secure base from which to explore the environment. Secure attachment is theorized to be an important foundation for psychological development later in childhood, adolescence, and adulthood.

13. **dismissing/avoidant attachment** An insecure attachment category in which individuals de-emphasize the importance of attachment. This category is associated with consistent experiences of rejection of attachment needs by caregivers.

14. **preoccupied/ambivalent attachment** An insecure attachment category in which adolescents are hypertuned to attachment experiences. This is thought to occur mainly because parents are inconsistently available to the adolescents.

15. **unresolved/disorganized attachment** An insecure category in which the adolescent has an unusually high level of fear and is disoriented. This may result from such traumatic experiences as a parent's death or abuse by parents.

16. **boundary ambiguity** The uncertainty in stepfamilies about who is on or out of the family and who is performing or responsible for certain tasks in the family system.

KEY PEOPLE
IN SECTION

1. E   2. A   3. B   4. D   5. C
6. F

"DR. DETAIL'S"
LIBRARY EXERCISE

Individual answers will vary, but most should report changes in the size of the family and mobility of the family. Other issues could be income, divorce rates, etc.

THE NATURE OF FAMILY PROCESSES
SECTION REVIEW

1. Reciprocal socialization is the process by which children and adolescents socialize parents just as parents socialize them.

2. Synchrony refers to the carefully coordinated interaction between the parent and the child or adolescent, in which, often unknowingly, they are attuned to each other's behavior.

3. The continuity view emphasizes the role that early parent-child relationships play in constructing a basic way of relating to people throughout the life span. The discontinuity view emphasizes change and growth in relationships over time.

4. Twain felt that as adolescents grow older, they come to understand their parents better.

5. Adolescents today are required to function in a more anonymous, larger environment with multiple and varying teachers.

6.   The primary difference found is that the fathers are warmer and communicate better with their children.

7.   During its height, the depression produced economic deprivation, adult depression and discontent, marital conflict, inconsistent child-rearing, and unhealthy behaviors (e.g., drinking).

8.   Cognitive processes are increasingly believed to be central to understanding socialization in the family.

KEY PEOPLE
IN SECTION

Alan Sroufe—Found in his research support for continuity.

Andrew Collins—In his longitudinal study, he found evidence for the discontinuity view of relationships.

Mark Twain—Once remarked that when he was 14 his father was so ignorant he could hardly stand to have the man around, but when Twain turned 21, he was astonished at how much his father had learned in those seven years.

Margaret Mead—Described subtle changes in a culture that have significant influences on the family.

PARENT-ADOLESCENT RELATIONSHIPS
SECTION REVIEW

1.   Matching Answers:

1.	J	2.	G	3.	B	4.	E	5.	F
6.	A	7.	C	8.	D	9.	H	10.	I
11.	K								

2.   The reasons are numerous. Some escape poverty, abuse, overcontrolling parents and still others are just simply adventure-seeking.

KEY PEOPLE
IN SECTION

Diana Baumrind—Believes that parents should be neither punitive nor aloof from their adolescents, but rather should develop rules and be affectionate with them.

Judith Smetana—Believes that parent-adolescent conflict can be better understood by considering the adolescent's changing social cognitive abilities.

Reed Larson—Recently spent six months in India studying middle-SES adolescents and their families. He observed that in India there is little parent-adolescent conflict and many would fit Baumrind's model of 'authoritarian.'

John Bowlby—Argued that secure attachment in infancy is central to the development of social competence.

Mary Ainsworth—Argued that secure attachment in infancy is central to the development of social competence.

SIBLING RELATIONSHIPS
SECTION REVIEW

1.   Sibling relationships show a higher degree of conflict than with relationships with other social agents (parents, peers, teachers, and romantic partners).

2.   Later-borns usually enjoy better relations with peers than first-born children.

3.   Contrary to public opinion of 'spoiled brat,' most research suggests goal orientation and many positive personality traits.

THE EFFECTS OF DIVORCE, STEPFAMILIES, AND WORKING PARENTS
SECTION REVIEW

1.   Most research suggests that adolescents from divorced families show poorer adjustment, such as externalizing disorders.

2.   One of the biggest adjustments following divorce is lower SES. There is a greater decline if the child lives with the mother.

3.   They matter a lot. When divorced parents have a harmonious relationship, the children do much better.

4.   a. stepfather, b. stepmother, and c. blended or complex families

5.   Yes. Their adjustment problems are very similar to those of kids in divorced families.

6.   Abusing siblings, stealing, vandalizing, using substances, etc.

7.   Deprived adolescents show less positive peer interaction.

KEY PEOPLE
IN SECTION

James Bray—Found that over time stepfamilies often fall into three types based on their relationships: neo-traditional, matriarchal, and romantic.

E. Mavis Hetherington—Prominent researcher regarding the effects of divorce on children.

Lois Hoffman—A leading authority on maternal employment. She says it's a fact of life.

Nancy Galambos—Studied the effects of parents' work overload on their relationships with their adolescent on the adolescent's development.

Thomas and Lynette Long—Concluded that a slight majority of latchkey children had negative experiences.

Joan Lipsitz—Called the lack of adult supervision of children and adolescents in the after-school hours one of the nation's major problems.

UNDERSTANDING CULTURE, ETHNICITY, GENDER, AND PARENTING
SECTION REVIEW

1. Ethnic minority families differ from White American families in their size, structure, reliance on kinship networks, level of income, and education.

2. Mothers tend to get little of the credit for their children's successes and much of the blame for their failures.

3. During the Industrial Revolution, fathers gained the role of breadwinner, although moral role model has also been a historic part of the father's role as well.

4. Today's fathers spend only a small portion of their time with their children. As little as 1/3 what mothers do.

KEY PEOPLE
IN SECTION

Frank Furstenburg and Kathleen Harris—Documented how nurturant fathering can overcome children's difficult life circumstances.

SOCIAL POLICY AND FAMILIES
SECTION REVIEW

1. Show them warmth and respect; demonstrate sustained interest in their lives; recognize and adapt to their changing cognitive and socioemotional development; communicate expectations for high standards of conduct and achievement; display authoritative, constructive ways of dealing with problems and conflict.

EXPLORATIONS
IN ADOLESCENCE

Both ethnic groups tend to "stick together." African-American grandmothers are a great resource for mothers and infants. Mothers of adolescents who have good relationships with their mothers pass that on to their children. Family support has been directly related to adolescent school success and self-reliance. In Mexican-American families the father is the undisputed authority but the mother is the main source of affection and care. These families exist more for each other, rather than for themselves. Self-reliance is not valued as highly as it is in African-American (and White) families.

COGNITIVE CHALLENGE

1.   Example: Parents and adolescent should set aside a time when the teen first indicates an interest in dating to discuss only this issue. Each come to the "meeting" with a list of what they feel they "must" have and what they would "like" to have. Beginning with the "must" have list, they should discuss and negotiate, then move on to the "like" to have list. They should come up with a written agreement that both are comfortable with signing. The agreement could have a method for resolving disputes that arise about dating, such as submitting the issue to a respected and neutral party (such as an aunt or uncle).

2.   Example: Parents should tell their child as soon as the separation is decided upon. Both parents should be present and should make it clear that they respect each other and love their child, and that the separation is no fault of the child's. The teenager should be consulted about which parent he or she wishes to live with and the arrangements for visiting the other parent. The teen should be given the opportunity to ask questions and express his or her feelings.

ADOLESCENCE IN RESEARCH

The researcher assessed 139 boys and girls 14 years of age and their parents. The hypothesis was that parents with problems would be more likely to have adolescents with problems. The results supported the hypothesis. The adolescents were very directly impacted by the adjustment levels of the parents.

⊠ COMPREHENSIVE REVIEW

1.	d	2.	c	3.	c	4.	b	5.	b
6.	a	7.	b	8.	c	9.	b	10.	d
11.	b	12.	d	13.	b	14.	a	15.	c
16.	b	17.	d	18.	d	19.	c	20.	a
21.	b	22.	b	23.	d	24.	b	25.	b
26.	c	27.	b	28.	a				

Chapter 6   Peers

Learning Goals with Key Terms and Key People in Boldface

1.0   DISCUSS PEER GROUP FUNCTIONS AND FAMILY-PEER LINKAGES

A.   Peer Group Functions

1.1   What are peers, and how are they important to adolescent social development?

1.2   How do peers provide a basis for social comparison and a source of information about the world outside the family?

1.3   Why are good peer relations necessary for normal social development?

1.4   What do adolescents do when they are with their peers?

1.5   How can peer relations be either positive or negative?

1.6   What did Jean Piaget and Harry Stack Sullivan stress about peer relations?

1.7   According to Willard Hartup, in what ways do peer relations vary?

B.   Family-Peer Linkages

1.8   How do healthy family relations promote healthy peer relations?

1.9   What are some of the ways in which the worlds of parents and peers connected?

1.10   What is the main difference between the quality of adolescent's relations with their peers and parents?

1.11   How does culture affect the influence peers have in relationships with parents?

2.0   DISCUSS PEER CONFORMITY, PEER STATUSES, AND OTHER DIMENSIONS

A.   Peer Conformity

2.1   What is the difference between **conformity, nonconformity**, and **anticonformity**?

2.2   At what point does conformity to antisocial peers peak?

B.   Peer Statuses

2.3   How would you describe **popular children?**

2.4   What is the peer status of **neglected children**?

2.5   How well do **rejected children** fare among their peers?

2.6   Where do **controversial children** fit in with their peer group?

C.   Social Cognition

2.7   How is social knowledge associated with improved peer relations?

2.8   How do good information processing skills improve peer relations?

2.9   What are the five steps children go through in processing information about their social world?

D.   Emotional Regulation in Peer Relations

2.10   What part does the ability to regulate emotion in successful peer relations?

E.   Conglomerate Strategies for Improving Social Skills

2.11   How do **conglomerate strategies** improve social skills?

F.   Bullying

2.12   What are the short-term and long-term effects of bullying on its victims?

2.13   What are some strategies that teachers can use to reduce bullying?

3.0 THE SIGNIFICANCE OF FRIENDSHIP FOR ADOLESCENT DEVELOPMENT

A. Importance of Friendship

3.1 What are the six functions that friendship play in adolescence?

B. Harry Stack Sullivan's Ideas

3.2 How does research support or refute Sullivan's ideas?

C. Intimacy and Similarity

3.3 What are the key aspects of friendship?

3.4 Are friendships of adolescent girls more intimate than the friendships of adolescent boys?

D. Mixed-Age Friendships

3.5 What happens to adolescents who become close friends with older individuals?

3.6 Are there gender differences in mix-group friendships and their effects on younger adolescents?

4.0 ADOLESCENT GROUPS

A. Group Function and Formation

4.1 How do groups satisfy adolescents' personal needs, reward them, provide information, raise their self-esteem, and give them an identity?

4.2 How do **norms** and **roles** play a part in any group?

4.3 What are group **norms**?

4.4 What are group **roles**?

B. Children Groups and Adolescent Groups

4.5 In what ways do children's groups differ from those of adolescents?

4.6 What did Dexter Dunphy learn about adolescent groups?

C. Ethnic and Cultural Variations

4.7 What are some features of lower-socioeconomic status groups?

4.8 Why do ethnic minority adolescents often have two sets of peers?

4.9 Why do ethnic minority adolescents turn to peer groups more than White adolescents?

5.0 DISCUSS CLIQUES, CROWDS, AND YOUTH ORGANIZATIONS

A. Cliques and Crowds

5.1 What is the difference between a **clique** and a **crowd**?

5.2 What different cliques are found in most secondary schools?

5.3 With what type of cliques is membership associated with high self-esteem?

5.4 What is the main feature distinguishing a **crowd**?

5.5 What are Brown's conclusions about adolescent crowds?

B. Youth Organizations

5.6 In what way do youth organizations influence adolescent development?

5.7 What is the mission of Boys' Clubs and Girls' Clubs?

6.0 DATING IN ADOLESCENCE

A. Functions of Dating

6.1 What is dating and what are its functions?

6.2 What eight functions can be served by dating?

B. Types of Dating and Developmental Changes

6.3 At what age do adolescents start to hang out together in heterosexual groups?

6.4 What is the difference between hooking up, seeing each other, and going out?

6.5 What is cyberdating?

Exercises

KEY TERMS
COMPLETION EXERCISE

Each key term is presented in the form of an incomplete sentence. Compare each sentence by either defining the term or giving an example. Compare your definitions with those given at the end of the study guide chapter.

1. To adolescents, **peers** are

    _____

    _____

2. **Conformity** means to

    _____

    _____

3. **Nonconformity** means to

    _____

    _____

4. In contrast with conformity and nonconformity, **anticonformity** means

    _____

    _____

5. **Popular children** are those who

    _____

    _____

6. **Neglected children** are very likely to

    _____

    _____

7. **Rejected children** often

    _____

    _____

8. **Controversial children** are those who

    _____

    _____

9. **Conglomerate strategies** are meant to

    _____

    _____

10. **Intimacy in friendship** is exemplified by

    _____

    _____

11. Examples of **norms** are

    _____

    _____

12. The importance of **roles** is

    _____

    _____

13. **Cliques** are meant to

    _____

    _____

14. **Crowds** are seen when

    _____

    _____

15. **Dating scripts** are used by

    _____

    _____

16. An example of **romantic love** is

    _____

    _____

17.   An example of **affectionate love** is

_____

_____

KEY PEOPLE
IN THE STUDY OF ADOLESCENCE

_____	1. Reed Larson	A. Studied conformity
_____	2. Thomas Berndt	B. Studied nature and function of adolescent and children's groups, emphasizing change in sexual make-up
_____	3. John Coie and Kenneth Dodge	C. Studied role of attachment patterns in adolescent romantic relationships
_____	4. William Hartup	D. Studied role of peers in romantic involvement
_____	5. Harry Stack Sullivan	E. Encouraged structured volunteer activities as a way to develop initiative
_____	6. Candice Feiring	F. Studied the impact of insecure attachment on dating relationships
_____	7. Dexter Dunphy	G. Psychoanalytical theorist who emphasized importance of friendship for adolescents
_____	8. Wyndol Furman	H. Studied nature of child and adolescent friendships
_____	9. Bradford Brown	I. Studied role of peer influences in child and adolescent aggression and antisocial behavior
_____	10. Jennifer Connolly	J. Found that males and females bring different motivations to the dating experience

PEER GROUP FUNCTIONS AND FAMILY-PEER LINKAGES
SECTION REVIEW

1.   How they are seen by peers is the most important aspect of many adolescents' lives. Why?

_____

_____

2.   What do adolescents do when they are with their peers?

_____

_____

3.   How important are good peer relationships for normal social development in adolescence?

_____

_____

4.   What are some of the ways the worlds of parents and peers are connected?

_____

_____

5.   How are Japanese adolescents different than American adolescents in relating to their parents?

_____

_____

KEY PEOPLE
IN SECTION

Anna Freud—

_____

_____

Jean Piaget and Harry Stack Sullivan—

_____

_____

PEER CONFORMITY, PEER STATUSES, AND OTHER DIMENSIONS
OF PEER RELATIONS
SECTION REVIEW

1.   What is conformity?

_____

_____

2.   What is nonconformity?

_____

_____

3.   What is anticonformity?

_____

_____

4. According to developmentalists, what are three types of children who have a different status than popular children?

_____

_____

5. How can neglected children and adolescents be trained to interact more effectively with their peers?

_____

_____

6. In peer relations, what role is played by appropriate cognitive skills?

_____

_____

7. How can conglomerate strategies be used to improve adolescents' social skills?

_____

_____

8. What is the outcome of being a victim of bullying?

_____

_____

9. What are some strategies for teachers to use to reduce bullying?

_____

_____

KEY PEOPLE
IN SECTION

Thomas Berndt—

_____

_____

James Coleman—

_____

_____

Kenneth Dodge—

_____

_____

FRIENDSHIPS IN ADOLESCENCE
SECTION REVIEW

1. What six functions do adolescent friendships serve?

    _____

    _____

2. List and give an example of five appropriate strategies for making friends.

    _____

    _____

3. List and give examples for three inappropriate strategies for making friends.

    _____

    _____

4. Are the friendships of girls more intimate than the friendships of adolescent boys?

    _____

    _____

5. How important is similarity in forming friendships?

    _____

    _____

KEY PEOPLE
IN SECTION

Harry Stack Sullivan—

_____

_____

Willard Hartup—

_____

_____

ADOLESCENT GROUPS
SECTION REVIEW

1.   Why does an adolescent join a group?

_____

_____

2.   What two things do all groups have in common?

_____

_____

KEY PEOPLE
IN SECTION

Dexter Dunphy—

_____

_____

CLIQUES, CROWDS, AND YOUTH ORGANIZATIONS
SECTION REVIEW

1.   Describe what Dunphy found to be the five stages of progression of peer group relations in adolescence.

_____

_____

2.   Summarize the conclusions of Bradford Brown and colleagues' most recent research on cliques.

_____

_____

3.   Compare and contrast cliques and crowds.

_____

_____

4.   What impact can youth organizations have on adolescents?

_____

_____

KEY PEOPLE
IN SECTION

Bradford Brown—

_____

_____

Jane Lohr—

_____

_____

Reed Larson—

_____

_____

DATING IN ADOLESCENCE
SECTION REVIEW

1.   What eight functions are served by dating?

_____

_____

2.   a.   Describe the three main activities involved in the male dating script and give an example of each.

_____

_____

     b.   Describe the three main activities involved in the female dating script and give an example of each.

_____

_____

KEY PEOPLE
IN SECTION

Candice Feiring—

_____

_____

ROMANTIC LOVE AND ITS CONSTRUCTION
SECTION REVIEW

1.   What is romantic love?

        _____

        _____

2.   What is affectionate love?

        _____

        _____

KEY PEOPLE
IN SECTION

Wyndol Furman and Elizabeth Wehner—

        _____

        _____

Peter Blos—

        _____

        _____

Mavis Heatherington—

        _____

        _____

Harry Stack Sullivan—

        _____

        _____

Jennifer Connolly—

        _____

        _____

EXPLORATIONS
IN ADOLESCENCE

1. What did the 1995 Search Institute study find regarding barriers to participation in youth programs?

_____

_____

COGNITIVE
CHALLENGE

1. How did your relationship with your parents affect your peer relationships and friendships in adolescence? How did your parents influence your choice of peers and friends? How did your parents' marital relationship affect your dating and romantic relationships?

_____

_____

2. Think back over your adolescent dating experiences. How were your experiences different when you were 13, 15, and 17? What would you do differently if you could begin anew today? What advice would you offer today's teenagers of those ages?

_____

_____

ADOLESCENCE
IN RESEARCH

Concerning Brown and Lohr's 1987 research dealing with the self-esteem of students in grades 7 through 12, state the hypothesis, the research methods (if known), the research conclusions, and the implications and applications for adolescent development.

_____

_____

COMPREHENSIVE REVIEW

1. Jason is a sixth-grader who spends a lot of time with his peers. Statistically speaking, in which activity is he most likely engaging?
    a. Going to stores
    b. Watching television
    c. Team sports
    d. Girl-watching

2. A(n) _____ is a person who purposively diverges from the expectations of the group.
    a. anticonformist
    b. independent
    c. nonconformist
    d. leader

3. Participating in a newspaper drive with one's club because the club wants everyone to be involved in this activity is an example of _____ conformity.
    a. negative
    b. positive
    c. independent
    d. responsible

4. Thomas Berndt found that adolescent conformity to antisocial, peer-endorsed behavior _____ in late high school years, and _____ agreement between parents and peers begins to occur in some areas.
    a. decreases; greater
    b. decreases; lesser
    c. increases; greater
    d. increases; lesser

5. The adolescent who does not have significant interactions with peers is likely to be
    a. handicapped.
    b. antisocial.
    c. neglected.
    d. mature and independent.

6. Kenneth Dodge indicates that adolescents go through five steps when processing information about their social world. Which of the following is NOT one of these steps?
    a   Response search
    b. Selecting an optimal response
    c. Decoding of social cues
    d. Elaboration of possibilities

7. Your teenage son Jeremy has a friend who brags about his clothes, jewelry, and his athletic accomplishment. Jeremy's friend
    a. is probably well liked by his peers.
    b. would probably be called an anticonformist.
    c. probably compliments others for their accomplishments.
    d. might need coaching to gain peer group acceptance.

8.   Children who are frequently nominated as a best friend and are rarely disliked by their peers are
     a.   popular children.
     b.   neglected children.
     c.   rejected children.
     d.   controversial children.

9.   Children who are infrequently nominated as a best friend but are not disliked by their peers are
     a.   popular children.
     b.   neglected children.
     c.   rejected children.
     d.   controversial children.

10. Children who are infrequently nominated as a best friend and are actively disliked by their peers are
     a.   popular children.
     b.   neglected children.
     c.   rejected children.
     d.   controversial children.

11. Children who are frequently nominated both as a best friend and as being disliked are
     a.   popular children.
     b.   neglected children.
     c.   rejected children.
     d.   controversial children.

12. Which of the following is NOT one of the six functions served by friendship?
     a.   Intimacy/affection.
     b.   Personal gain.
     c.   Ego support.
     d.   Stimulation.

13. Rules that apply to all members of a group are
     a.   Mandates.
     b.   Roles.
     c.   Values.
     d.   Norms.

14. _____ are small groups that range from two to about twelve individuals and average about five to six individuals.
     a.   Cliques
     b.   Chumships
     c.   Crowds
     d.   Youth organizations

15. Which of the following is not among the six functions of friendship?
     a.   Physical support
     b.   Skill-streaming
     c.   Social comparisons
     d.   Intimacy

16. Which theorist stressed the importance of friendship to adolescent development?
    a. Kenneth Dodge
    b. Erik Erikson
    c. Muzafer Sherif
    d. Harry Stack Sullivan

17. As the parent of an adolescent male, you are concerned about his friends who are 3–5 years older than he is. Your concern is
    a. not justified.
    b. not justified, because he will probably not drop out of school.
    c. justified because his friend is probably a drug user.
    d. justified because your son will likely engage in deviant behavior.

18. In social groups, all members are expected to
    a. assume roles.
    b. conform to norms.
    c. discriminate against outsiders.
    d. maintain secrecy about group activities.

19. Compared to adolescent groups, children's groups
    a. are not as formalized.
    b. include a broader array of members.
    c. have well-defined rules and regulations.
    d. are composed of large cliques.

20. In formal groups, such as athletic teams and student councils,
    a. racial and ethnic cliques predominate.
    b. socially active collegiates predominate.
    c. the greatest mixture of social class and ethnicity occurs.
    d. lower-class students have gained parity with middle-class students.

21. Sarah is 16 years old and does not want to belong to any clique. She does her own thing and is good at what she does. Her level of self-esteem is likely
    a. the same as the *jocks*.
    b. lower than the *populars*.
    c. lower than the *normal*s.
    d. the same as the *nobodies*.

22. Which of the following is NOT a main function of adolescent dating?
    a. Recreation
    b. Status
    c. Socialization
    d. Procreation

23. What percent of adolescents have had at least one date by the time they are 16 years old?
    a. 20
    b. 50
    c. 75
    d. 90

24. In dating, boys and girls
    a.   seek sexual intimacy on most dates.
    b.   self-disclose at about the same rate.
    c.   conform to cultural patterns and norms.
    d.   want to go steady to avoid anxiety.

25. That adolescents enjoy being with people who are similar to them in values and beliefs is predicated by the principle called
    a.   the matching hypothesis.
    b.   identity narcissism.
    c.   value matching.
    d.   consensual validation.

26. In mate selection, the matching hypothesis suggests that we often pair up with someone who is like us in
    a.   attractiveness.
    b.   intelligence.
    c.   key personality factors.
    d.   intimacy.

ADOLESCENCE ON THE SCREEN

- *Diner* follows a group of friends during high school and graduation.

- *Breakfast Club* depicts how students who must spend Saturday morning in detention develop into a cohesive group.

- *Trainspotting* involves a group of friends whose lives revolve around using drugs.

- *Romeo and Juliet*, a Shakespearean classic about romantic love, appeals to today's adolescents.

ADOLESCENCE IN BOOKS

- *Just Friends*, by Lillian Rubin (HarperCollins: NY, 1985), explores the nature of friends and intimacy.

Answer Key

KEY TERMS

1.   **peers** Children or adolescents who are of about the same age or maturity level.

2.   **conformity** This occurs when individuals adopt the attitudes or behaviors of others because of real or imagined pressure from them.

3.   **nonconformity** This occurs when individuals know what people around them expect but do not use these expectations to guide their behavior.

4.   **anticonformity** This occurs when individuals react counter to a group's expectations and deliberately move away from the actions or beliefs the group advocates.

5.   **popular children** Children who are frequently nominated as a best friend and are rarely disliked by their peers.

6.   **neglected children** Children who are infrequently nominated as a best friend but are not disliked by their peers.

7.   **rejected children** Children who are infrequently nominated as a best friend and are actively disliked by their peers.

8.   **controversial children** Children who are frequently nominated both as being a best friend and as being disliked.

9.   **conglomerate strategies** Involves the use of a combination of techniques, rather than a single approach, to improve adolescents' social skills.

10.   **intimacy in friendship** In most research, this is defined narrowly as self-disclosure or sharing of private thoughts.

11.   **norms** Rules that apply to all members of a group.

12.   **roles** Certain positions in a group that are governed by rules and expectations. Roles define how adolescents should behave in those positions.

13.   **cliques** These units are smaller, involve more intimacy, and are more cohesive than crowds. They are, however, larger and involve less intimacy than friendships.

14.   **crowd** The largest, most loosely defined, and least personal unit of adolescent peer society. Crowds often meet because of their mutual interest in an activity.

15. **dating scripts** The cognitive models that adolescents and adults use to guide and evaluate dating interactions.

16. **romantic love** Also called passionate love or Eros, this love has strong sexual and infatuation components, and it often predominates in the early part of a love relationship.

17. **affectionate love** Also called companionate love, this love occurs when an individual wants to have another person near and has a deep, caring affection for that person.

KEY PEOPLE
IN THE STUDY OF ADOLESCENCE

1.	E	2.	A	3.	I	4.	H	5.	G
6.	J	7.	B	8.	F	9.	C	10.	D

PEER GROUP FUNCTIONS AND FAMILY-PEER LINKAGES
SECTION REVIEW

1. To be excluded means stress, frustration, and sadness. So many will do most anything to be included.

2. For boys (more so than girls) a lot of time was spent doing sports activities. General play and going places was common for both sexes.

3. Good peer relationships might be necessary for normal social development.

4. Parents choose where they will work, live, churches, school districts, etc. All impact the children.

5. Japanese adolescents spend less time outside of the home, have less leisure time, and are involved in fewer extracurricular activities than American adolescents.

KEY PEOPLE
IN SECTION

Anna Freud—Studied peer attachment with six children from different families whose parents were killed in WWII.

Jean Piaget and Harry Stack Sullivan—Were influential theorists who stressed that it is through peer interaction that children and adolescents learn the symmetrical reciprocity mode of relationships.

PEER CONFORMITY, PEER STATUSES, AND OTHER DIMENSIONS OF PEER RELATIONS
SECTION REVIEW

1. When individuals adopt the attitudes or behavior of others because of real or imagined pressure from them.

2. When individuals know what people around them expect but do not use those expectations to guide their behavior.

3. When individuals react counter to a group's expectations and deliberately move away from the actions or beliefs the group advocates.

4. Neglected children, rejected children, and controversial children.

5. Train them to hold their attention by asking questions, listening in a warm and friendly way, and by saying things about themselves that might be of interest.

6. They help generate correct interpretations of situations, which lessens the likelihood of conflict.

7. Refers to coaching to improve an adolescent's social skills.

8. Both short-term and long-term negative effects in relationships suffer.

9. Get older peers to serve as monitors for bullying; develop schoolwide rules and sanctions against bullying; form friendship groups for adolescents who are regularly bullied; spread the anti-bullying message around the community.

KEY PEOPLE
IN SECTION

Thomas Berndt—Focused on the negative, neutral, and positive aspects of peer conformity.

James Coleman—Pointed out that for adolescents in the average range, there is little or no relation between physical attractiveness and popularity.

Kenneth Dodge—Found that aggressive boys are more likely to perceive another child's actions as hostile when the peer's intentions are ambiguous.

FRIENDSHIPS IN ADOLESCENCE
SECTION REVIEW

1. Companionship; stimulation; physical support; ego support; social comparison; intimacy/affection.

2. Initiate interaction; be nice; engage in prosocial behavior; show respect for self and others; provide social support.

3. Using psychological aggression, having a negative self-presentation; engaging in antisocial behavior.

4. Girls refer to intimate conversations and faithfulness more than boys do.

5. Friends are generally similar in terms of age, sex, ethnicity, and other factors.

KEY PEOPLE
IN SECTION

Harry Stack Sullivan—Was the most influential theorist to discuss the importance of friendship.

Willard Hartup—Studied peer relations across four decades, recently concluding that children and adolescents often use friends as cognitive and social resources.

ADOLESCENT GROUPS
SECTION REVIEW

1. Groups satisfy adolescents' personal needs, reward them, provide information, raise self-esteem, and give them an identity.

2. Norms and roles.

KEY PEOPLE
IN SECTION

Dexter Dunphy—Indicated that opposite-sex participation in groups increases during adolescence.

CLIQUES, CROWDS, AND YOUTH ORGANIZATIONS
SECTION REVIEW

1. a. Precrowd stage of isolated, unisex groups
    b. Beginning of the crowd; unisex groups start group-group interaction
    c. Crowd in structural transition; unisex groups are forming mixed-sex groups
    d. Fully developed crowd; mixed-sex groups are closely associated
    e. Crowd begins to disintegrate as loosely associated groups of couples pair off

2.   a.   The influence of cliques is not entirely negative
      b.   The influence of cliques is not uniform for all adolescents
      c.   Development changes occur in cliques

3.   Cliques are small groups that range from two to about 12 individuals and average about five. Crowds are a larger group structure than cliques. Adolescents are usually members of a crowd based on reputation.

4.   Youth organizations can have an important influence on the adolescent's development, depending on which they are.

KEY PEOPLE IN SECTION

Bradford Brown—Researched the role of crowds in adolescence.

Jane Lohr—Examined self-esteem of adolescents.

Reed Larson—Felt that structured activities, such as selling Girl Scout cookies, is especially well-suited for the development of initiative.

DATING IN ADOLESCENCE SECTION REVIEW

1.   Dating can be a form of recreation. Dating is a source of status and achievement. Dating is part of the socialization process in adolescence. Dating involves learning about intimacy and serves as an opportunity to establish a unique, meaningful relationship with a person of the opposite sex. Dating can be a context for sexual experimentation. Dating can provide companionship through interaction and shared activities. Dating experiences contribute to identity formation and development. Dating can be a means of mate sorting and selection.

2.   a.   (1) Initiating the date; (2) controlling the public domain; and (3) initiating physical contact.
      b.   (1) Concern for the private domain; (2) participating in structure of the date; and (3) responding to sexual gestures.

KEY PEOPLE IN SECTION

Candice Feiring—Found that male and female adolescents bring different motivations to the dating experience.

ROMANTIC LOVE AND ITS CONSTRUCTION
SECTION REVIEW

1.   Also called passionate love or Eros; it has strong sexual and infatuation components and often predominates in the early parts of a relationship.

2.   Also called companionate love; occurs when individuals desire to have another person near and have a deep, caring affection for that person.

KEY PEOPLE
IN SECTION

Wyndol Furman and Elizabeth Wehner—discussed how specific insecure attachment styles might be related to adolescents' romantic relationships.

Peter Blos—noted that at the beginning of adolescence, boys and girls try to separate themselves from opposite-sex parents as a love object.

Mavis Heatherington—found that divorce was associated with a stronger heterosexual orientation of adolescent daughters.

Harry Stack Sullivan—believed that it is through intimate friendships that adolescents learn a mature form of love he referred to as "collaborative."

Jennifer Connolly—documented the role of peers in the emergence of romantic involvement in adolescence.

EXPLORATIONS
IN ADOLESCENCE

This study, based in Minneapolis, found that more than 50 percent of the youth said they don't participate in any type of youth program in a typical week. More than 40 percent reported no participation in youth programs during the summer months.

COGNITIVE
CHALLENGE

No answers. Individual activity.

ADOLESCENCE
IN RESEARCH

Two hundred twenty-one adolescents were either associated with major cliques (jocks, populars, normals, druggies/toughs, and nobodies) or not associated with any clique. The self-esteem of the jocks and populars was the highest, whereas that of the nobodies was the lowest. Those involved with no clique—the independents—had self-esteem equivalent to the jocks and the populars.

⊠ COMPREHENSIVE REVIEW

1.	c	2.	a	3.	b	4.	a	5.	c
6.	d	7.	d	8.	a	9.	b	10.	c
11.	d	12.	b	13.	d	14.	a	15.	b
16.	d	17.	d	18.	b	19.	a	20.	c
21.	a	22.	d	23.	d	24.	c	25.	c
26.	a								

Chapter 7   Schools

Learning Goals with Key Terms and Key People in Boldface

1.0   WHAT ARE APPROACHES TO EDUCATING STUDENTS?
  A.   **Approaches to Educating Students**
    1.1   How have secondary schools changed since the nineteenth century?
    1.2   What is the comprehensive high school?
    1.3   What functions of secondary schools are being debated today?
    1.4   What is the **back-to-basics movement**?
    1.5   What arguments are being made for schools to fulfill more comprehensive functions?
    1.6   How do American schools compare with those in other countries?
    1.7   What is **direct instruction approach** to student learning?
    1.8   What are **cognitive constructivist approaches** to student learning?
    1.9   What are **social constructivist approaches** to student learning?
    1.10 What is the American Psychological Association's learner centered psychological principles?

2.0   KNOW ABOUT SCHOOLS' CHANGING SOCIAL DEVELOPMENTAL CONTEXTS
    2.1   What are the Carnegie Council on Adolescent Development's eight principles for transforming adolescent's educational experiences?
    2.2   How do the social context of schools differ at the preschool, elementary school, and secondary school levels?

3.0   EVALUATE TRANSITIONS IN MIDDLE SCHOOL/JUNIOR HIGH
  A.   **Transition to Middle or Junior High School**
    3.1   What is the origin of junior high schools?
    3.2   What were the justifications for junior high schools?
    3.3   How has the role of ninth grade been resolved over time?
    3.4   Why have middle schools become more popular than the junior high model?
    3.5   How are middle schools related to pubertal development?
    3.6   Is the transition to sixth- through eight-grade middle schools easier for students than the transition to traditional junior highs (7–9)?
    3.7   Why is the transition to middle- or junior-high school stressful?
    3.8   What is the **top-dog phenomenon**?
  B.   **Successful Middle Schools**
    3.9   According to Lipsitz, what makes a middle school successful?
    3.10 What did the Carnegie Foundation recommend about the redesign of middle schools?

4.0   TRANSITION FROM HIGH SCHOOL TO COLLEGE
  A.   **High School to College**
    4.1   How does the transition from high school to college parallel the transition from elementary to middle-junior high school?
    4.2   What happens to parental interaction with the transition?
    4.3   What are the effects of discontinuity between high school and college?
    4.4   Why are today's college freshmen suffering from more depression and stress than in the past?

B.   High School Dropouts and Noncollege Youth

4.5   Over the past 40 years, what has been the reason for the drop in the numbers of dropouts?

4.6   What educational deficiencies do students who dropout experience in adulthood?

4.7   What are the extent and characteristics of ethnic minority students who drop out?

4.8   What factors are associated with dropping out?

4.9   What approaches can be used to reduce the rate of dropping out and improve student experiences?

5.0   UNDERSTANDING SCHOOLS, CLASSROOMS, TEACHERS, AND PARENTS

A.   Size and Climate

5.1   What are the most desirable classroom and school size?

5.2   What are some benefits of a small school?

5.3   What are some of the drawbacks of large schools?

5.4   What are some benefits of a large school?

5.5   Which class size best benefits student learning?

5.6   What are the components of a positive classroom climate?

5.7   What is the **authoritative strategy of classroom management**?

5.8   What is the **authoritarian strategy of classroom management**?

5.9   What is the **permissive strategy of classroom management**?

5.10   To what variables are classroom climate generally linked?

5.11   What is the effect of school climate on student achievement?

B.   Person-Environment Fit and Aptitude-Treatment Interaction

5.12   What happens when the schools do not meet the adolescent's needs?

5.13   What is meant by **aptitude-treatment interaction**?

C.   Teachers and Parents

5.14   Can a profile of a competent teacher be compiled?

5.15   How does parental involvement with schools change as students move into adolescence?

5.16   Why do student-teacher relationships often deteriorate after the transition to junior high?

5.17   Why is greater collaboration between schools, families, and communities needed?

5.18   What is Epstein's framework for improving parent involvement in adolescents' schooling?

6.0   THE EFFECTS OF SOCIOECONOMIC STATUS AND ETHNICITY IN SCHOOLS

A.   Socioeconomic Status and Ethnicity in Schools

6.1   What is the effect of poverty on student learning?

6.2   What are the characteristics of schools in low-income neighborhoods?

B.   Ethnicity

6.3   How does ethnicity impact on school experiences?

6.4   What is the role of teacher's positive expectations of ethnic students?

6.5   What are some effective teaching strategies for improving relations with ethnically diverse students?

6.6   What is a **jigsaw** classroom?

6.7   How can the concept of the **jigsaw** classroom be used to improve American schools?

6.8   What has been the evaluation of the effectiveness of the Comer schools?

6.9   What are some social policy recommendations for improving schools for adolescents?

7.0   ADOLESCENTS WITH DISABILITIES.

A.   Who Are Adolescents with Disabilities?

7.1   How many U.S. students receive special education services?

7.2   What percentage of students receiving special education has **learning disabilities**?

B.   Learning Disabilities
    7.3   What are the characteristics of a **learning disability**?
    7.4   How are **learning disabilities** defined?
    7.5   What is the most common problem for students with a learning disability?

C.   Attention Deficit/Hyperactivity Disorder (ADHD)
    7.6   How is **ADHD** defined?
    7.7   What is the controversy related to the diagnosis and treatment of **ADHD**?
    7.8   What interventions are recommended for children and adolescents with **ADHD**?

D.   Educational Issues Involving Adolescents with a Disability
    7.9   What is **Public Law 92–142**?
    7.10   What is **The Individuals with Disabilities Act (IDEA)**?
    7.11   What does **least restrictive environment (LRE)** mean?
    7.12   What is meant by **inclusion**?

8.0   GIFTED ADOLESCENTS

A.   Adolescents Who Are Gifted
    8.1   What are the criteria for giftedness?
    8.2   According to Winner, what are the three characteristics of adolescents who are gifted?
    8.3   What are some characteristics that characterize **gifted adolescents**?
    8.4   What program options exist for students who are gifted?

Exercises

KEY TERMS
COMPLETION EXERCISE

Each key term is presented in the form of an incomplete sentence. Complete each sentence by either defining the term or giving an example. Compare your definitions with those given at the end of the study guide chapter.

1. According to the **back-to-basics movement**

    _____

    _____

2. A benefit of the **direct instruction approach** is

    _____

    _____

3. The **cognitive constructivist approaches** emphasize

    _____

    _____

4. **Social constructivist approaches** focus on

    _____

    _____

5. You typically see evidence of the **top-dog phenomenon** in

    _____

    _____

6. The benefits of an **authoritative strategy of classroom management** are

    _____

    _____

7. The benefits of an **authoritarian strategy of classroom management** are

    _____

    _____

8.   A **permissive strategy of classroom management** can lead to

_____

_____

9.   The **aptitude-treatment interaction (ATI)** stresses the importance of

_____

_____

10.   I can tell Jovan is in a **jigsaw classroom** because

_____

_____

11.   Having a **learning disability** means

_____

_____

12.   Having an **attention deficit/hyperactivity disorder (ADHD)** suggests

_____

_____

13.   With the institution of **Public Law 94–142** came

_____

_____

14.   The **Individuals with Disabilities Education Act (IDEA)** is

_____

_____

15.   Placement in the **least restrictive environment** means

_____

_____

16.   **Inclusion** means

_____

_____

17.   **Adolescents who are gifted** are

_____

_____

KEY PEOPLE
IN THE STUDY OF ADOLESCENCE

Match the person with the concept of adolescent development with which they are associated.

_____	1. Joan Lipsitz	A.	Believed teachers should help students achieve industry
_____	2. Jacqueline Eccles	B.	Pioneered research on the jigsaw classroom
_____	3. Erik Erikson	C.	Studied how developmentally appropriate school environments could meet students' needs
_____	4. Joyce Epstein	D.	Conducted research into what makes a good middle school
_____	5. Jonathan Kozol	E.	Believes that parents needs to be more involved in schools
_____	6. John Ogbu	F.	Anthropologist who says American schools exploit minority students
_____	7. Eliot Aronson	G.	Author of *Savage Inequities*
_____	8. Ellen Winner	H.	Believes that a community, team approach is the best way to educate students
_____	9. James Comer	I.	Conducted research about gifted children

"DR. DETAIL'S"
MATCHING EXERCISE

Match the person with his/her contribution to the understanding of adolescents.

_____	1. Arthur Powell, Eleanor Farrar, and David Cohen	A.	Searched the nation finding and describing the best middle schools.
_____	2. Roberta Simmons and Dale Blyth	B.	Philanthropist who donated money to start the I Have A Dream Program.
_____	3. Joan Lipsitz	C.	Studied self-esteem in students participating in varied numbers of extracurricular activities.
_____	4. Donna Smith	D.	Developed the metaphor of the "shopping mall" high school
_____	5. Eugene Lang	E.	Has been working at schools on the Neah Bay Indian Reservation as a school psychologist.
_____	6. Diana Baumrind	F.	Described the effective teacher as one secure in his/her own identity and sexuality.
_____	7. Jacob Kounin	G.	Provided the original idea of an authoritative classroom management strategy.
_____	8. Stephanie Feeney	H.	Studied classroom management styles to identify effective teachers.
_____	9. Dr. Henry Gaskins	I.	Started an after-school tutorial program for ethnic minority students in 1983.

APPROACHES TO EDUCATING STUDENTS
SECTION REVIEW

1. How have secondary schools changed since the nineteenth century?

   _____

   _____

2. What is the comprehensive high school?

   _____

   _____

3. What functions of secondary schools are being debated today?

   _____

   _____

4. What is the back-to-basics movement?

   _____

   _____

5. What is the direct instruction approach to student learning?

   _____

   _____

6. What are cognitive constructivist approaches to student learning?

   _____

   _____

7. What are social constructivist approaches to student learning?

   _____

   _____

8.   Match the APA Learner-Centered Psychological Principle with its description.

Cognitive and Metacognitive Factors

_____	1. nature of the learning process	A.	Successful learners can create a repertoire of thinking and reasoning strategies to achieve complex goals.
_____	2. goals of the learning process	B.	Successful learners can create meaningful, coherent representations of knowledge.
_____	3. construction of knowledge	C.	Higher order strategies for selecting and monitoring mental operations facilitate creative and critical thinking.
_____	4. strategic thinking	D.	The learning of complex subject matter is more effective when it is an intentional process of constructing meaning and experience.
_____	5. thinking about thinking	E.	Successful learners can link new information with existing knowledge in meaningful ways.
_____	6. context of learning	F.	Learning is influenced by environmental factors, including culture, technology, and instructional practices.

Motivational, Instructional, Developmental, Social, and Individual Difference Factors

_____	1. motivational and emotional influences on learning	A.	The learner's creativity, higher order thinking, and natural curiosity all contribute to motivation to learn.
_____	2. intrinsic motivation to learn	B.	Acquiring complex knowledge and skills requires extended learner effort and guided practice. Without learners' motivation to learn, the willingness to exert this effort is unlikely without coercion.
_____	3. effects of motivation on effort	C.	What and how much is learned is influenced by the learner's motivation, which, in turn, is influenced by the learner's emotional states, beliefs, interests, goals, and habits of thinking.
_____	4. developmental influences on learning	D.	Setting appropriately high and challenging standards and assessing the learner and learning progress are integral aspect of the learning experience.
_____	5. social influences on learning	E.	Learning is influenced by social interactions, interpersonal relations, and communication with others.
_____	6. individual differences in learning	F.	Learners have different strategies, approaches, and capabilities for learning that are a function of prior experience and heredity.
_____	7. learning and diversity	G.	Learning is most effective when differential development within and across physical, cognitive, and socioemotional domains is taken into account.
_____	8. standards and assessment	H.	Learning is most effective when differences in learner's linguistic, cultural, and social backgrounds are considered.

SCHOOLS' CHANGING SOCIAL DEVELOPMENTAL CONTEXTS
SECTION REVIEW

1. What are the Carnegie Council on Adolescent Development's eight principles for transforming adolescent's educational experiences?

    _____

    _____

    _____

    _____

2. How do the social context of schools differ at the preschool, elementary school, and secondary school levels?

    _____

    _____

EVALUATE TRANSITIONS IN MIDDLE SCHOOL/JUNIOR HIGH
SECTION REVIEW

1. What is the origin of junior high schools?

    _____

    _____

2. How has the role of ninth grade been resolved over time?

    _____

    _____

3. Why have middle schools become more popular than the junior highs?

    _____

    _____

4. Is the sixth- through eight-grade middle school transition easier than the transition to junior highs?

    _____

    _____

5. Why is the transition to middle- or junior-high school stressful?

    _____

    _____

6. What is the top-dog phenomenon?

    _____

    _____

7. According to Lipsitz, what makes a middle school successful?

    _____

    _____

8. What did the Carnegie Foundation recommend about the redesign of middle schools?

    _____

    _____

TRANSITION FROM HIGH SCHOOL TO COLLEGE
SECTION REVIEW

1. How does the transition from high school to college parallel the transition from elementary to middle-junior high school?

    _____

    _____

2. Why are today's college freshmen suffering from more depression and stress than in the past?

    _____

    _____

3. Over the past 40 years, what has accounted for the drop in the numbers of dropouts?

    _____

    _____

4. What educational deficiencies do students who drop out experience in adulthood?

    _____

    _____

5.   What factors are associated with dropping out of school?

_____

_____

6.   What approaches can be used to reduce the rate of dropping out and improve students' experiences?

_____

_____

UNDERSTANDING SCHOOLS, CLASSROOMS, TEACHERS, AND PARENTS SECTION REVIEW

1.   What is the most desirable classroom/school size?

_____

_____

2.   What are some benefits of a small school?

_____

_____

3.   What are some benefits of a large school?

_____

_____

4.   What are the components of a positive classroom climate?

_____

_____

5.   What is the authoritative strategy of classroom management?

_____

_____

6.   What is the authoritarian strategy of classroom management?

_____

_____

7.   What is the permissive strategy of classroom management?

_____

_____

8.   What is meant by aptitude-treatment interaction?

_____

_____

9.   How does parental involvement with schools change as students get older?

_____

_____

10.   Why do student-teacher relationships often deteriorate after the transition to junior high?

_____

_____

11.   What is Epstein's framework for improving parent involvement in schooling?

_____

_____

12.   List three things teachers can do to improve the likelihood that students will cooperate with them in the classroom.

_____

_____

THE EFFECTS OF SOCIOECONOMIC STATUS AND ETHNICITY IN SCHOOLS SECTION REVIEW

1.   What is the effect of poverty on student learning?

_____

_____

2.   How does ethnicity impact on school experiences?

_____

_____

3.   What is a jigsaw classroom?

_____

_____

4.   What are some social policy recommendations for improving schools for adolescents?

_____

_____

ADOLESCENTS WITH DISABILITIES
SECTION REVIEW

1.   What are the characteristics of a learning disability?

_____

_____

2.   How are learning disabilities defined?

_____

_____

3.   How is ADHD defined?

_____

_____

4.   What is the controversy related to the diagnosis and treatment of ADHD?

_____

_____

5.   What interventions are recommended for adolescents with ADHD?

_____

_____

6.   What is Public Law 92–142?

_____

_____

7.   What is the Individuals with Disabilities Education Act (IDEA)?

_____

_____

8.   What does least restrictive environment mean?

_____

_____

9.   What is inclusion?

_____

_____

ADOLESCENTS WHO ARE GIFTED
SECTION REVIEW

1.   According to Winner, what are the three characteristics of adolescents who are gifted?

_____

_____

2.   What are some characteristics that characterize gifted adolescents?

_____

_____

3.   What program options exist for students who are gifted?

_____

_____

EXPLORATIONS
IN ADOLESCENT DEVELOPMENT

Compare and contrast the following aspects of secondary schools in Australia, Brazil, Germany, Japan, Russia, and the United States: (a) mandatory age: (b) number of levels; (c) role of sports; (d) entrance and exit exams; (e) content and philosophy; and (f) foreign language education.

_____

_____

COGNITIVE CHALLENGE

1. In three sections, list the things you 'liked most' about high school; 'liked least' about high school; and would change about school in general to make them more effective.

    liked most

    _____

    _____

    liked least

    _____

    _____

    would change

    _____

    _____

2. Think back on your high school classmates that were of diverse ethnic, religious, and socioeconomic background. How well did your school meet the social and educational needs of these students? Knowing what you know now, how would you have responded to the needs of these students if you had been a teacher at the school?

    _____

    _____

ADOLESCENCE IN RESEARCH

Describe two attributes which were found in adolescents of the 8–4 arrangement and researchers conclusions.

 ## COMPREHENSIVE REVIEW

1. In the 1970s, three independent panels that examined the benefits of secondary school for adolescents concluded that high schools
    a. increase adolescents' exposure to adults.
    b. restrict the transition to adulthood.
    c. decrease adolescents' sense of alienation.
    d. increase employment opportunities for adolescents.

2. Which kind of school has been referred to as "teenage warehouses?"
   a. Middle school
   b. Elementary school
   c. High school
   d. Military school

3. In which country are martial arts classes a standard?
   a. United States
   b. Russian
   c. Brazil
   d. Japan

4. A major current concern among educators regarding middle schools or junior highs is that
   a. there are not enough of them to accommodate the growing population.
   b. they are becoming "watered down" versions of high school.
   c. the curriculum is too basic for the growing needs of children of that age.
   d. there is a shortage of teachers for these schools.

5. According to the back-to-basics movement, the main function of schools should be to
   a. provide extracurricular activities.
   b. enhance the social and emotional development of adolescents.
   c. be comprehensive and provide a multifaceted curriculum.
   d. develop an intellectually mature person by emphasizing training in basic subject.

6. The major rationale for the establishment of junior high schools in the 1920s–1930s was that
   a. early adolescents experience many changes at this time and need to be segregated.
   b. the poor economic conditions put pressure upon the schools to provide more "baby-sitting" space.
   c. too many older adolescents were fighting with the young adolescents.
   d. high schools were "upgraded" and reorganized to encourage students to go on to college or university.

7. The top-dog phenomenon refers to
   a. the superior formal operational reasoning of high school students compared to junior high students.
   b. the dating advantage that junior high school girls have over junior high school boys.
   c. the self-perceptions of junior high school students who attend supportive and stable schools.
   d. the lowered status experienced by students when they move from elementary to junior high school.

8. Darren has been complaining about not being able to make good grades. He says he used to feel good in school, but now feels like a little fish in a big pond. Darren
   a. probably have the same school crises as girls of his age.
   b. is struggling with the transition to junior high school.
   c. is becoming self-conscious because of the emergence of formal operational thought.
   d. probably has developed the underdog adjustment disorder associated with junior high entry.

9.   Effective schools for young adolescents have all of the following characteristics EXCEPT
    a.   similar methods of grouping students.
    b.   emphasis on the school context as a community.
    c.   curricula emphasizing self-exploration and definition.
    d.   responsiveness to their community political milieus.

10.   In which country would you find a *juku* or *cramming school*?
    a.   United States
    b.   Australia
    c.   Germany
    d.   Japan

11.   Freddy is the oldest boy in his middle school and the best athlete. Which of the following is likely true about Freddy?
    a.   He is probably very unpopular.
    b.   He is probably a poor student.
    c.   He is probably a *top dog*.
    d.   He is probably truant.

12.   Which of the following is NOT a recommendation by the 1989 Carnegie Council on Adolescent Development?
    a.   Involving parents and community leaders in the schools
    b.   Boosting students' health and fitness with more in-school programs and helping students who need public health care get it
    c.   Merging multiple small school districts into larger districts so as to offer more programs and better utilize resources
    d.   Lowering student-to-counselor rations from several hundred-to-1 to 10 to 1

13.   The report from the Carnegie Commission encourages
    a.   disbanding middle schools in favor of a longer stay in elementary school.
    b.   eliminating high schools and moving from junior high directly to college prep schools.
    c.   arranging middle school students in smaller groups.
    d.   eliminating middle schools in favor of junior high schools.

14.   The students least likely to complete high school are
    a.   African American.
    b.   from single-parent homes.
    c.   Native Americans.
    d.   Urban Hispanics.

15.   About 50 percent of the dropouts do so for school-related reasons, whereas another 20 percent drop out of high school
    a.   for economic reasons.
    b.   because they are unable to read and write well.
    c.   because they are in trouble with law-enforcement authorities.
    d.   are Native Americans.

16. Small schools are more likely to
    a.   be associated with prosocial behavior than large schools.
    b.   provide fewer opportunities for school participation than large schools.
    c.   promote better academic achievement than large schools.
    d.   promote more antisocial behavior than large schools.

17. The _____ classroom is characterized by teachers who serve as facilitators of student learning rather than teaching in the traditional manner.
    a.   open
    b.   new wave
    c.   multi-dimensional
    d.   California

18. Young adolescents appear to respond well to teachers who
    a.   let the students set the limits in the classroom.
    b.   are pals.
    c.   are insensitive to student criticism.
    d.   use natural authority.

19. A teacher says to a student, "Thank you for being quiet in class today for a change." With which type of student is this more likely to occur?
    a.   A "trouble-maker"
    b.   A White-American student
    c.   An African-American student
    d.   The "best" student in the class

20. Among minority youth who stay in school, poor academic performance is linked to
    a.   the refusal of other students to study with them.
    b.   the unwillingness to engage in cooperative learning.
    c.   the language barriers.
    d.   coming from a poor, single-parent family.

21. The Education for All Handicapped Children Act mandated that all states do which of the following for all handicapped children?
    a.   Provide free health care
    b.   Provide educational programs for their parents
    c.   Provide free testing programs
    d.   Provided individualized educational programs

22. Inclusion refers to
    a.   teaching handicapped children in public schools.
    b.   assigning handicapped children to regular classrooms.
    c.   giving handicapped children a high educational priority.
    d.   assuring handicapped children interact with nonhandicapped children whenever possible.

23. Shawna, a second grader, has no trouble with math, science, or art; but she cannot spell, read, or write. It is likely that Shawna has a(n)
    a. visual impairment.
    b. speech handicap.
    c. learning disability.
    d. attention deficit.

24. Timothy is suffering from attention-deficit hyperactivity disorder. He is most likely to be experiencing all but one of the following symptoms?
    a. short attention span.
    b. easily distracted.
    c. below-normal intelligence.
    d. high levels of physical activity.

25. What type of drug is used to control attention-deficit hyperactivity disorder?
    a. Stimulants
    b. Depressant
    c. Tranquilizers
    d. Relaxants

26. The I Have a Dream program (IHAD) was created by Eugene Lang to help in
    a. alleviating the school violence problem in America.
    b. to boost student literacy rates.
    c. to decrease the likelihood of a child dropping out of school.
    d. to get troubled kids off of the streets.

27. What is the best school size?
    a. 500 to 600 or fewer
    b. 800 to 1000
    c. 1000 to 1500
    d. 2000 or more

28. _____ is the only country in the world that has high school athletics and sports as an integral part of the educational system.
    a. South Africa
    b. Japan
    c. Italy
    d. The United States

ADOLESCENCE ON THE SCREEN

- *To Sir, With Love* is the story of a black engineer who takes a job in a rough London school.

- *The Breakfast Club* portrays how students in a Saturday detention class coalesce as a group.

- *Dangerous Minds* depicts a female teacher struggling to deal with tough inner city teenagers.

■ *Dead Poet's Society* stars Robin Williams playing an English teacher, who tries to change the way students learn literature.

■ *Middle School Confessions* (HBO) is a documentary that portrays in shocking detail the crisis in today's middle schools in America.

ADOLESCENCE IN BOOKS

■ *Adolescence in the 1990s,* edited by Ruby Takanishi (Teachers College Press, 1993), features a number of experts on adolescence addressing the risks and opportunities for adolescents in today's world. Many chapters focus on improving the quality of schooling for adolescents.

■ *Successful Schools for Young Adolescents*, by Joan Lipsitz (Transaction Books: NJ, 1984), is a classic resource for people involved in middle school education.

■ *Endangered Minds*, by Jane M. Healy (Simon and Schuster: NY, 1999) depicts clearly the problems existing in our schools and makes specific suggestions on how to change things.

■ *Failure to Connect: How Computers Affect Our Children's Minds, and What We Can Do About It*, by Jane M. Healy (Simon and Schuster: NY, 1999) presents a very strong case "against" the use of computers in modern classrooms.

ADOLESCENCE IN RESEARCH

Concerning Simmons' and Blyth's 1987 study comparing school systems with a 6–3–3 arrangement and those with an 8–4 arrangement, state the hypothesis, the research methods (if known), the research conclusions, and the implications and applications for adolescent development.

_____

_____

Answer Key

KEY TERMS

1. **back-to-basics movement** This philosophy stresses that the function of schools should be the rigorous training of intellectual skills through such subjects as English, mathematics, and science.

2. **direct instruction approach** A teacher-centered approach that is characterized by teacher direction and control, mastery of academic skills, high expectations for students' progress, and maximum time spent on learning tasks.

3. **cognitive constructivist approaches** Emphasizes the adolescent's active, cognitive construction of knowledge and understanding; an example of this approach is Piaget's theory.

4. **social constructivist approach** Focus on collaboration with others to produce knowledge and understanding; an example of this approach is Vygotsky's theory.

5. **top-dog phenomenon** The circumstance of moving from the top position (in elementary school, the oldest, biggest, and most powerful students) to the lowest position (in middle or junior high school, the youngest, smallest, and least powerful).

6. **authoritative strategy of classroom management** Encourages students to be independent thinkers and doers but still involves effective monitoring. Authoritative teachers engage students in considerable verbal give-and-take and show a caring attitude toward them. However, they still declare limits when necessary.

7. **authoritarian strategy of classroom management** Is restrictive and punitive. The focus is mainly on keeping order in the classroom rather than on instruction and learning.

8. **permissive strategy of classroom management** Offers students considerable autonomy but provides them with little support for developing learning skills or managing their behavior.

9. **aptitude-treatment interaction (ATI)** This interaction stresses the importance of both the attitudes and the characteristics of the adolescent, such as academic potential or personality traits, and the treatments or experiences, such as the educational techniques that the adolescent receives. *Aptitude* refers to such characteristics as the academic potential and personality characteristics on which students differ; *treatment* refers to educational techniques, such as structured versus flexible classrooms.

10. **jigsaw classroom** Students from different cultural backgrounds are placed in a cooperative group in which they have to construct different parts of a project to reach a common goal.

11. **learning disability** Describes individuals who 1) are of normal intelligence or above, 2) have difficulties in a least one academic area and usually several, and 3) their difficulties cannot be attributed to any other diagnosed problem or disorder, such as mental retardation.

12. **attention deficit/hyperactivity disorder (ADHD)** Is a disability in which children and adolescents show one or more of the following characteristics over a period of time: 1) inattention, 2) hyperactivity, and 3) impulsivity.

13. **Public Law 94–142** The Education for All Handicapped Children Act, which requires all students with disabilities to be given a free, appropriate education and provides the funding to help implement this education.

14. **Individuals with Disabilities Education Act (IDEA)** This spells out broad mandates for services to all children and adolescents with disabilities. These include evaluation and eligibility determination, appropriate education and the Individualized Education Program (IEP), and least restrictive environment.

15. **least restrictive environment** A setting that is as similar as possible to the one in which the children, or adolescents without a disability are educated; under the Individuals with Disabilities Education Act, the child or adolescent must be educated in this setting.

16. **inclusion** Educating a child or adolescent with special education needs full-time in a general school program.

17. **adolescents who are gifted** They are characterized by having above average intelligence (usually defined as an IQ of 120 or higher) and/or superior talent in some domain such as art, music, or mathematics.

KEY PEOPLE
IN THE STUDY OF ADOLESCENCE

1.	D	2.	C	3.	A	4.	E	5.	G
6.	F	7.	B	8.	I	9.	H		

"DR. DETAIL'S"
MATCHING EXERCISE

1.	D	2.	C	3.	A	4.	E	5.	B
6.	G	7.	H	8.	F	9.	I		

APPROACHES TO EDUCATING STUDENTS
SECTION REVIEW

1. In the late 1800s, most states passed laws prohibiting child labor. These coincided a move toward compulsory secondary education.

2. This is the popular notion of the 1970s to build high schools that offered some of everything, like shopping malls.

3. The basis of the debate is between frills or back to the basics.

4. This is the movement to focus more on basic curriculum, e.g., math, reading, and science.

5. A teacher-centered approach that is characterized by teacher direction and control, mastery of skills, high expectations for students' progress, and maximum time spent on learning tasks.

6. These emphasize the adolescent's active, cognitive construction of knowledge, and understanding.

7. These focus on collaboration with others to produce knowledge and understanding.

8. ***Cognitive and Metacognitive Factors***

1. D	2. B	3. E	4. A	5. C
6. F				

Motivational, Instructional, Developmental, Social, and Individual Difference Factors

1. C	2. A	3. B	4. G	5. E
6. F	7. H	8. D		

SCHOOLS' CHANGING SOCIAL DEVELOPMENTAL CONTEXTS
SECTION REVIEW

1. Create communities for learning; teach a core of common knowledge; provide an opportunity for all students to succeed; strengthen teachers and principals; prepare teachers for the middle grades; improve academic performance through better health and fitness; engage families in the education of adolescents; connect schools with communities.

2. They start out as protected environments and become increasingly more complex, especially socially.

EVALUATE TRANSITIONS IN MIDDLE SCHOOL/JUNIOR HIGH
SECTION REVIEW

1. Junior highs were justified on the basis of physical, cognitive, and social changes that characterize early adolescence.

2. Middle schools appear to better suite the maturation rates of children, so ninth grade has slowly become part of high school again.

3. Again, sixth to eighth grade seems to cover a phase of maturation and the transition to high school is easier in the ninth grade. In junior high, one problem is that ninth graders are far more mature than the other children.

4. The sixth through eighth transition generally goes well, but can be complicated by the fact that this period encompasses much of puberty for the average child.

5. Because of the onset of puberty.

6. The circumstance of moving from the top, power position to the lowest position, due to changing schools.

7. These schools emphasize the importance of creating an environment that was positive for the adolescent's social and emotional development.

8. Develop smaller communities; lower student-to-counselor ratios; involve parents and community leaders; develop curriculum that produces competent students; have teachers team-teach in more flexible curriculum blocks; boosting students' health and fitness.

TRANSITION FROM HIGH SCHOOL TO COLLEGE
SECTION REVIEW

1.   Both involve change and possible stress.

2.   Many report that they feel overwhelmed.

3.   Laws requiring more time in school have been passed and there is a general consensus that a high school diploma is the basis for finding a good job.

4.   They have lower grades, especially in reading.

5.   Reasons can be school-related, economic, family-related, peer-related, and personal.

6.   Approaches that bridge the gap between school and work, such as the "I Have a Dream" foundation.

UNDERSTANDING SCHOOLS, CLASSROOMS, TEACHERS, AND PARENTS
SECTION REVIEW

1.   Classrooms about 20, schools 500–600.

2.   Safe, personalized climate.

3.   More course offerings.

4.   Teachers who more carefully monitor activities have the better classroom climates.

5.   Encourages students to be independent thinkers and doers but still involves effective monitoring. Authoritative teachers involve students in considerable verbal give and take.

6.   This is restrictive and punitive to maintain order.

7.   This offers students considerable autonomy but provides them with little support for developing learning skills or managing their behavior.

8.   This stresses the importance of both adolescents' characteristics and motivation and the treatments or experiences they receive in schools.

9.   Parents are often active in early education, but become less involved when children grow into adolescents.

10.   Part of the problem appears to be higher self-confidence and self-efficacy found in teachers of children in lower grades, as opposed to those teaching seventh grade or above.

11.   a.   Parents need to be knowledgeable about adolescent health and safety issues.
      b.   Schools need to communicate with families about school programs and the individual progress of the adolescents.
      c.   Parents need to be more involved in schools assisting teachers.
      d.   Parents need to be involved in their children's homework.
      e.   Parents need to be involved in decision making at school.
      f.   Schools need to collaborate with community organizations.

12. a. Develop a positive relationship with students.
     b. Get students to share and assume responsibility.
     c. Reward appropriate behavior.

THE EFFECTS OF SOCIOECONOMIC STATUS AND ETHNICITY IN SCHOOLS
SECTION REVIEW

1. Adolescents from backgrounds of poverty have more difficulties on average.

2. Ethnicity and poverty tend to go hand-in-hand with fewer educational opportunities and poorer schools for those children from impoverished backgrounds.

3. Where students from different cultural backgrounds are placed in cooperative groups in which they have to construct different parts of a project to reach a common goal.

4. Comer recommends (1) a governance and management team that develops a comprehensive school plan, (2) a mental health or school support team, and (3) a parents program.

ADOLESCENTS WITH DISABILITIES
SECTION REVIEW

1. Normal intelligence versus sub-normal performance.

2. Adolescents with a learning disability are of normal intelligence and have difficulties in a least one academic area and usually several, and their difficulty cannot be attributed to any other diagnosed problem.

3. ADHD is a disability in which children and adolescents show one or more of the following characteristics over a period of time: inattention, hyperactivity, and impulsivity.

4. The controversy is that in many parts of the country it is over-diagnosed and over-medicated.

5. Many recommend a combination of academic, behavioral, and medical interventions to help students.

6. The Education for All Handicapped Children Act.

7. IDEA spells out broad mandates for services to all children and adolescents with disabilities.

8. A setting that is similar as possible to the one in which the children without a disability are educated.

9. Inclusion used to be called mainstreaming. It means educating a child or adolescent with special education needs full-time in a general school program.

ADOLESCENTS WHO ARE GIFTED
SECTION REVIEW

1. (a) precocity, (b) marching to their own drummer, and (c) a passion for mastery.

2. Above average intelligence and/or superior talent in some domain, such as art, music or math.

3.   (a) Special classes, (b) acceleration and enrichment in the regular classroom setting, (c) mentor and apprenticeship programs, (d) work/study and community service programs.

EXPLORATIONS IN ADOLESCENT DEVELOPMENT

1.   Brazil—14; Russia—17; Germany, Japan, Australia, and U.S.—15 to 16.

2.   Most schools have two or more levels (elementary, junior/middle, and high school), but Germany has three ability tracks.

3.   U.S. is the only country in the world that has integrated sports into the public school system. Private schools in other countries may have organized sports.

4.   Japanese secondary schools have entrance exam, but other five countries do not; only Australia and Germany have exit exams.

5.   Russia emphasizes preparation for work, but gifted students attend special schools; Brazil requires that students take four foreign languages, due to the country's international characters; Australian students take courses in sheep husbandry and weaving, activities important to the country's economics and culture; Japanese students take courses in Western languages, literature, physical education, and art.

COGNITIVE CHALLENGE

1.   No answer provided. Individual activity.

2.   No answer provided. Individual activity.

ADOLESCENCE IN RESEARCH

The adolescents in the 8–4 arrangement had higher self-esteem and participated more in extracurricular activities than the adolescents in the 6–3–3 arrangement, who had to change schools twice. The researchers concluded that the earlier the school transitions occur in adolescence, the more difficult it likely is for students.

⊠ COMPREHENSIVE REVIEW

1.	b	**2.**	c	**3.**	d	**4.**	b	**5.**	d
6.	a	**7.**	d	**8.**	b	**9.**	a	**10.**	d
11.	c	**12.**	c	**13.**	c	**14.**	c	**15.**	a
16.	a	**17.**	a	**18.**	d	**19.**	c	**20.**	d
21.	d	**22.**	d	**23.**	b	**24.**	c	**25.**	c
26.	c	**27.**	c	**28.**	a	**29.**	d		

Chapter 8   Culture

Learning Goals with Key Terms and Key People in Boldface

1.0   THE RELATIONSHIP BETWEEN CULTURE AND ADOLESCENCE
    A.   **Culture**
        1.1   What is culture?
    B.   **The Relevance of Culture to the Study of Adolescence**
        1.2   What is the relevance of culture to the study of adolescence in the twenty-first century?
    C.   **Cross-Cultural Comparisons**
        1.3   What are **cross-cultural studies**?
        1.4   In what context did the study of adolescence emerge in **cross-cultural** comparisons?
    D.   **Models of Cultural Change**
        1.5   What four models have been used to understand cultural changes within and between cultures?
        1.6   What is **assimilation**?
        1.7   What is **acculturation**?
        1.8   What is **alternation model**?
        1.9   What is the multiculturalism?
        1.10   What is the advantage of using the **multicultural model**?
    E.   **Rites of Passage**
        1.11   What is meant by **rites of passage**?
        1.12   How are rites of passage different for American and primitive cultures?

2.0   SOCIOECONOMIC STATUS (SES) AND POVERTY
    A.   **The Nature of Socioeconomic Status**
        2.1   What is meant by socioeconomic status?
        2.2   What is the significance of socioeconomic status for adolescent development?
    B.   **Socioeconomic Variations in Families, Neighborhoods, and Schools**
        2.3   How does socioeconomic status affects the families, neighborhoods, and schools of adolescents?
        2.4   What effect do socioeconomic variables in families, neighborhoods, and schools have on adolescent development?
        2.5   How do low-socioeconomic parents differ from their middle-SES counterparts?

3.0   THE ROLE OF POVERTY IN ADOLESCENT DEVELOPMENT
    A.   **Poverty**
        3.1   What is poverty?
        3.2   What percentage of U.S. children lives in poverty?
        3.3   What is the nature of the subculture of the poor?
        3.4   What is meant by the **feminization of poverty**?
        3.5   What effects do persistent and long-lasting poverty have on development?

4.0 THE EFFECT OF ETHNICITY ON ADOLESCENT DEVELOPMENT?

A. Domains and Issues
4.1   What is ethnicity?

4.2   How do history, the economy, and social experiences produce legitimate differences between ethnic minority groups and between ethnic minority groups and the White majority?

4.3   What is **ethnocentrism**?

4.4   Are ethnic differences often interpreted as deficits?

4.5   How does failure to recognize diversity lead to stereotyping?

4.6   What is **prejudice?**

4.7   In what ways do ethnic minority adolescents experience prejudice, discrimination, and bias?

4.8   Why is adolescence a critical juncture in the development of ethnic minority individuals?

5.0 ETHNIC MINORITY ADOLESCENTS

A. African-American Adolescents
5.1   What are some defining characteristics of African-American adolescents?

5.2   Why is low SES a problem among black youth?

B. Latino Adolescents
5.3   Where are national origins of Latino adolescents?

5.4   What is a **Chicano**?

5.5   What roles do families play in the lives of Latino youth?

C. Asian-American Adolescents
5.6   What countries do Asian American adolescents represent?

5.7   What accounts for the strong achievement orientation of Asian American youth?

D. Native American Adolescents
5.8   What discriminations have Native American adolescents endured?

E. The United States and Canada: Nations with Many Cultures
5.9   How is American a cultural mosaic?

5.10   What are included in Canadian cultures?

5.11   How do adolescents in Canada compare to adolescents in the United States?

5.12   What are the main ethnic ties of Canadian adolescents?

6.0 TELEVISION AND OTHER MEDIA

A. Functions and Use of Media
6.1   What are the functions of media?

6.2   How do adolescents use media?

B. Television
6.3   What are the functions of television for adolescents?

6.4   What are the special concerns raised by television today?

6.5   How strongly does televised violence influence a person's behavior?

6.6   What impact is television having on the sexual behaviors of youth?

C. The Media and Music
6.7   How important is music to adolescents?

6.8   How do adolescent's music tastes change during the course of adolescence?

6.9   What adolescent needs does music fulfill?

D. **Technology, Computers, and the Internet**
  6.10 How is the technological revolution affecting teenagers today?
  6.11 What is the **Internet**?
  6.12 What are some concerns surrounding **Internet** regulation?
  6.13 What is **E-mail**?
  6.14 What is the importance of **E-mail** for adolescents?
  6.15 What inequities might arise as a result of the technological revolution?
  6.16 How have computers impacted schools?
  6.17 What is the relationship between technology and adolescent learning?
E. **Social Policy and Media**
  6.18 What social policy recommendations concerning the media would benefit adolescents?

Exercises

KEY TERMS
COMPLETION EXERCISE

Each key term is presented in the form of an incomplete sentence. Complete each sentence by either defining the term or giving an example. Compare your definitions with those given at the end of the study guide chapter.

1.   **Culture** is the

    _____

    _____

2.   A person's **socioeconomic status (SES)** is

    _____

    _____

3.   Because of Juan's **ethnicity,** he often

    _____

    _____

4.   **Ethnocentrism** leads to

    _____

    _____

5.   **Cross-cultural studies** are used in order to

    _____

    _____

6.   **Assimilation** is seen when

    _____

    _____

7.   **Acculturation** results from

    _____

    _____

8.   The **alternation model** assumes that

_____

_____

9.   The **multicultural model** promotes

_____

_____

10.   **Rites of passage** are evidenced in

_____

_____

11.   **Feminization of poverty** refers to

_____

_____

12.   An example of **prejudice** is

_____

_____

13.   The term **Chicano** means

_____

_____

14.   The **Internet** is the

_____

_____

15.   **E-mail** is used for

_____

_____

KEY PEOPLE
IN THE STUDY OF ADOLESCENCE

Match the person with the concept of adolescent development with which they are associated.

_____ 1. Richard Brislin   A. Asian American researcher who studies prejudice and discrimination

_____ 2. Vonnie McLoyd   B. A cross-cultural psychologist who argues that intimate contact reduces conflict between individuals from different ethnic backgrounds

_____ 3. Stanley Sue   C. Psychologist who observed that one function of education is to rearrange prejudice

_____ 4. James Jones   D. Studied the effect on children of ethnic minority mothers' poverty and stress

_____ 5. Sandra Calvert   E. Co-director of the Harvard Immigration Projects

_____ 6. Carola Suárez-Orozco   F. Studies the role of the technological revolution in adolescent development

"DR. DETAIL'S"
PUZZLE EXERCISE

Across

1. A dimension of culture based on heritage, nationality, race, religion, and language.
2. Cultural change that occurs with first-hand contact between two cultural groups.
3. An unjustified negative attitude towards a person due to his/her membership in a group.
4. The name politically conscious Mexican American adolescents give themselves.
5. The core of computer-mediated communication.

Down

1. The behavior, patterns, and beliefs of a particular group of people.
2. Absorption of ethnic minority groups into a dominant group.
3. Stands for electronic mail.

CULTURE AND ADOLESCENT DEVELOPMENT
SECTION REVIEW

1.   List the seven features of culture according to Richard Brislin (1993).

    a. _____

    _____

    b. _____

    _____

    c. _____

    _____

    d. _____

    _____

    e. _____

    _____

    f. _____

    _____

    g. _____

    _____

2.   List five common features of ethnocentrism present in all cultures.

    a. _____

    _____

    b. _____

    _____

    c. _____

    _____

    d. _____

       _____

    e. _____

       _____

3.   What are cross-cultural studies?

    _____

    _____

4.   What four models have been used to understand cultural changes within and between cultures?

    _____

    _____

5.   What is alternation model?

    _____

    _____

6.   What is multiculturalism?

    _____

    _____

7.   What is meant by rites of passage?

    _____

    _____

SOCIOECONOMIC STATUS AND ADOLESCENCE
SECTION REVIEW

1.   According to Richards and colleagues (1994), what three negative experiences are worse for adolescents living in poverty than their middle-class counterparts?

    a. _____

    b. _____

    c. _____

2.   What is meant by socioeconomic status?

_____

_____

POVERTY IN ADOLESCENT DEVELOPMENT
SECTION REVIEW

1.   What is the most common marker of poverty?

_____

_____

2.   Compare the poverty rate of adolescents in the United States to those living in Canada and Sweden.

_____

_____

3.   Compare the poverty rate of African American and Latino adolescents with the overall adolescent poverty rate in the United States.

_____

_____

4.   Give three explanations for why poverty is so high among American youth?

   a.   _____

   _____

   b.   _____

   _____

   c.   _____

   _____

5.   What is meant by the feminization of poverty?

_____

_____

ISSUES RELATED TO ETHNICITY
SECTION REVIEW

1. What is ethnicity?

_____

_____

2. Are ethnic differences often interpreted as deficits?

_____

_____

3. How does failure to recognize diversity lead to stereotyping?

_____

_____

4. What is prejudice?

_____

_____

ETHNIC MINORITY ADOLESCENTS
SECTION REVIEW

1. What are some defining characteristics of African-American adolescents?

_____

_____

2. Why is low SES a problem among black youth?

_____

_____

3. Where are the national origins of Latino adolescents?

_____

_____

4. What is a Chicano?

_____

_____

5. What role does families play in the lives of Latino youth?

_____

_____

6. What accounts for the strong achievement orientation of Asian American youth?

_____

_____

7. What discriminations have Native American adolescents endured?

_____

_____

TELEVISION AND OTHER MEDIA
SECTION REVIEW

1. What are the six functions of media for adolescents?

_____

_____

2. How strongly does television influence a child's negative behavior?

_____

_____

3. What impact is television having on the sexual behaviors of youth?

_____

_____

4. How important is music to adolescents?

_____

_____

5. What is the Internet?

_____

_____

6.   What is the relationship between technology and adolescent learning?

          _____

          _____

7.   What social policy recommendations were made by the Carnegie Council on Adolescent Development regarding the effects of the media?

          _____

          _____

COGNITIVE CHALLENGE

1.   Take a moment to imagine how your life might have been different if you were of another race or ethnic background. Would your friends be the same? Would you live in the same neighborhood? How might your family be different? Would your attitude towards education be different?

          _____

          _____

ADOLESCENCE IN RESEARCH

Concerning the evaluation of the Quantum Opportunities Program, comparing mentored students with a nonmentored control group, state the hypothesis, the research methods (if known), the research conclusions, and the implications and applications for adolescent development.

          _____

          _____

⊠ COMPREHENSIVE REVIEW

1.   The learning and shared behavioral patterns, beliefs, and values of a group of people that are passed on from one generation to the next is known as
   a.   culture.
   b.   minority.
   c.   ethnicity.
   d.   socioeconomic status.

2.   Family income is a good measure of
   a.   ethnicity.
   b.   social class.
   c.   culture.
   d.   ethnocentrism.

3.   _____ is a tendency to favor one's own group over others.
   a.   ethnicity
   b.   social class
   c.   culture
   d.   ethnocentrism

4.   In comparison to adolescents from other cultures, American adolescents are often described as more
   a.   passive.
   b.   Rebellious.
   c.   achievement-oriented.
   d.   mentally healthy.

5.   Of the different ethnic groups living in America, which is the most achievement oriented?
   a.   African-American.
   b.   Asian American.
   c.   Latino.
   d.   Anglo-American.

6.   The melting pot belief in the United States assumes which process of cultural change?
   a.   Assimilation
   b.   Acculturation
   c.   Accommodation
   d.   Cultural schema shifting

7.   Which of the following is NOT an adolescent rite of passage?
   a.   Experimentation with alcohol.
   b.   Participation in athletics.
   c.   Experimentation with sex.
   d.   Gaining independence from parents.

8.   By the end of adolescence, what percentage of youth have had sexual intercourse?
   a.   30%.
   b.   90%.
   c.   50%.
   d.   70%.

9.   Children from low-SES backgrounds are at high risk for all but one of the following?
   a.   Depression
   b.   Peer conflict
   c.   Academic success
   d.   Low self-confidence

10.   Which of the following is LEAST likely to make use of the extended family unit?
    a.   African American.
    b.   Anglo-American.
    c.   Latino.
    d.   Asian American.

11.   According to research by Lee, successful African-American students are most likely to have mentioned _____ as having an important influence on their lives.
    a.   their father
    b.   Bill Clinton
    c.   Jesus Christ
    d.   Jessie Jackson

12.   Rituals such as bar mitzvah and confirmation are examples of
    a.   rites of passage.
    b.   cultural transitions of sexuality.
    c.   evidence of ethnocentrism.
    d.   family traditions.

13.   The most common rite of passage for American adolescents is probably
    a.   a religious ceremony.
    b.   going off to college.
    c.   graduating from high school.
    d.   buying the first car.

14.   _____ percent of the children in the United States live in poverty.
    a.   Eleven
    b.   Thirty-three
    c.   Sixteen
    d.   Twenty

15.   The adolescent raised in a single-parent, female-headed household is more likely than not to be
    a.   sexually active.
    b.   promiscuous.
    c.   in trouble with the law.
    d.   poor.

16.   When an adolescent has a negative attitude about another individual because that individual belongs to a particular group, the adolescent is exhibiting
    a.   values.
    b.   an opinion.
    c.   prejudice.
    d.   cognitive narrowing.

17. El Puente is a social program for _____ Latinos.
    a. low-income
    b. female
    c. Protestant
    d. English-speaking

18. Which ethnic minority adolescent group has the highest suicide rate in the United States?
    a. African American
    b. Hispanic
    c. Native American
    d. Asian

19. Compared to the United States, the ethnic subcultures of Canadian adolescents tend to be organized along the lines of
    a. economic power.
    b. political affiliation.
    c. religious participation.
    d. gender differences.

20. Adolescents spend approximately _____ of their waking hours with some form of mass media.
    a. one-eighth
    b. one-third
    c. one-half
    d. two-thirds

21. Television has been criticized for all of the following EXCEPT
    a. teaching adolescents that problems are easily resolved.
    b. declining national achievement test scores.
    c. increasing the leisure activities of adolescents.
    d. creating passive learners.

22. Which is the most accurate conclusion about the long-term effects of watching television violence?
    a. Watching television violence causes crime
    b. Watching television violence has no relationship to crime
    c. Watching television violence may be associated with violence in some young people
    d. Watching television violence makes young people less afraid of being a victim.

ADOLESCENCE ON THE SCREEN

- *Saturday Night Fever* highlights the disco era.

- *Pulp Fiction* is a parody of drug-use, violence, and down-and-out diner bandits.

- *Woodstock* captures the drug and rock culture of the 1960s.

- *Fresh* Shows the challenges faced by a 12-year-old trying to grow up in one of America's roughest neighborhoods.

ADOLESCENCE
IN BOOKS

- *The Adolescent & Young Adult Fact Book*, by Janet Simons, Belva Finlay, and Alice Yang (Children's Defense Fund, 1991), describes the role of poverty and ethnicity in adolescent development.

- *Children's Journey Through the Information Age*, by Sandra Calvert (McGraw-Hill: IA, 1999), covers topics related to the information age, including television and computers.

- *Understanding Culture's Influence on Behavior*, by Richard Brislin (Harcourt Brace: FL, 1993), details the role of culture in behavior and development.

- *Failure to Connect: How Computers Affect Our Children's Minds, and What We Can Do About It*, by Jane M. Healy (Simon and Schuster: NJ, 1999) presents a very strong case "against" the use of computers in modern classrooms.

Answer Key

KEY
TERMS

1.   **culture** The behavior, patterns, beliefs, and all other products of a particular group of people that are passed on from generation to generation.

2.   **socioeconomic status (SES)** A grouping of people with similar occupational, educational, and economic characteristics.

3.   **ethnicity** A dimension of culture based on cultural heritage, nationality, race, religion, and language.

4.   **ethnocentrism** A tendency to favor one's own group over other groups.

5.   **cross-cultural studies** Studies that compare a culture with one or more other cultures. Such studies provide information about the degree to which adolescent development is similar, or universal, across cultures, or about the degree to which it is culture specific.

6.   **assimilation** The absorption of ethnic minority groups into the dominant group, which often means the loss of some or virtually all of the behavior and values of the ethnic minority group.

7.   **acculturation** Cultural change that results from continuous, first-hand contact between two distinctive cultural groups.

8.   **alternation model** This model assumes that it is possible for an individual to know and understand two different cultures. It also assumes that individuals can alter their behavior to fit a particular social context.

9.   **multicultural model** This model promotes a pluralistic approach to understanding two or more cultures. It argues that people can maintain their distinctive identities while working with others from different cultures to meet common national or economic needs.

10.   **rites of passage** Ceremonies or rituals that mark an individual's transition from one status to another, especially into adulthood.

11.   **feminization of poverty** The fact that far more women than men live in poverty. Likely causes are women's low income, divorce, and the resolution of divorce cases by the judicial system, which leaves women with less money than they and their children need to adequately function.

12.   **prejudice** An unjustified negative attitude toward an individual because of her or his membership in a group.

13.   **Chicano** The name politically conscious Mexican American adolescents give themselves, reflecting the combination of their Spanish-Mexican-Indian heritage and Anglo influence.

14.   **Internet** The core of computer-mediated communication. The Internet is worldwide and connects thousands of computer networks, providing an incredible array of information adolescents can access.

15.   **e-mail** Stands for electronic mail and is a valuable way the Internet can be used. Written messages can be sent to and received by individuals as well as large numbers of people.

KEY PEOPLE
IN THE STUDY OF ADOLESCENCE

1. B   2. D   3. A   4. C   5. F
6. E

"DR. DETAIL'S"
PUZZLE EXERCISE

Across   *Down*
1. ethnicity   1. culture
2. acculturation   2. assimilation
3. prejudice   3. e-mail
4. Chicano
5. Internet

CULTURE AND ADOLESCENT DEVELOPMENT
SECTION REVIEW

1.   a.   Culture is made up of ideals, values, and assumptions about life that guide people's behaviors.
        b.   Culture is made by people.
        c.   Culture is transmitted from generation to generation.
        d.   Culture's influence is noticed most in well-meaning clashes between people from very different cultural backgrounds.
        e.   Despite compromises, cultural values still remain.
        f.   People react emotionally when their cultural values are violated or when their cultural expectations are ignored.
        g.   People accept a cultural value at one point in their life and reject it at another.

2.   a.   People believe that what happens in their culture is natural and correct and that what happens in other cultures is unnatural and incorrect.
        b.   People perceive their cultural customs as universally valid, that is, good for everyone.
        c.   People behave in ways that favor their own cultural group.
        d.   People feel proud of their cultural group.
        e.   People feel hostile toward other cultural groups.

3.   These involve the comparison of a culture with one or more other cultures, which provides information about the degree to which adolescent development is similar, or universal, across cultures, or the degree to which it is culture-specific.

4.   (1) assimilation, (2) acculturation, (3) alternation, and (4) multiculturalism.

5.   This model assumes that it is possible for an individual to know and understand two different cultures.

6.   This model promotes a pluralistic approach to understanding two or more cultures.

7.   These are ceremonies or rituals that mark an individual's transition from one status to another, especially into adulthood.

SOCIOECONOMIC STATUS AND ADOLESCENCE
SECTION REVIEW

1.   a.   physical punishment and lack of structure at home
      b.   violence in the neighborhood
      c.   domestic violence in their homes

2.   The grouping of people with similar occupational, educational, and economic characteristics.

POVERTY IN ADOLESCENT DEVELOPMENT
SECTION REVIEW

1.   Its most common marker is the federal poverty threshold.

2.   The overall poverty rate for American adolescents is 17 percent. In Canada it is 9 percent, whereas in Sweden it is only 2 percent.

3.   The overall poverty rate is 17 percent. The poverty rate for African American and Latino adolescents is 40 percent.

4.   a.   Economic changes have eliminated many blue-collar jobs that paid reasonably well.
      b.   Increase in the percentage of youth living in single-parent families headed by the mother.
      c.   Reduction of government benefits during the 1970s and 1980s.

5.   This refers to the fact that far more women than men live in poverty.

ISSUES RELATED TO ETHNICITY
SECTION REVIEW

1.   Ethnicity is race and cultural background and tradition.

2.   Traditionally, this has been the case, but it depends on the situation.

3.   Stereotyping discounts individuality. By lumping someone inextricably to an ethnic group and discounting individuality, one increases the likelihood of both positive and negative stereotyping.

4.   Prejudice is an unjustified negative attitude toward an individual because of the individual's membership in a group.

ETHNIC MINORITY ADOLESCENTS
SECTION REVIEW

1.   The majority stay in school, do not take drugs, do not prematurely get married or become parents, are employed, are not involved in crime, and grow up to be very productive despite disadvantage.

2.   Low SES places people in worse neighborhoods and at poorer schools. This leads to many other problems.

3.   Most are from Mexico.

4.   Chicano is the name politically conscious Mexican American adolescents give themselves to reflect the combination of their Spanish-Mexican-Indian heritage and Anglo influences.

5.   Church and family are very important in the lives of Latino youth.

6.   There is a general expectation for success that places pressure on these kids to perform at a high level.

7.   Native Americans have experienced an inordinate amount of discrimination. Terrible abuse and punishment, among other things.

TELEVISION AND OTHER MEDIA
SECTION REVIEW

1.   a.   Entertainment
      b.   Information
      c.   Sensation
      d.   Coping
      e.   Gender-role modeling
      f.   Youth culture identification

2. Adolescents spend a third or more of their waking hours with some form of mass-media, most often TV. Research has suggested that the amount of TV watched at age 8 is directly correlated with problem behaviors in adulthood.

3. Adolescents like to watch TV with much sexual content. It tends to lead them to make errors in judgment with regards to what typical sexual activity is.

4. Very important. Two-thirds of all records and tapes are purchased by those 10- to 24-years old.

5. The core of computer mediated communication.

6. The numbers of computers in schools has increased dramatically, but it has not impacted adolescent learning.

7. (a) Encourage socially responsible programming, (b) support public efforts to make the media more adolescent friendly, (c) encourage media literacy programs as part of school curricula, youth and community organizations, and family life, (d) increase media presentations of health promotions, (e) expand opportunities for adolescents' views to appear in the media.

COGNITIVE CHALLENGE

1. No answer provided. Individual activity

ADOLESCENCE IN RESEARCH

An evaluation of the Quantum project compared the mentored students with a nonmentored control group. The methods were experimental. The hypothesis was that the features of the Quantum project would help overcome the intergenerational transmission of poverty and its negative outcomes. The mentored students were involved in academic-related activities, community service projects, and cultural enrichment and personal development activities. Students also received financial incentives for participating, including bonuses for every 100 hours of education. Sixty-three percent of the mentored students graduated from high school, but only 42 percent of the control group did. Forty-two percent of the mentored group is currently enrolled in college, but only 16 percent of the control group. The control-group students were twice as likely as mentored students to receive food stamps or be on welfare and they had more arrests. The conclusion is that programs like the Quantum project have the potential to help overcome the intergenerational transmission of poverty and its negative outcomes.

⊠ COMPREHENSIVE REVIEW

1.	a	**2.**	b	**3.**	d	**4.**	c	**5.**	b
6.	a	**7.**	b	**8.**	d	**9.**	c	**10.**	b
11.	c	**12.**	a	**13.**	c	**14.**	d	**15.**	d
16.	c	**17.**	a	**18.**	c	**19.**	a	**20.**	b
21.	c	**22.**	c							

SECTION IV
SOCIAL, EMOTIONAL, AND PERSONALITY DEVELOPMENT

Chapter 9   The Self and Identity

Learning Goals with Key Terms and Key People in Boldface

1.0   EVALUATE THE ADOLESCENT'S SELF-UNDERSTANDING
A.   The Self
    1.1   How is self-understanding defined?
B.   The Dimensions of Adolescents' Self-Understanding
    1.2   What are the dimensions of adolescents' **self-understanding**?
    1.3   What is the difference between the real and ideal self, and the true and false self?
    1.4   What is meant by **possible self**?
    1.5   What is social comparison?
    1.6   What does it mean to be self-conscious and self-protective?
    1.7   What is self-integration?
C.   Self-Understanding and Social Concepts
    1.8   What is meant by adolescents having multiple selves?

2.0   THE ADOLESCENT'S SELF-ESTEEM AND SELF-CONCEPT
A.   Self-Esteem and Self-Concept
    2.1   What is **self-esteem**?
    2.2   What is **self-concept**?
B.   Measuring Self-Esteem and Self-Concept
    2.3   How do you measure an adolescent's self-esteem?
    2.4   What is Harter's Self-Perception Profile for Adolescents?
    2.5   Why is it good to use multiple measures to assess self-esteem?
C.   Are Some Domains More Salient than Others to the Adolescent's Self Esteem?
    2.6   How important is perceived physical appearance to an adolescent's self-esteem?
    2.7   What role does peer acceptance play in the self-esteem of adolescents?
D.   Parental and Peer Influences
    2.8   What parental influences and behaviors are associated with boy's self-esteem?
    2.9   What role do peer judgments play in self-esteem?
    2.10   Is classmate support more strongly linked to self-esteem than close-friend support?

E. **Consequence of Low Self-Esteem**

    2.11   What is the consequence of low self-esteem for most adolescents?

    2.12   What are the ramifications for some adolescents when low self-esteem persists?

    2.13   What can happen if self-esteem is compounded by difficult school transitions?

F. **Increasing Adolescents' Self-Esteem**

    2.14   What are four ways that adolescents' self-esteem can be improved?

    2.15   Why should adolescents be taught to value competence?

3.0 DISCUSS ERIKSON'S IDEAS ON IDENTITY, IDENTITY STATUSES, AND DEVELOPMENTAL CHANGES

A. **Erikson's Ideas on Identity**

    3.1   What is the meaning and significance of Erikson's fifth stage, **identity versus identity confusion**?

    3.2   What is **psychosocial moratorium** as it relates to identity development?

    3.3   What is revealed by Erikson's insights?

B. **Personality and Role Experimentation**

    3.4   According to Erikson, what do personality and role exploration have to do with identity development?

C. **Some Contemporary Thoughts on Identity**

    3.5   What are some contemporary views of identity development?

    3.6   How long does identity development take?

    3.7   Is identity development complex?

D. **The Four Statuses of Identity**

    3.8   What is Marcia's view of identity?

    3.9   What are the four statuses of identity?

    3.10   What are the characteristics of **identity diffusion** and **identity foreclosure**?

    3.11   How is **crisis** identified?

    3.12   How is **commitment** identified?

    3.13   What is **identity moratorium**?

    3.14   What does Marcia mean by **identity achievement**?

    3.15   What is the role of crisis and **commitment** in Marcia's theory of identity statuses?

    3.16   What are the criticisms of Marcia's identity statuses?

E. **Developmental Changes**

    3.17   What three aspects of the young adolescent's development are important in identity formation?

    3.18   What are "MAMA" cycles?

4.0 LINKS BETWEEN IDENTITY AND FAMILY INFLUENCE, CULTURE AND ETHNICITY, AND GENDER

A. **Family Influence**

    4.1   How do parents influence adolescents' identity development?

    4.2   What is **individuality**?

    4.3   What is **connectedness**?

    4.4   What family processes promote adolescent identity development?

    4.5   What do adolescent **individuality** and **connectedness** have to do with identity development?

B. Cultural and Ethnic Aspects of Identity

4.6 What emphasis did Erikson place on the role of culture in identity development?

4.7 What is meant by **ethnic identity**?

4.8 Why is adolescence a special juncture in the identity development of ethnic minority individuals?

4.9 What is Helms' Model of Ethnic Identity Development?

C. What Role Does Gender Play In Identity?

4.10 Do ethnic minority individuals have bicultural gender identities?

4.11 Do adolescent males have a stronger vocational identity than females?

4.12 Do female adolescents have a stronger social identity than males?

5.0 EXPLAIN IDENTITY AND INTIMACY

A. Intimacy

5.1 What are the features of Erikson's sixth stage, **intimacy versus isolation**?

5.2 What are the characteristics of Orlofsky's **intimate style, preintimate style, stereotyped style, pseudointimate style,** and **isolated style** of intimate interaction?

5.3 What is the difference between White's **self-focused level, role-focused level,** and **individuated-connected** level of relationship maturity?

B. Loneliness

5.4 When are adolescents most likely to feel lonely?

5.5 What is loneliness associated with?

5.6 According to Weiss, what is the difference between **emotional isolation** and **social isolation**?

5.7 How can individuals reduce their loneliness?

Exercises

KEY TERMS
COMPLETION EXERCISE

Each key term is presented in the form of an incomplete sentence. Complete each sentence by either defining the term or giving an example. Compare your definitions with those given at the end of the study guide chapter.

1. **Self-understanding** is seen in the

   _____

   _____

2. Jacob is ponding his **possible self.** This means he is

   _____

   _____

3. **Self-esteem** is presented as a measure of

   _____

   _____

4. A person's **self-concept** is

   _____

   _____

5. In proposing **identity versus identity confusion,** Erikson was suggesting

   _____

   _____

6. **Psychosocial moratorium** is Erikson's term for

   _____

   _____

7. **Crisis** is represented by

   _____

   _____

8. Johnny is showing **commitment** to his schoolwork as evidenced by

    _____

    _____

9. According to Marcia, **identity diffusion** is when

    _____

    _____

10. **Identity foreclosure** is an adolescent state

    _____

    _____

11. While in **identity moratorium,** a person is likely

    _____

    _____

12. **Identity achievement** suggests

    _____

    _____

13. Evidence of expressing **individuality** is seen in

    _____

    _____

14. **Connectedness** consists of two dimensions:

    _____

    _____

15. A sense of **ethnic identity** is seen

    _____

    _____

16. **Intimacy versus isolation** according to Erikson is

    _____

    _____

17. **Intimate style** is reflected in Bobby's and Amanda's relationship because

_____

_____

18. **Preintimate style** is evidenced by

_____

_____

19. **Stereotyped style** is marked by relationships that are

_____

_____

20. **Pseudointimate style** suggests a lack of

_____

_____

21. People with an **isolated style**

_____

_____

22. The **self-focused level** of a relationship is

_____

_____

23. When in the **role-focused level** individuals are

_____

_____

24. The **individuated-connected level** is highlighted by

_____

_____

25. **Emotional isolation** is a type of

_____

_____

26. **Social isolation** is a type of

_____

_____

KEY PEOPLE
IN THE STUDY OF ADOLESCENCE

Match the person with the concept of adolescent development with which they are associated.

_____	1.	Susan Harter	A. Most famous for his theory of identity development
_____	2.	Robert Weiss	B. Developed an assessment for adolescent self-esteem
_____	3.	Erik Erikson	C. Expanded on Erikson's identity development theory
_____	4.	James Marcia	D. Distinguished two forms of loneliness
_____	5.	Alan Waterman	E. Developed a model of relationship maturity
_____	6.	Catherine Cooper	F. Conducted research on ethnic identity
_____	7.	Stuart Hauser	G. Believes that ethnic minority youth must bridge multiple worlds in constructing identity
_____	8.	Jean Phinney	H. Developed a classification of five styles of intimate interaction
_____	9.	Jacob Orlofsky	I. Illuminated family processes that promote adolescent identity development
_____	10.	Kathleen White	J. Conducted research on timing of identity achievement

"DR. DETAIL'S"
IDENTITY STATUS EXERCISE

What is your identity status? Think about your exploration and commitment in the areas listed below. For each area, check whether your identity status is diffused, foreclosed, moratorium, or achieved. If you check "diffused" or "foreclosed" for any areas, take some time to think about what you need to do to move into a moratorium identity status in those areas.

Identity Component	Diffused	Foreclosed	Moratorium	Achieved
Vocational (career)				
Political				
Religious				
Relationship				
Achievement				
Sexual				
Gender				
Ethnic/Cultural				
Interests				
Personality				
Physical				

ADOLESCENT SELF-UNDERSTANDING
SECTION REVIEW

1. List and give an example or explanation for Harter's five ways an adolescent's sense of self differs from that of a child.

    a. _____

    _____

    b. _____

    _____

    c. _____

    _____

    d. _____

    _____

    e. _____

    _____

2. What are the dimensions of adolescents' self-understanding?

    _____

    _____

3. What is meant by possible self?

    _____

    _____

4. What is social comparison?

    _____

    _____

5. What is self-integration?

    _____

    _____

SELF-ESTEEM AND SELF-CONCEPT
SECTION REVIEW

1. Complete the chart by filling in the positive and negative behavioral indicators of self-esteem

Positive Indicators	Negative Indicators

2. What is self-esteem?

_____

_____

3. What is self-concept?

_____

_____

4. What is Harter's Self-Perception Profile for adolescents?

_____

_____

5. How important is perceived physical appearance to an adolescent's self-esteem?

_____

_____

6. What role does peer judgments play in self-esteem?

_____

_____

7. What are four ways that adolescents' self-esteem can be improved?

_____

_____

ERIKSON'S IDEAS ON IDENTITY, IDENTITY STATUSES, AND DEVELOPMENTAL CHANGES
SECTION REVIEW

1. What is the meaning and significance of Erikson's fifth stage, identity versus identity confusion?

   _____

   _____

2. What is psychosocial moritorium as it relates to identity development?

   _____

   _____

3. How long does identity development take?

   _____

   _____

4. What are the four statuses of identity?

   _____

   _____

5. What are some characteristics of identity diffusion and identity foreclosure?

   _____

   _____

6. Differentiate between crisis and commitment.

   _____

   _____

7. What three aspects of the young adolescent's development are important in identity formation?

   _____

   _____

8. What are "MAMA" cycles?

   _____

   _____

LINKS BETWEEN IDENTITY AND FAMILY INFLUENCE, CULTURE AND ETHNICITY, AND GENDER
SECTION REVIEW

1. What is individuality?

_____

_____

2. What is connectedness?

_____

_____

3. What family processes promote adolescent identity development?

_____

_____

4. What is meant by ethnic identity?

_____

_____

5. What is Helms' Model of Ethnic Identity Development?

_____

_____

6. Contrast the vocational identity and social identity of males versus females.

_____

_____

IDENTITY AND INTIMACY
SECTION REVIEW

1. What are the features of Erikson's sixth stage, intimacy versus isolation?

_____

_____

2. What are the characteristics of Orlofsky's intimate style, preintimate style, stereotyped style, pseudointimate style, and isolated style of intimate interaction?

_____

_____

3. What is the difference between White's self-focused level, role-focused level, and individuated-connected level of relationship maturity?

_____

_____

4. According to Weiss, what is the difference between emotional isolation and social isolation?

_____

_____

COGNITIVE CHALLENGE

1. Think about what your future selves might be. Which of your prospective selves do you think will make you the happiest? Which of your prospective selves might have negative possibilities?

_____

_____

_____

_____

_____

_____

ADOLESCENCE IN RESEARCH

Concerning the research about boys' self-esteem by Coopersmith (1967), state the hypothesis, the research methods (if known), the research conclusions, and the implications and applications for adolescent development.

_____

_____

☒ COMPREHENSIVE REVIEW

1. Bernie describes himself as in control, masculine, and intelligent when he is with his girlfriend; but when he is with his buddies, he describes himself as fun loving and spontaneous. Bernie is
   a. two-faced.
   b. differentiated.
   c. schizophrenic.
   d. lacking an identity.

2. _____ felt that when the real and ideal selves are too discrepant, it is a sign of maladjustment.
    a. Susan Harter
    b. Erik Erikson
    c. Carl Rogers
    d. Jean Phinney

3. Adolescents are more likely than children to
    a. use social comparison.
    b. be self-conscious.
    c. be preoccupied with understanding.
    d. All of the above.

4. Which of the following is NOT one of Marcia's phases describing changes in adolescence?
    a. Reconstruction
    b. Deconstruction
    c. Self-understanding
    d. Consolidation

5. Joyce is on a date with someone she wants to impress. She uses large words that she does not normally use and exaggerates her intellectual ability. She is exhibiting her
    a. negative possible self
    b. positive possible self.
    c. ideal self.
    d. false self.

6. _____ involves domain-specific evaluations of the self.
    a. Self-esteem
    b. Self-concept
    c. Positive possible self
    d. Negative possible self

7. _____ is the global evaluative dimension of the self.
    a. Self-esteem
    b. Self-concept
    c. Positive possible self
    d. Negative possible self

8. _____ refers to an individuals' beliefs that they can master a situation and produce positive outcomes.
    a. Self-esteem
    b. Self-concept
    c. Self-efficacy
    d. Self-reference

9. Adolescents understand that there may be an unconscious aspect of the self because they have
    a. formal operations.
    b. concrete knowledge of the unconscious.
    c. better education about unconscious influences.
    d. a broad world-view.

10. An adolescent who starts to admit inconsistencies in his behavior is achieving
    a.   his ideal self.
    b.   egocentrism.
    c.   self-reference
    d.   self-integration.

11. Using two instruments to measure self-esteem is considered by developmental psychologists as
    a.   likely to lead to confusion.
    b.   likely to give inconsistent results.
    c.   likely to reflect the richness of the self.
    d.   unethical.

12. Which of the following parental characteristics is associated with self-esteem in children?
    a.   Expression of affection
    b.   Setting permissive rules
    c.   Conflicted family environments
    d.   Parental intelligence

13. Rodney's parents don't set any limits on his behavior. The family seems to always be in a state of chaos. Research indicates that Rodney's self-esteem will likely be
    a.   low.
    b.   high.
    c.   unconscious.
    d.   differentiated.

14. Programs that emphasize both academic and social skills are likely to enhance
    a.   identity achievement.
    b.   patience.
    c.   self-esteem.
    d.   harmonious family relationships.

15. Which is the most accurate statement of Erikson's views on identity development?
    a.   Losing your identity in a crowd is a form of identity confusion.
    b.   Running away and dropping out of school indicates moratorium.
    c.   The identity crisis is unrelated to earlier psychosocial stages.
    d.   Experimenting with different roles and personalities indicates a negative identity.

16. According to James Marcia and others, identity formation
    a.   is a lifetime activity.
    b.   should occur after intimacy.
    c.   is much easier than Erikson made it out to be.
    d.   does not require advanced thinking skills.

17. Karen, who is in a state of identity foreclosure,
    a.   has not experienced any crisis or made any commitment.
    b.   has made a commitment but has not experienced a crisis.
    c.   is in the midst of a crisis.
    d.   has undergone a crisis and made a commitment.

18. Jackson came home with green spiked hair. _____ is the least adequate explanation for his behavior?
    a. Identity moratorium
    b. Negative identity
    c. Identity confusion
    d. Identity foreclosure

19. Which of the following is NOT one of Helms' stages of Ethnic Development?
    a. Preencounter
    b. Immersion
    c. Encounter
    d. Conversation

20. Which of the following is NOT one of Marcia's four statuses of identity?
    a. Identity moratorium
    b. Negative identity
    c. Identity diffusion
    d. Identity foreclosure

21. According to Cooper and her colleagues, the two dimensions of connectedness are
    a. bonding and respect.
    b. mutuality and sensitivity.
    c. self- and other-connectedness.
    d. mutuality and permeability.

22. Adolescence may be a particularly difficult time for minority individuals because this is the time they
    a. are subject to the most intense discrimination.
    b. also confront their own ethnicity.
    c. have the fewest resources to achieve identity.
    d. become aware of other people's resources.

23. Gender differences in identity formation
    a. are a backlash against the women's movement.
    b. are greater now because of the New Age movement.
    c. have decreased in the last twenty years.
    d. are the same as they have always been.

24. Erikson believed that intimacy should come after one has established
    a. identity.
    b. trust.
    c. generativity.
    d. Industry.

25. Jacob Orlofsky discovered that college students who had a stable sense of identity were more likely to achieve _____ status.
    a. stereotyped
    b. preintimacy
    c. pseudointimacy
    d. intimacy

26.   _____-focused is the first level of relationship maturity.
    a. Role
    b. Image
    c. Self
    d. Parent

27. Robert Weiss distinguished between
    a. emotional and social isolation.
    b. individuation and connectedness.
    c. intimate and isolated relationships.
    d. situational and chronic loneliness.

28. The Boston Compact Youth Incentive Program provides troubled adolescents with
    a. good-paying jobs.
    b. birth control counseling.
    c. day care centers.
    d. food stamps.

ADOLESCENCE ON THE SCREEN

- *The Cider House Rules* A young boy born and raised in an orphanage breaks away from his surrogate-father who runs the orphanage and charts his own course in life.

- *King Gimp* Two University of Maryland professors won the Academy Award in 2000 for best documentary short subject with this film spanning the adolescence and young adulthood of Dan Keplinger, a young man suffering from a highly disabling form of cerebral palsy, as he searches for identity in a world that shuns him.

- *Shine* Based on the true story of Australian pianist David Helfgott, the movie chronicles Helfgott's search for an identity. He has to overcome an abusive childhood, loss of his family in concentration camps, and mental illness before he finds himself as a concert pianist.

- *Simon Birch* Simon Birch, age 12, believes that God made him for a special purpose. The movie presents his quest to fulfill the destiny he believes in.

ADOLESCENCE IN BOOKS

- *Gandhi*, by Erik Erikson (Norton: NY, 1966), the Pulitzer Prize-winning biography of Mahatma Gandhi, emphasizes Gandhi's identity crisis.

- *Identity's Architect: A Biography of Erik H. Erikson*, by Lawrence J. Friedman (Scribner: NY, 1999), traces Erik Erikson's own identity crises, which contributed to the development of his psychosocial theory.

- *Intimate Connections*, by David D. Burns (William Morrow: NY, 1985), presents a program for overcoming loneliness.

Answer Key

KEY TERMS

1. **self-understanding** The adolescent's cognitive representation of the self, the substance and content of the adolescent's self-conceptions.

2. **possible self** What individuals might become, what they would like to become, and what they are afraid of becoming.

3. **self-esteem** The global evaluative dimension of the self. Self-esteem is also referred to as self-worth or self-image.

4. **self-concept** Domain-specific evaluations of the self.

5. **identity versus identity confusion** Erikson's fifth developmental stage, which individuals experience during the adolescent years. At this time, individuals are faced with finding out who they are, what they are all about, and where they are going in life.

6. **psychosocial moratorium** Erikson's term for the gap between childhood security and adult autonomy that adolescents experience as part of their identity exploration.

7. **crisis** A period of identity development during which the adolescent is choosing among meaningful alternatives.

8. **commitment** The part of identity development in which adolescents show a personal investment in what they are going to do.

9. **identity diffusion** Marcia's term for the state adolescents are in when they have not yet experienced a crisis or made any commitments.

10. **identity foreclosure** Marcia's term for the state adolescents are in when they have made a commitment but have not experienced a crisis.

11. **identity moratorium** Marcia's term for the state of adolescents who are in the midst of a crisis, but whose commitments are either absent or are only vaguely defined.

12. **identity achievement** Marcia's term for having undergone a crisis and made a commitment.

13. **individuality** An important element in adolescent identity development. It consists of two dimensions: self-assertion, the ability to have and communicate a point of view; and separateness, the use of communication patterns to express how one is different from others.

14. **connectedness** An important element in adolescent identity development. It consists of two dimensions: mutuality, sensitivity to and respect for others' views; and permeability, openness to others' views.

15. **ethnic identity** An enduring, basic aspect of the self that includes a sense of membership in an ethnic group and the attitudes and feelings related to that membership.

16. **intimacy versus isolation** Erikson's sixth developmental stage, which individuals experience during the early adulthood years. At this time, individuals face the developmental task of forming intimate relationships with others.

17. **intimate style** The individual forms and maintains one or more deep and long-lasting love relationships.

18. **preintimate style** The individual shows mixed emotions about commitment, an ambivalence reflected in the strategy of offering love without obligations.

19. **stereotyped style** The individual has superficial relationships that tend to be dominated by friendship ties with same-sex rather than opposite-sex individuals.

20. **pseudointimate style** The individual maintains a long-lasting sexual attachment with little or no depth or closeness.

21. **isolated style** The individual withdraws from social encounters and has little or no attachment to same or opposite-sex individuals.

22. **self-focused level** The first level of relationship maturity, at which one's perspective of another or of a relationship is concerned only with how it affects oneself.

23. **role-focused level** The second or intermediate level of relationship maturity, at which perceiving others as individuals in their own right begins to develop. However, at this level the perspective is stereotypical and emphasizes social acceptability.

24. **individuated-connected level** The highest level of relationship maturity, at which there is evidence of an understanding of oneself, as well as consideration of others' motivations and anticipation of their needs. Concern and caring involve emotional support and individualized expression of interest.

25. **emotional isolation** A type of loneliness that arises when a person lacks an intimate attachment relationships; single, divorced, and widowed adults often experience this type of loneliness.

26. **social isolation** A type of loneliness that occurs when a person lacks of sense of integrated involvement. Being deprived of participation in a group or community involving companionship, shared interests, organized activities, and meaningful roles causes a person to feel alienated, bored, and uneasy.

KEY PEOPLE
IN THE STUDY OF ADOLESCENCE

1. B	**2.** D	**3.** A	**4.** C	**5.** J
6. G	**7.** I	**8.** F	**9.** H	**10.** E

"DR. DETAIL'S"
IDENTITY STATUS EXERCISE

Individual answers may vary.

ADOLESCENT SELF-UNDERSTANDING
SECTION REVIEW

1. Individual answers may vary.
    a. **Abstract and idealistic**: A teenager is more apt to describe himself/herself in abstract terms, such as saying that he/she is compassionate and caring.
    b. **Differentiated**: An adolescent is likely to describe himself/herself as having one set of characteristics in relationship to his/her families and another in relationship to his/her peers and friends.
    c. **Fluctuating**: Adolescents' sense of themselves changes over short periods of time. They can be self-confident one moment, and anxious the next.
    d. **Contradictions within the self**: Adolescents' self-descriptions show contradictions. They may think of themselves as both attractive and unattractive.
    e. **Real and ideal selves**: Depression and self-doubt can arise when an adolescent feels that they are not living up to their idea sense of self.

2. (a) abstract and idealistic, (b) differentiated, (c) the fluctuating self, (d) contradictions within the self, (e) real and ideal, true and false selves.

3. What individuals might become, what they would like to become, and what they are afraid of becoming.

4. They ways in which adolescents evaluate themselves.

5. In adolescence, self-understanding becomes more integrative, with the disparate parts of the self more systematically pieced together, especially in late adolescence.

SELF-ESTEEM AND SELF-CONCEPT
SECTION REVIEW

1.

Positive Indicators	Negative Indicators
Gives others directives or commands	Puts down others by teasing, name-calling, or gossiping
Uses voice quality appropriate for situation	Uses gestures that are dramatic or out of context
Expresses opinions	Engages in inappropriate touching or avoids physical contact
Sits with others during social activities	Gives excuses for failures
Works cooperatively in a group	Glances around to monitor others
Faces others when speaking or being spoken to	Brags excessively about achievements, skills, appearance
Maintains eye contact during conversation	Verbally puts self down; self-deprecation
Initiates friendly contact with others	Speaks too loudly, abruptly, or in a dogmatic tone
Maintains comfortable space between self and others	Does not express views or opinions, especially when asked
Little hesitation in speech, speaks fluently	Assumes a submissive stance

2. Self-esteem is the global evaluative dimension of the self.

3. Self-concept involves domain-specific evaluations of the self.

4. Scholastic competence, athletic competence, social acceptance, physical appearance, behavioral conduct, close friendship, romantic appeal, and job competence.

5. Very important. It's the foundation of adolescent self-perception.

6. Peer judgments gain greater importance among older children and adolescents.

7. (a) identifying the causes of low esteem and the domains of competence important to the self, (b) emotional support and social approval, (c) achievement, and (d) coping.

ERICKSON'S IDEAS ON IDENTITY, IDENTITY STATUSES, AND DEVELOPMENT CHANGES
SECTION REVIEW

1. Its Erikson's fifth developmental stage, which individuals experience during the adolescent years. Adolescents examine who they are, what they are all about, and where they are going in life.

2. Erikson's term for the gap between childhood security and adult autonomy that adolescents experience as part of their identity exploration.

3. It's a lengthy process that neither begins or ends in adolescence.

4. (a) identity diffusion, (b) identity foreclosure, (c) identity moratorium, and (d) identity achievement.

5. Identity diffusion is Marcia's term for the state adolescents are in when they have not yet experienced a crisis or made any commitments. Identity foreclosure is Marcia's term for the state adolescents are in when they have made a commitment but have not experienced a crisis.

6. Crisis is defined as a period of identity development during which the adolescent is choosing among meaningful alternatives. Commitment is a part of identity development in which adolescents show a personal investment in what they are going to do.

7. Young adolescents must be confident that they have parental support, must have an established sense of industry, and must be able to adopt a self-reflective stance toward the future.

8. "MAMA" cycles are moratorium-achievement-moratorium-achievement.

LINKS BETWEEN IDENTITY AND FAMILY INFLUENCE, CULTURE AND ETHNICITY, AND GENDER
SECTION REVIEW

1. Individuality consists of two dimensions: self-assertion, the ability to have and communicate a point of view; and separateness, the use of communication patterns to express how one is different from others.

2. Connectedness consists of mutuality, sensitivity to and respect for others' views; and permeability, openness to others' views.

3. Parents who explain, accept, and give empathy foster development.

4. An enduring, basic aspect of the self that includes a sense of membership in an ethnic group and the attitudes and feelings related to that membership.

5. Helm's model consists of four stages: (a) preencounter, (b) encounter, (c) immersion/emersion, and (d) internalization/commitment.

6. In recent decades, differences that once existed have now begun to disappear as females close the gap.

IDENTITY AND INTIMACY
SECTION REVIEW

1. In Erikson's sixth stage, individuals experience during early adulthood. At this time, individuals face the task of forming intimate relationships with others.

2. Intimate style—the individual forms and maintains one or more deep and long-lasting love relationships. Preintimate style—the individual shows mixed emotions about commitment. Stereotyped style—the individual has superficial relationships that tend to be dominated by friendship ties with same-sex rather than opposite-sex individuals. Pseudointimate style—the individual maintains a long-lasting sexual attachment with little depth. Isolated style—the individual withdraws from social encounters and has little or no attachment to same- or opposite-sex individuals.

3. Self-focused is the first level of relationship maturity, at which one's perspective of another or a relationship is concerned only with how it affects oneself. The role-focused level is the second or intermediate level of relationship maturity, at which perceiving others as individuals in their own right begins to develop. The individual-connected level is the highest level of relationship maturity, at which there is evidence of self-understanding, as well as consideration of others' motivations and anticipation of their needs.

4. Emotional isolation is a type of loneliness that arises when a person lacks an intimate attachment relationship. Social isolation is a type of loneliness that occurs when a person lacks a sense of integrated involvement.

COGNITIVE
CHALLENGE

1. No answers provided. Individual activity

ADOLESCENCE
IN RESEARCH

The hypothesis was that relationships with parents and peers contribute to adolescents' self-esteem. Coopersmith administered a self-esteem assessment to boys, and also interview boys and their mothers about their family relationships. The methods were assessment instrument and interviews. The study was correlational. The conclusions were that the following parenting attributes were associated with high self esteem: expression of affection, concern about the boys' problems, harmony in the home, participation in joint family activities, giving boys competent, organized help when needed, setting and abiding by clear and fair rules, and allowing boys freedom within prescribed limits. The research is important because it establishes parenting factors that may be related to self-esteem.

⊠ COMPREHENSIVE REVIEW

1.	b	**2.**	c	**3.**	d	**4.**	c	**5.**	d
6.	b	**7.**	a	**8.**	c	**9.**	a	**10.**	d
11.	c	**12.**	a	**13.**	a	**14.**	c	**15.**	a
16.	a	**17.**	b	**18.**	d	**19.**	d	**20.**	b
21.	d	**22.**	b	**23.**	c	**24.**	a	**25.**	d
26.	c	**27.**	a	**28.**	a						

Chapter 10 Gender

Learning Goals with Key Terms and Key People in Boldface

1.0 KNOW WHAT IS MEANT BY GENDER

A. What is Gender?

1.1 What is the nature of gender?

1.2 What is meant by one's **gender role**?

2.0 BIOLOGICAL, SOCIAL, AND COGNITIVE INFLUENCES ON GENDER

A. Biological Influences

2.1 How strong are the biological influences on gender?

2.2 What is the role of sexuality in adolescent gender development?

2.3 How do Freud and Erikson's ideas promote the premise that anatomy is destiny?

2.4 How do today's developmentalists believe that biological and environmental influences affect gender?

2.5 What are some criticisms of the anatomy-is-destiny view?

2.6 What is the evolutionary psychology view of gender development?

B. Social Influences

2.7 How do social roles impact gender development?

2.8 What roles do gender hierarchy and sexual division of labor play in sex-differentiated behavior?

2.9 According to the **social cognitive theory of gender**, what role do parents play in the development of gender-appropriate behavior?

2.10 How do peers reward gender-appropriate behavior?

2.11 How has the increase in the number of working mothers in recent years impacted adolescents?

2.12 What evidence suggests that gender inequity still exists in education?

2.13 How does television program to specifically male and females audiences, and what impact does it have?

2.14 How are men portrayed on television?

C. Cognitive Influences

2.15 What was **Kohlberg's** theory of gender development?

2.16 What is a **schema**?

2.17 What does the **gender schema theory** state about individual gender development?

3.0 DESCRIBE GENDER STEREOTYPES, SIMILARITIES, AND DIFFERENCES

A. Gender Stereotyping

3.1 What is the nature of **gender stereotypes** today?

3.2 How common is stereotyping?

3.3 How widespread is feminine and masculine stereotyping?

3.4 What is **sexism**?

B. Gender Similarities and Differences

3.5 What are the physical and biological differences that characterize male and female comparisons?

3.6 Have male/female differences been exaggerated?

Exercises

KEY TERMS
COMPLETION EXERCISE

Each key term is presented in the form of an incomplete sentence. Complete each sentence by either defining the term or giving an example. Compare your definitions with those given at the end of the study guide chapter.

1.   Simply put, **gender** refers to

_____

_____

2.   **Gender role** refers to one's

_____

_____

3.   **Cognitive developmental theory of gender** states

_____

_____

4.   **Social cognitive theory of gender** states

_____

_____

5.   A good example of a **schema** is

_____

_____

6.   A **gender schema** is a

_____

_____

7.   **Gender schema theory** suggests that

_____

_____

8.   **Gender stereotypes** can be seen in

_____

_____

9.   **Sexism** is seen in situations where

_____

_____

10.   Jill uses **rapport talk** when she is

_____

_____

11.   Bart uses **report talk** because

_____

_____

12.   A sure sign of **androgyny** is when

_____

_____

13.   **Gender-role transcendence** is a belief that

_____

_____

14.   The **gender intensification hypothesis** states that

_____

_____

KEY PEOPLE
IN THE STUDY OF ADOLESCENCE

Match the person with the concept of adolescent development with which they are associated.

_____	1. Sigmund Freud	A.	An evolutionary psychologist
_____	2. Erik Erikson	B.	Proposed the cognitive developmental theory of gender
_____	3. Alice Eagly	C.	Developed an assessment instrument for androgyny
_____	4. Eleanor Maccoby	D.	Believes that males and females have a different style of "talk"
_____	5. Myra Sadker and David Sadker	E.	Worked with Eleanor Maccoby and concluded that males have better math and visuospatial abilities
_____	6. Lawrence Kohlberg	F.	Believes that women have a different "voice"
_____	7. Carol Jacklin	G.	Believed that male and female psychological differences are related to genital structure
_____	8. Janet Shibley Hyde	H.	Believed that gender and sexual behavior are unlearned and instinctual
_____	9. Deborah Tannen	I.	Proponent of the male role-strain perspective
_____	10. David Buss	J.	Studied gender discrimination in schools
_____	11. Sandra Bem	K.	Says that psychological sex differences arise from social roles of men and women
_____	12. Joseph Pleck	L.	Believes that cognitive differences between females and males have been exaggerated
_____	13. Carol Gilligan	M.	Now believes that differences in male and female verbal ability have virtually disappeared

WHAT IS MEANT BY GENDER
SECTION REVIEW

1. What is gender?

_____

_____

2. What is meant by one's gender role?

_____

_____

BIOLOGICAL, SOCIAL, AND COGNITIVE INFLUENCES ON GENDER
SECTION REVIEW

1. How strong are biological influences on gender?

_____

_____

2.   Compare Freud's and Erikson's theories related to gender and explain how they promote the notion that anatomy is destiny.

_____

_____

3.   To what extent do hormones play a role in the sexual activities of boys and girls?

_____

_____

4.   What is the evolutionary view of gender development?

_____

_____

5.   What roles do gender hierarchy and sexual division of labor play in sex-differentiated behavior?

_____

_____

6.   According to the social cognitive theory of gender, what role do parents play in the development of gender-appropriate behavior?

_____

_____

7.   How does television program to specifically male and female audiences, and what impact does it have?

_____

_____

8.   How are men portrayed on television?

_____

_____

9.   Compare and contrast male and female helping behavior and display of emotions.

_____

_____

10.   What was Kohlberg's theory of gender development?

_____

_____

11. What is a schema?

_____

_____

12. What does gender schema theory state about individual gender development?

_____

_____

GENDER STEREOTYPES, SIMILARITIES, AND DIFFERENCES
SECTION REVIEW

1. What is the nature of gender stereotypes today?

_____

_____

2. How common is stereotyping?

_____

_____

3. How widespread is feminine and masculine stereotyping?

_____

_____

4. What is sexism?

_____

_____

5. Differentiate between 'old fashioned' and 'modern' sexism.

_____

_____

6. Using Tannen's model, distinguish between rapport talk and report talk.

_____

_____

GENDER CONTROVERSY AND GENDER IN CONTEXT
SECTION REVIEW

1.   What is David Buss's hypothesis regarding how gender differences develop?

        _____

        _____

2.   Why is context an important factor in understanding gender?

        _____

        _____

TRADITIONAL GENDER ROLES AND ANDROGYNY
SECTION REVIEW

1.   Do gender roles vary around the world?

        _____

        _____

2.   When did alternatives to traditional masculinity and femininity begin to develop?

        _____

        _____

3.   How do androgynous individuals compare with either masculine or feminine individuals?

        _____

        _____

4.   Are there ethical concerns associated with regard to teaching children and adolescents to depart from socially approved behavior patterns?

        _____

        _____

POSSIBLE PROBLEMS WITH MASCULINITY
AND EXPLAIN GENDER-ROLE TRANSCENDENCE
SECTION REVIEW

1.   According to the role-strain view, what are some areas where men's roles can cause considerable strain?

_____

_____

2.   According to Levant, what steps can be taken to reconstruct masculinity in more positive ways?

_____

_____

3.   What is the premise of gender-role transcendence?

_____

_____

DEVELOPMENTAL CHANGES AND JUNCTURES
SECTION REVIEW

1.   What is the gender intensification hypothesis?

_____

_____

2.   Is early adolescence a critical juncture for females?

_____

_____

3.   What is Gilligan's belief about the critical juncture for adolescent females?

_____

_____

4.   What are some criticisms of Gilligan's beliefs and theories?

_____

_____

EXPLORATIONS
IN ADOLESCENCE DEVELOPMENT

How widespread is gender stereotyping today? Generate two lists; one for males and one for females, of all of the current gender stereotypes you can think of.

_____

_____

_____

_____

ADOLESCENCE
IN RESEARCH

Describe the attitudes towards masculinity as given by Pleck and colleagues.

COGNITIVE
CHALLENGE

1.   Make up a list of words that you associated with masculinity and femininity. Identify those words that have negative connotations for males and/or females. Then replace them with words that have more positive connotations.

_____

_____

2.   How will you attempt to raise your children, in terms of gender roles? Will you try to raise gender-neutral children? Or will you encourage more traditional gender distinctions?

_____

_____

3.   What factors during your childhood led you to develop your gender role?

_____

_____

COMPREHENSIVE REVIEW

1. _____ refers to a set of expectations about sex-appropriate behavior.
   a. Stereotype
   b. Gender role
   c. Gender intensification
   d. Sexism

2. According to Udry, which of the following has the greatest impact on sexual activity for adolescent girls?
   a. Levels of the hormone estrogen
   b. Levels of the hormone androgen
   c. The type of friends they affiliated with
   d. The SES of their family

3. According to Freud and Erikson, this is a largest single factor regarding gender behavior of adolescents.
   a. temperament
   b. religion
   c. attitudes of the parents
   d. genitals they are born with

4. Erik Erickson and Sigmund Freud believed that the differences between males and females
   a. was the result of females' ability and males' inability to articulate their feelings.
   b. resulted from prenatal hormonal influences.
   c. resulted from anatomical differences.
   d. were gender stereotypes rather than gender differences.

5. An adolescent mother can reduce the sex-role stereotypes of her children by
   a. dressing them all the same.
   b. withholding praise for their physical appearance.
   c. holding a job outside the home.
   d. divorcing their father.

6. According to contemporary views of evolutionary psychology, which of the following is NOT an evolved disposition of men?
   a. Violence
   b. Competition
   c. Risk taking
   d. Compassion

7. On the playground, girls teach girls and boys teach boys about their gender behaviors. This is known as
   a. gender socialization.
   b. gender intensification.
   c. peer socialization.
   d. peer generalization.

8.   Sadker and Sadker (1994) noted that in some ways both boys and girls might not receive a fair education. Which is NOT one of their listed concerns?
        a.   Girl's learning problems are not identified as often as boys' learning problems.
        b.   Boys are given the lion's share of attention in school.
        c.   Pressure to achieve is more likely to be heaped on boys than on girls.
        d.   More girls than boys come from families living in poverty.

9.   School curriculum planners decide in which grades algebra, history, and science are to be taught. These decisions are based mainly upon the
        a.   cognitive developmental norms for children.
        b.   social-emotional developmental norms for children.
        c.   developmental norms for males.
        d.   developmental norms for females.

10.   Adolescent females watching television are likely to find
        a.   fewer role models than their brothers will.
        b.   accurate representations of women's roles.
        c.   important lessons on managing relationships.
        d.   little to identify with in terms of sexual intimacy.

11.   A boy recognizes that he is a male and then starts doing "male" things. This description is consistent with the _____ theory of gender.
        a.   socialization
        b.   genderization
        c.   cognitive-developmental
        d.   intensification

12.   Television directed at adolescents might be the most extreme in its portrayal of
        a.   violence.
        b.   sexual behavior.
        c.   teenage girls.
        d.   teenage boys.

13.   According to Kohlberg, the main changes in gender development occur
        a.   in infancy.
        b.   in adolescence.
        c.   in childhood.
        d.   as young adults.

14.   Gender schema theory predicts that adolescents are drawn to sources of information that enable them to
        a.   conform to stereotypes.
        b.   learn about sexuality.
        c.   learn about relationships.
        d.   think idealistically.

15. On which of the following tasks is an adolescent girl likely to outperform an adolescent boy?
    a.   Spelling the word commitment
    b.   Calculating the area of a triangle
    c.   Selecting a picture from among six others than matches a standard
    d.   Finding a hidden object in a picture

16. Pat gets embarrassed when making a mistake in public and experiences episodes of jealousy and passion. What gender is Pat likely to be?
    a.   Male
    b.   Female
    c.   Equally likely to be male or female
    d.   There is no research on which to base an answer.

17. According to the Bem Sex-Role Inventory, an adolescent is androgynous if she scores
    a.   high on masculinity and high on femininity.
    b.   high on masculinity and low on femininity.
    c.   low on femininity and low on masculinity.
    d.   half-way between masculinity and femininity.

18. The concept of _____ involves the notion that an individual's competence should not be conceptualized along the lines of gender orientation, but rather, the emphasis should be on the individual.
    a.   gender-neutrality
    b.   humanism
    c.   gender-role transcendence
    d.   critical feminism

19. The gender intensification hypothesis indicates that behavioral differences between males and females become greater during adolescence as a result of
    a.   hormones.
    b.   pressures to conform to stereotypes.
    c.   television commercials.
    d.   the development of a new schema.

20. The concept of _____ refers to the fact that the amount, timing, and intensity of gender socialization are different for girls and boys.
    a.   gender intensification
    b.   asymmetric gender socialization
    c.   gender role transcendence
    d.   sex difference

21. According to Tannen, which of the following is NOT an example of 'report talk'?
    a.   Joking
    b.   Storytelling
    c.   Lecturing
    d.   Relationship oriented conversation

22. According to Tannen, which of the following is an example of 'rapport talk'?
    a. Joking
    b. Story telling
    c. Lecturing
    d. Relationship oriented conversation

23. Carol Gilligan has suggested that girls
    a. are better than boys.
    b. are equal to boys.
    c. are different than boys.
    d. are none of the above.

24. According to many studies, adolescent girls are likely to suffer from declines in
    a. intelligence.
    b. self-esteem.
    c. verbal fluency.
    d. social skills.

ADOLESCENCE IN RESEARCH

Concerning Pleck and colleagues' 1994 National Survey of Adolescent Males, state the hypothesis, the research methods (if known), the research conclusions, and the implications and applications for adolescent development.

_____

_____

ADOLESCENCE ON THE SCREEN

- *Boys Don't Cry* Hilary Swank won an academy award for her portrayal of the true story of a boy with gender identity disorder who was murdered when his biological sex was revealed.

- *The Crying Game* A shocking ending reveals that one of the main characters is a transsexual.

- *Mr. and Mrs. Bridges* Joanne Woodward and Paul Newman as an upper-class couple in the American Midwest of the 1940s who embody the male and female stereotypical roles of the time.

- *Ma Vie En Rose (My Life in Pink)* A French movie (with English subtitles) about a boy with gender identity disorder who dresses and lives as a girl.

- *Antigonia's Line* A longitudinal portrayal of the transformation from adolescence to womanhood and the life's decisions involved.

- *The Body Beautiful* This film is a generative example of how our various bodily and social identities are built and given meaning concurrently.

- *Daughters of the Dust* Life and development on a barrier island amongst the Gullah Subculture. An isolated African-American culture off the coast of South Carolina.

ADOLESCENCE IN BOOKS

- *A New Psychology of Men*, by Ronald Levant and William Pollack (Basic Books, 1995), is a collection of essays on men's issues and male gender roles.

- *As Nature Made Him*, by John Colapinto (HarperCollins: NY, 2000), is the true story of one of identical twins whose penis was accidentally severed during circumcision and who was given female hormones and raised as a girl until his parents revealed the accident. He then had penile reconstructive surgery and hormone treatments and resumed life as a man.

- *Stiffed: The Betrayal of the American Man*, by Susan Faludi (William Morrow: NY, 1999), examines the problems of men in modern life, emphasizing the stress and strain of male sex roles.

- *You Just Don't Understand*, by Deborah Tannen (Ballantine: NY, 1990), explores the differences in male and female communication styles.

Answer Key

KEY TERMS

1. **gender** The sociocultural dimension of being male or female.

2. **gender role** A set of expectations that prescribes how females and males should think, act, and feel.

3. **social cognitive theory of gender** This theory emphasizes that children's and adolescents' gender development occurs through observation and imitation of gender behavior, and through rewards and punishments they experience for gender-appropriate and -inappropriate behavior.

4. **cognitive developmental theory of gender** In this view, children's gender-typing occurs after they have developed a concept of gender. Once they begin to consistently conceive of themselves as male or female, children often organize their world on the basis of gender.

5. **schema** A cognitive structure of network of associations that organizes and guides an individual's perception.

6. **gender schema** A cognitive structure that organizes the world in terms of male and female.

7. **gender schema theory** According to this theory, an individual's attention and behavior are guided by an internal motivation to conform to gender-based sociocultural standards and stereotypes.

8. **gender stereotypes** Broad categories that reflect our impressions and beliefs about females and males.

9. **sexism** Prejudice and discrimination against an individual because of his or her sex.

10. **rapport talk** Is the language of conversation and a way of establishing connections and negotiating relationships.

11. **report talk** Is talk that gives information. Public speaking would be an example.

12. **androgyny** The presence of a high degree of desirable feminine and masculine characteristics in the same individual.

13. **gender-role transcendence** The belief that, when an individual's competence is at issue, it should be conceptualized not on the basis of masculinity, femininity, or androgyny but, rather, on a person basis.

14. **gender intensification hypothesis** This hypothesis states that psychological and behavioral differences between boys and girls become greater during early adolescence because of increased socialization pressures to conform to masculine and feminine gender roles.

KEY PEOPLE IN THE STUDY OF ADOLESCENCE

1.	H	2.	G	3.	K	4.	M	5.	J
6.	B	7.	E	8.	L	9.	D	10.	A
11.	C	12.	I	13.	F				

WHAT IS MEANT BY GENDER
SECTION REVIEW

1.   Gender refers to the psychological and sociocultural dimensions of being male or female.

2.   Gender role is a set of expectations that prescribes how females or males should think, act, and feel.

BIOLOGICAL, SOCIAL, AND COGNITIVE INFLUENCES ON GENDER
SECTION REVIEW

1.   Hormones and pubertal change contributes to an increased incorporation of sexuality in the gender attitudes and behavior of adolescents.

2.   Both felt that genitals were the primary source of influence on gender behavior.

3.   Androgen levels are related to sexual activity in boys, but girls were more likely to be influenced by the kinds of friends they hung out with.

4.   Evolutionary psychologists argue that men and women faced different evolutionary pressures in primeval environments, and adapted to these.

5.   From the perspective of social influences, gender hierarchy and sexual division of labor are important causes of sex-differentiated behavior.

6.   Emphasizes that childrens' and adolescents' gender development occurs through observation and imitation of gender behavior, and through rewards and punishments they experience for gender-appropriate and—inappropriate behavior.

7.   Television targets teens, in particular teenage girls in its depiction of females on TV.

8.   Males are more often seen in work roles, cars, or in sports. Females get much less TV time and are more likely to be seen in the home.

9.   Males are more likely to help in contexts in which a perceived danger is present and they feel competent to help. Females are more likely to help when a child or personal problem is involved. Males are more likely to show anger toward strangers and other males to discuss emotion in terms of interpersonal relationships and to express fear and sadness.

10.   Children's gender-typing occurs after they have developed a concept of gender. Once they begin to consistently conceive of themselves as male or female, children often organize their world on the basis of gender.

11.   A schema is a cognitive structure, a network of associations that organizes and guides an individual's perceptions.

12.   Gender Schema Theory state that an individual's attention and behavior are guided by an internal motivation to conform to gender-based sociocultural standards and stereotypes.

GENDER STEREOTYPES, SIMILARITIES, AND DIFFERENCES
SECTION REVIEW

1. These are broad categories that reflect our impressions and beliefs about females and males.

2. They are so general that they are often ambiguous.

3. According to college students in 30 countries, it is very common.

4. Sexism is prejudice and discrimination against an individual because of her or his sex.

5. Old-fashioned is characterized by endorsement of traditional gender roles, differential treatment for men and women with the assumption that women are less competent then men. Modern sexism is characterized by the denial that there is still discrimination and lack of support for policies designed to help women.

6. Rapport talk is the language of conversation and a way of establishing connections and negotiating relationships. Report talk is talk that gives information (e.g., public speaking).

GENDER CONTROVERSY AND GENDER IN CONTEXT
SECTION REVIEW

1. Buss argues that men and women differ psychologically in those domains in which they have faced different adaptive problems across their evolutionary history.

2. Context determines what males and females are likely to do in particular circumstances when they encounter specific problems.

TRADITIONAL GENDER ROLES AND ANDROGYNY
SECTION REVIEW

1. Yes. Many cultures have quite different views regarding the roles of men and women.

2. Alternatives were introduced in the 1960s and 1970s.

3. Androgynous individuals are described as more flexible and more mentally healthy.

4. Ethical concerns are raised when the program involves teaching children and adolescents to depart from socially approved behavior patterns.

POSSIBLE PROBLEMS WITH MASCULINITY
AND EXPLAINING GENDER-ROLE TRANSCENDENCE
SECTION REVIEW

1. Health; male-female relationships; male-male relationships

2. (a) reexamine his beliefs about manhood, (b) separate out the valuable aspects of the male role, and (c) get rid of those parts of the masculine role that are destructive.

3. The belief that when an individual's competence is at issue, it should not be conceptualized on the basis of masculinity, femininity, or androgyny, but rather on a person basis.

DEVELOPMENTAL CHANGES AND JUNCTURES
SECTION REVIEW

1. This states that psychological and behavioral differences between boys and girls become greater during early adolescence because of increased socialization pressures to conform to traditional masculine and feminine gender roles.

2. Yes. Much is learned from the age of 6 through 18.

3. Gilligan suggests that the critical juncture for the development of little girls is around 11–12 years of age.

4. Critics argue that Gilligan overemphasized differences in gender.

EXPLORATIONS
IN ADOLESCENCE DEVELOPMENT

No answers provided. Individual activity.

ADOLESCENCE
IN RESEARCH

Pleck and colleagues hypothesized that problem behaviors in adolescent males are associated with their attitudes toward masculinity. They also examined the risk and protective influences for problem behaviors. They studied 1,680 15- to 19-year-old males. Their findings supported their hypothesis. Males who had traditional beliefs about masculinity were more likely to have difficulty in school, use drugs and alcohol, be sexually active, and participate in delinquent activities. Risk factors for problem behaviors included low parental education, being the son of a teenage mother, living in a mother-headed household or having no nonmaterial family member in the home, lenient family rules, and infrequent church attendance. Protective factors included strict family rules and frequent church attendance.

COGNITIVE
CHALLENGE

1. No answers provided. Individual activity.
2. No answers provided. Individual activity.
3. No answers provided. Individual activity.

⊠ COMPREHENSIVE REVIEW

1.	b	**2.**	c	**3.**	d	**4.**	c	**5.**	c
6.	d	**7.**	c	**8.**	d	**9.**	a	**10.**	a
11.	c	**12.**	c	**13.**	c	**14.**	a	**15.**	a
16.	c	**17.**	a	**18.**	a	**19.**	b	**20.**	a
21.	d	**22.**	d	**23.**	c	**24.**	b		

Chapter 11 Sexuality

Learning Goals with Key Terms and Key People in Boldface

1.0 UNDERSTAND THAT SEXUALITY IS A NORMAL ASPECT OF ADOLESCENCE

A. A Normal Aspect of Development

1.1 Do cultures differ in how they view adolescent sexuality?

1.2 What other chapters in the text serve as a backdrop for understanding adolescent sexuality?

B. The Sexual Culture

1.3 What is the nature of adolescent sexuality in today's culture?

1.4 Is there more tension related to sexuality between adolescents and parents in the United States than in other cultures?

C. Developing a Sexual Identity

1.5 What is involved in forming a sexual identity?

1.6 What is an adolescent's sexual preference?

D. Obtaining Information about Adolescent Sexuality

1.7 Who is most likely to respond to a sex survey?

1.8 Why is it difficult to obtain valid information about adolescent sexuality?

2.0 KNOW ABOUT SEXUAL ATTITUDES AND BEHAVIOR

A. Heterosexual Attitudes and Behaviors

2.1 What is the progression of sexual behaviors?

2.2 Are some adolescents more vulnerable to irresponsible sexual behavior than others?

2.3 Have the number of females engaging in intercourse increased more rapidly than that of males?

2.4 Are there ethnic and racial differences in sexual activity?

2.5 What is the current profile of sexual activity of adolescents?

B. Adolescent Female and Male Sexual Scripts

2.6 What are the common male and female adolescent **sexual scripts**?

C. Risk Factors for Sexual Problems

2.7 What are some of the risks faced by adolescents who are sexually active?

2.8 What are specific risk factors for sexual problems in adolescence?

3.0 DESCRIBE ADOLESCENT HOMOSEXUAL ATTITUDES AND BEHAVIOR

A. Homosexual Attitudes and Behavior

3.1 What is the attitude today about sexual orientation?

3.2 What do we know about adolescent's same-sex attractions?

3.3 What is the continuum of sexual orientation?

B. Gay or Lesbian Identity in Adolescence

3.4 What conclusions can be reached about adolescents who disclose their gay or lesbian identity?

3.5 What is meant by homophobia?

3.6 What is a harmful aspect of the stigmatization of homosexuality?

4.0   DISCUSS SELF-STIMULATION AND EVALUATE CONTRACEPTIVE USE

A.   Self-Stimulation

4.1   What is the nature of sexual self-stimulation?

B.   Contraceptive Use

4.2   How many adolescents are using contraceptives?

4.3   Which adolescents are least likely to use contraceptives?

5.0   KNOW ABOUT ADOLESCENT PREGNANCY

A.   Adolescent Pregnancy

5.1   How many American adolescents become pregnant each year?

5.2   How many adolescent births are unintended?

5.3   Is adolescent pregnancy increasing or decreasing?

5.4   What cultural changes have taken place in the last forty years regarding adolescent sexuality and pregnancy?

B.   Consequences of Adolescent Pregnancy

5.5   What are the health risks for mother and offspring?

5.6   How does adolescent pregnancy affect a mother's school and work opportunities?

C.   Cognitive Factors in Adolescent Pregnancy

5.7   How does the personal fable impact on pregnancy prevention efforts?

D.   Adolescents as Parents

5.8   What infant risks are associated with being born to an adolescent mother?

5.9   What kind of mothers do adolescents make?

5.10   What is the nature of adolescent fatherhood?

E.   Reducing Adolescent Pregnancy

5.11   What are Congers four recommendations for reducing adolescent pregnancy?

5.12   What programs have worked to reduce adolescent pregnancy?

5.13   What is the Teen Outreach Program?

6.0   DESCRIBE SEXUALLY TRANSMITTED DISEASES (STDS)?

A.   Types

6.1   What are sexually transmitted diseases (STDs)?

6.2   How are STDs contracted?

6.3   What is gonorrhea?

6.4   What is syphilis?

6.5   What is chlamydia?

6.6   What is genital herpes?

B.   AIDS

6.7   What is **AIDS**?

6.8   What is the rate of AIDS in adolescence?

6.9   How does the long incubation period affect adolescents who may have been infected with the AIDS virus as teenagers?

6.10   Where is the region of most concern regarding the spread of HIV/AIDS?

6.11   How is AIDS transmitted?

6.12   How is AIDS prevented?

7.0   FORCIBLE SEXUAL BEHAVIOR AND SEXUAL HARASSMENT

A.   Forcible Sexual Behavior

7.1   What is the nature and incidence of **rape**?

7.2   What is **date, or acquaintance, rape**?

7.3   What is sexual harassment?

7.4   How prevalent is adolescent sexual harassment?

7.5   What is **quid pro quo sexual harassment**?

7.6   What is the nature of **hostile environment sexual harassment**?

8.0 EVALUATE SEXUAL KNOWLEDGE AND SEX EDUCATION

A. Sexual Knowledge

8.1   How much do American adolescents and adults know about sex?

B. Sources of Sex Information

8.2   What is the nature or source of most sex information?

8.3   What are the sources of sex information?

C. Sex Education in the Schools

8.4   What is the incidence and nature of sex education in the schools?

8.5   Why do some experts believe that school-linked sex education tied to community health centers is a promising strategy?

8.6   How is sex education changing?

8.7   What are some criticisms of school-linked sex education?

9.0 EXPLORE SEXUAL WELL-BEING, SOCIAL POLICY, AND ADOLESCENTS

A. Sexual Well-Being and Development Transitions

9.1   What are the five issues related to adolescent sexuality that need examination?

9.2   What might be considered some healthy sexual pathways?

B. Social Policy and Adolescent Sexuality

9.3   What social policy initiatives do we need concerning sex education?

9.4   What initiatives are needed to reduce adolescent pregnancy?

9.5   What did the Carnegie Foundation's report "Starting points: Meeting the needs of our youngest children" emphasize?

Exercises

KEY TERMS
COMPLETION EXERCISE

Each key term is presented in the form of an incomplete sentence. Complete each sentence by either defining the term or giving an example. Compare your definitions with those given at the end of the study guide chapter.

1.   A **sexual script** is

_____

_____

2.   John is **bisexual,** which means he

_____

_____

3.   People must learn about **sexually transmitted diseases (STDs)** because

_____

_____

4.   The symptoms of **gonorrhea** are

_____

_____

5.   The symptoms of **syphilis** are

_____

_____

6.   The symptoms of **chlamydia** are

_____

_____

7.   The symptoms of **genital herpes** are

_____

_____

8. **AIDS** is a pseudonym standing for

    _____

    _____

9. The description of **rape** is

    _____

    _____

10. **Date, or acquaintance, rape** occurs when

    _____

    _____

11. **Quid pro quo sexual harassment** occurs when

    _____

    _____

12. **Hostile environment sexual harassment** occurs when

    _____

    _____

KEY PEOPLE
IN THE STUDY OF ADOLESCENCE

Match the person with the concept of adolescent development with which they are associated.

_____	1. Shirley Feldman	A.	Director of Kinsey Institute for Sex, Gender, and Reproduction
_____	2. Alfred Kinsey	B.	Views sexuality as a normal aspect of adolescent development
_____	3. Richard Savin-Williams	C.	Studies developmental issues in adolescent sexuality
_____	4. Simon LeVay	D.	Early and famous sex researcher
_____	5. P. Lindsay Chase-Lansdale	E.	Studied the brains of gay men for clues to causes of homosexuality
_____	6. June Reinisch	F.	Researched the pattern of gay and lesbian adolescents' disclosure of sexual orientation
_____	7. Jeanne Brooks-Gunn	G.	Studies contraceptive patterns in American adolescents and adolescents in foreign countries

263

"DR. DETAIL'S"
MATCHING EXERCISE

Match the STD with the associated features.

_____ 1. Syphilis	A. Commonly called the "drip" or "clap."
_____ 2. Chlamydia	B. Caused by a large family of viruses with many different strains.
_____ 3. Genital herpes	C. Destroys the body's immune system.
_____ 4. Gonorrhea	D. Is caused by the bacterium Treponema pallidum.
_____ 5. AIDS	E. Is the most common of all sexually transmitted diseases.

SEXUALITY AS A NORMAL PART OF ADOLESCENCE
SECTION REVIEW

1. Do cultures differ in how they view adolescent sexuality?

    _____

    _____

2. What other chapter in the text serve as a backdrop for understanding adolescent sexuality?

Chapter	Concept
3: Biological Differences	
4: Cognitive Differences	
5: Families	
6: Peers	
7: Schools	
8: Culture	
9: The Self and Identity	
10: Gender	

3. What is the nature of adolescent sexuality in today's culture?

    _____

    _____

4.   What is involved in forming a sexual identity?

_____

_____

5.   Who is most likely to respond to a sex survey?

_____

_____

SEXUAL ATTITUDES AND BEHAVIORS
SECTION REVIEW

1.   What is the typical progression of sexual behaviors?

_____

_____

2.   Have the number of females engaging is intercourse increased more rapidly than males?

_____

_____

3.   Are there ethnic and racial differences in sexual activity?

_____

_____

4.   What is the current profile of sexual activity of adolescents?

_____

_____

5.   What are the common male and female adolescent sexual scripts?

_____

_____

6.   What are some of the risk factors faced by adolescents who are sexually active?

_____

_____

ADOLESCENT HOMOSEXUAL ATTITUDES AND BEHAVIOR
SECTION REVIEW

1.   What is the continuum of sexual orientation?

_____

_____

2.   What is meant by homophobia?

_____

_____

3.   What is a harmful aspect of the stigmatization of homosexuality?

_____

_____

4.   What four conclusions did Savin-Williams (1998) make about adolescents who disclose their gay or lesbian identity?

_____

_____

KEY PEOPLE
IN SECTION

Alfred Kinsey—

_____

_____

Simon LeVay—

_____

_____

SELF-STIMULATION AND CONTRACEPTIVE USE
SECTION REVIEW

1.   What is the nature of sexual self-stimulation?

_____

_____

2.   How many adolescents are using contraceptives?

_____

_____

3.   Which adolescents are least likely to use contraceptives?

_____

_____

ADOLESCENT PREGNANCY
SECTION REVIEW

1.   How many adolescent births are unintended?

_____

_____

2.   What cultural changes have taken place in the last forty years regarding adolescent sexuality and pregnancy?

_____

_____

3.   What are the health risks for mother and child of adolescent pregnancy?

_____

_____

4.   How does adolescent pregnancy affect a mother's school and work opportunities?

_____

_____

5.   How does the *personal fable* impact on pregnancy prevention efforts?

_____

_____

6.   What infant risks are associated with teenage pregnancy?

_____

_____

7.   What is the nature of adolescent fatherhood?

_____

_____

8.   What are Conger's four recommendations for reducing adolescent pregnancy?

_____

_____

9.   What is the Teen Outreach Program?

_____

_____

KEY PEOPLE IN SECTION

John Conger—

_____

_____

SEXUALLY TRANSMITTED DISEASES (STDS) SECTION REVIEW

1.   What are sexually transmitted diseases?

_____

_____

2.   What is AIDS?

_____

_____

3.   Where is the region of most concern regarding the spread of HIV/AIDS?

_____

_____

4.   How is AIDS transmitted?

_____

_____

5.   How is AIDS prevented?

_____

_____

FORCIBLE SEXUAL BEHAVIOR AND SEXUAL HARASSMENT SECTION REVIEW

1.   What is the nature and incidence of rape?

_____

_____

2.   What is acquaintance rape?

_____

_____

3.   What is sexual harassment?

_____

_____

4.   What is quid pro quo sexual harassment?

_____

_____

5.   What is the nature of hostile environment sexual harassment?

_____

_____

SEXUAL KNOWLEDGE AND SEX EDUCATION
SECTION REVIEW

1.   How much do American adolescents and adults know about sex?

2.   What are the sources of most sex information?

3.   Why do some experts believe that school-linked sex education tied to community health centers is a promising strategy?

4.   What are some criticisms of school-linked sex education?

KEY PEOPLE
IN SECTION

June Reinisch—

SEXUAL WELL-BEING, SOCIAL POLICY, AND ADOLESCENTS
SECTION REVIEW

1.   What are the five issues related to adolescent sexuality that need examination?

2.   What might be considered some healthy sexual pathways?

3.   What initiatives are needed to reduce adolescent pregnancy?

_____

_____

4.   What did the Carnegie Foundation report emphasize?

_____

_____

KEY PEOPLE IN SECTION

Jeanne Brooks-Gunn and Roberta Paikoff—

_____

_____

COGNITIVE CHALLENGE

1.   Caroline contracted genital herpes from an old boyfriend. When she started dating Charles, she told him she had the herpes infection and he broke up with her. Now she is dating Jeff and she is afraid to tell him about the herpes because she thinks he will also break up with her. She thought maybe she should just tell him to use a condom so she won't get pregnant, and then she won't need to mention the herpes. What do you think Caroline should do?

_____

_____

2.   Based upon how you learned about sexuality, how do you expect to teach your children about sex? How do you want the schools to be involved in sex education for your children? Who other than parents and schools do you think should be involved in sex education?

_____

_____

ADOLESCENCE
IN RESEARCH

Buzwell & Rosenthal (1996) conducted an investigation of an adolescent's sexual identity, state the hypothesis, the research methods (if known), the research conclusions, and the implications and applications for adolescent development.

_____

_____

⊠ COMPREHENSIVE REVIEW

1. Sexual behaviors usually progress in the following order:
    a. kissing, oral sex, necking.
    b. petting, necking, kissing.
    c. intercourse, sexual adventure, oral sex.
    d. necking, petting, intercourse.

2. A _____ is a pattern involving stereotyped role prescriptions for how individuals should behave sexually.
    a. sexual bias
    b. sexual schema
    c. sexual role
    d. sexual script

3. Irresponsible sexual behavior such as unprotected intercourse is probably a reflection of
    a. cognitive immaturity.
    b. hostility against parental limits.
    c. vulnerability.
    d. parental stress or divorce.

4. An individual sexually attracted to both females and males is
    a. bisexual.
    b. homosexual.
    c. heterosexual.
    d. transsexual.

5. The most frequent sexual outlet for an adolescent is
    a. oral sex.
    b. sexual fantasy.
    c. masturbation.
    d. sexual intercourse.

6. As a drug store clerk, you are not at all surprised to find that condom sales are made most often to
    a.   older adolescents.
    b.   female adolescents.
    c.   younger adolescents.
    d.   sexually inactive adolescents.

7. Compared to those who wait to have children until they are in their mid- to late twenties, adolescent parents
    a.   have a better chance of staying married.
    b.   are less lonely.
    c.   have fewer children throughout their adult lives.
    d.   have lower incomes.

8. Infants born to adolescent mothers are more likely to
    a.   be overweight.
    b.   have an average survival rate.
    c.   bond with their mothers.
    d.   have low birth weights.

9. Sexually transmitted diseases are defined as those contracted through
    a.   vaginal intercourse.
    b.   vaginal intercourse and oral-genital contact.
    c.   oral-genital and anal-genital contact.
    d.   oral-genital and anal-genital contact and vaginal intercourse.

10. The most fatal sexually transmitted disease caused by a bacterium is
    a.   syphilis.
    b.   herpes.
    c.   AIDS.
    d.   gonorrhea.

11. The most common sexually transmitted disease among adolescents is
    a.   chlamydia.
    b.   herpes.
    c.   syphilis.
    d.   gonorrhea.

12. If you come into intimate sexual contact with an infected person, your risk of contracting the disease is greatest for
    a.   gonorrhea.
    b.   syphilis.
    c.   herpes.
    d.   AIDS.

13. According to comparative studies, the rate of AIDS among adolescents is
    a.   higher than adult rates.
    b.   about the same as adult rates.
    c.   lower than adult rates.
    d.   not directly compared with adult rates.

14. According to the text, the average time between contracting the HIV infection and development of illness is
    a. six months.
    b. ten years.
    c. five to seven years.
    d. three years.

15. _____ are usually the main source of an adolescent's sexual information.
    a. Parents
    b. Schools
    c. Peers
    d. Literature

16. Which of the following statements concerning sex education in the schools is accurate?
    a. The majority of adults in the United States do not approve of sex education in the schools.
    b. Sex education programs are more likely to appear in high schools and junior high schools than elementary schools.
    c. The emphasis in sex education classes is on contraception and variations in sexual behavior.
    d. Most sex education programs consist of full-semester courses on human sexuality.

17. Belinda's boyfriend used a variety of psychological ploys and physical behaviors to coerce her into having sex, even though she had said no to him. This is referred to as _____ rape.
    a. power
    b. sexual
    c. controlling
    d. acquaintance

18. The factor that is most important in facilitating the recovery from rape is
    a. physical health.
    b. retaliation against the rapist.
    c. resumption of consensual sexual relations.
    d. social support.

19. The Young Men's Sexuality Awareness program seeks to encourage
    a. affection without intercourse.
    b. intercourse with affection.
    c. fund raising for elective abortions.
    d. adolescent males to marry their sex partners.

20. The purpose of sex education programs in such countries as Holland and Sweden is to _____ the experience of adolescent sexuality.
    a. promote
    b. discourage
    c. demystify
    d. simplify

ADOLESCENCE
ON THE SCREEN

- *Chasing Amy* A young man is attracted to a girl who tells him that she is a lesbian. Actually she has had a wild heterosexual past and is manipulating the boy's attraction for her.

- *Taxi Driver* A New York City taxi driver tries to save a child prostitute.

- *The Summer of '42* A young boy has his first sexual experience with a kind, older women on whom he has a crush.

- *The Middle School Chronicles* [HBO] Startling view of sexuality and sex from very young children.

- *The Lost Kids of Rockdale County* [PBS Frontline] Chilling details regarding an epidemic of syphilis that raged threw the school in this quiet town. There is also discussion on school-related violence.

ADOLESCENCE
IN BOOKS

- *Boys and Sex*, by Wardell Pomery (Delacorte Press: NY, 1991), was written for adolescent boys and stresses the responsibility that comes with sexual maturity.

- *Girls and Sex*, by Wardell Pomery (Delacorte Press: NY, 1991), poses a number of questions that young girls often ask about sex and then answers them. Many myths that young girls hear about sex are also demystified.

Answer Key

KEY TERMS

1. **sexual script** A stereotypical pattern of role prescriptions for how individuals should behave sexually. Females and males have been socialized to follow different sexual scripts.

2. **bisexual** A person who is attracted to people of both sexes.

3. **sexually transmitted diseases (STDs)** Diseases that are contracted primarily through sexual contact. This contact is not limited to vaginal intercourse but includes oral-genital contact and anal-genital contact as well.

4. **gonorrhea** Reported to be one of the most common STDs in the United States, this sexually transmitted disease is caused by a bacterium called *gonococcus*, which thrives in the moist mucous membrane lining the mouth, throat, vagina, cervix, urethra, and anal tract. This disease is commonly called the "drip" or the "clap."

5. **syphilis** A sexually transmitted disease caused by the bacterium *Treponema pallidum*, a spirochete.

6. **Chlamydia** The most common of all sexually transmitted diseases, is named for Chlamydia trachomatis, an organism that infects both sexual partners.

7. **genital herpes** A sexually transmitted disease caused by a large family of viruses of different strains. These strains produce other, nonsexually transmitted diseases such as chicken pox and mononucleosis.

8. **AIDS** Acquired immune deficiency syndrome, primarily a sexually transmitted disease caused by the HIV virus, which destroys the body's immune system.

9. **rape** Forcible nonconsensual sexual intercourse.

10. **date or acquaintance rape** Coercive sexual activity directed at someone with whom the perpetrator is at least casually acquainted.

11. **quid pro quo sexual harassment** Occurs when a school employee threatens to base an educational decision (such as a grade) on a student's submission to unwelcome conduct

12. **hostile environment sexual harassment** Occurs when students are subjected to unwelcome sexual conduct that is so severe, persistent, or pervasive that it limits the students' ability to benefit from their education.

KEY PEOPLE
IN THE STUDY OF ADOLESCENCE

1.	B	**2.**	D	**3.**	F	**4.**	E	**5.**	G
6.	A	**7.**	C						

"DR. DETAIL'S"
MATCHING EXERCISE

1.	D	**2.**	E	**3.**	B	**4.**	A	**5.**	C

SEXUALITY AS A NORMAL PART OF ADOLESCENCE
SECTION REVIEW

1. Yes. In some societies women are escorted or get married before any sexual activity. Other societies are less concerned regarding sexual exploration.

2.

Chapter	Concept
3: Biological Differences	Early pubertal maturation in girls may lead to early dating and sexual activity.
4: Cognitive Differences	Adolescent egocentrism may lead to sexual risk-taking.
5: Families	Prolonged family conflict and lack of parental monitoring can lead to problems in sexuality
6: Peers	Peers and friends influence learning about and discussing sexual behavior.
7: Schools	Schools have a big role in sex education.
8: Culture	Sexuality in the media is often presented to adolescents in an unrealistic way.
9: The Self and Identity	Sexual identity is one dimension of identity.
10: Gender	Pubertal changes may lead to boys and girls conforming to traditional masculine and feminine behaviors.

3. Many Americans are ambivalent about sex. It is used to sell just about everything.

4. An adolescent's sexual identity involves an indication of sexual preference (homosexual, heterosexual, bisexual).

5. The most likely people to respond would be those least inhibited. So surveys may measure an extreme.

SEXUAL ATTITUDES AND BEHAVIORS
SECTION REVIEW

1.   Kissing preceded petting, which preceded sexual intercourse and oral sex.

2.   The proportion of female college students who report that they have had sexual intercourse has increased more rapidly than that of males.

3.   Male African Americans are more likely to have a less restrictive timetable for sexual behaviors than other groups, whereas Asian Americans are more likely to have a more restrictive one. Male African Americans and inner-city adolescents report being the most sexually active.

4.   Eight in 10 girls and seven in 10 boys are virgins at age 15. The probability that adolescents will have sexual intercourse increases steadily with age, but 1 in 5 individuals have not had intercourse by age 19. Initial sexual intercourse occurs in the mid- to late-adolescent years for a majority of teenagers. The majority of females' first sexual partners are similar in age.

5.   A sexual script is a stereotyped pattern of role prescriptions for how individuals should sexually behave. Females and males have been socialized to follow different sexual scripts.

6.   Pregnancy and sexually transmitted diseases.

ADOLESCENT HOMOSEXUAL ATTITUDES AND BEHAVIOR
SECTION REVIEW

1.   Exclusively heterosexual behavior; largely heterosexual; equal amounts of heterosexual and homosexual behavior; largely homosexual; exclusively homosexual behavior.

2.   Having irrational negative feelings against homosexuals.

3.   Self-devaluation.

4.   Parents are seldom the first to hear about the same-sex attraction. Mothers are usually told before fathers. Mothers are more likely than fathers to find out about son's same-sex attraction. Approximately 50 to 60 percent of gay adolescents have told a sibling. The first person told about same-sex attraction is usually a friend.

KEY PEOPLE
IN SECTION

Alfred Kinsey—described sexual orientation as a continuum on a six-point scale.

Simon LeVay—found that an area of the hypothalamus that governs sexual behavior is twice as large in heterosexual men as in homosexual men.

SELF-STIMULATION AND CONTRACEPTIVE USE
SECTION REVIEW

1. It's a way to deal with arousal.

2. Forty-eight to sixty-five percent.

3. Sexually active younger adolescents.

ADOLESCENT PREGNANCY
SECTION REVIEW

1. Forty-nine out of every 1000 girls.

2. More acceptance of sexual practice, contraception and abortion.

3. Adolescent mothers often drop out of school. Children are often of low birth weight, which is associated with a variety of problems later in life.

4. She is more likely to drop out of school and have a low skilled job.

5. "It won't happen to me."

6. Low birth weight, neurological problems and illness.

7. Most are uninvolved with their children.

8. (a) Sex education and family planning, (b) access to contraceptives, (c) the life options approach, and (d) broad community involvement and support.

9. It focuses on engaging adolescents in volunteer community service and stimulates enlightening discussions.

KEY PEOPLE
IN SECTION

John Conger—offered four recommendations for attacking the high rate of adolescent pregnancy.

SEXUALLY TRANSMITTED DISEASES (STDS)
SECTION REVIEW

1.   Diseases that are contracted primarily through sexual contact.

2.   Is a sexually transmitted disease that is caused by a virus, the human immunodeficiency virus, which destroys the body's immune system.

3.   Sub-Saharan Africa.

4.   Heterosexual sex, homosexual sex, blood transfusion, shared needles.

5.   Using condoms, not sharing needles, and screening blood donations.

FORCIBLE SEXUAL BEHAVIOR AND SEXUAL HARASSMENT
SECTION REVIEW

1.   Forcible sexual intercourse with a person who does not give consent.

2.   Coercive sexual activity directed at someone with whom the perpetrator is at least casually acquainted.

3.   Unwanted touch or harassing remarks.

4.   A school employee threatens to base an educational decision, such as a grade, on a student's submission to sex.

5.   Students are subjected to unwelcomed sexual conduct that is so severe, persistent, or pervasive that it limits the student's ability to benefit from their education.

SEXUAL KNOWLEDGE AND SEX EDUCATION
SECTION REVIEW

1.   According to June Reinisch, they know more about their cars than how their bodies function sexually.

2.   Peers.

3.   The attitude is that this can be more informative and reach more children in an unintrusive environment.

4.   Some feel that the knowledge is used to experiment with sexual behaviors, as opposed to abstaining.

KEY PEOPLE
IN SECTION

June Reinisch—feels that U.S. citizens know more about how their automobiles function than about how their bodies function sexually.

SEXUAL WELL-BEING, SOCIAL POLICY, AND ADOLESCENTS
SECTION REVIEW

1.   (a) Timing of behaviors associated with behavior, (b) co-occurrence of health-related behaviors, (c) the contexts of sexual behavior, (d) the timing of sexual experiences, and (e) gender and sexuality.

2.   (a) practicing abstinence, but having positive sexual attitudes, (b) engaging in sexual exploration as opposed to sexual intercourse, (c) engaging in sexual intercourse within the context of a committed relationship, and (d) participating in preintercourse behaviors with another individual early in adolescence.

3.   Teach kids responsibility before they become sexually active.

4.   The importance of preparing adolescents for responsible parenthood.

KEY PEOPLE
IN SECTION

Jeanne Brooks-Gunn and Roberta Paikoff—proposed five developmental issues that need to be examined more thoroughly in adolescent sexuality.

COGNITIVE
CHALLENGE

1.   Individual activity. No answer provided.

2.   Individual activity. No answer provided.

ADOLESCENCE
IN RESEARCH

The hypothesis was that adolescents, in choosing their sexual identity adopt different styles. They studied 470 tenth- to twelfth-grade Australian youth. Their results showed five different styles: Sexually naïve; sexually unassured; sexually competent; sexually adventurous; sexually driven.

⊠ COMPREHENSIVE REVIEW

1.	d	2.	d	3.	c	4.	a	5.	c
6.	c	7.	d	8.	d	9.	d	10.	a
11.	a	12.	c	13.	c	14.	c	15.	c
16.	b	17.	d	18.	d	19.	a	20.	c

Chapter 12   Moral Development, Values, and Religion

Learning Goals with Key Terms and Key People in Boldface

Learning Goals with Key Terms and Key People in Boldface

1.0   KNOW WHAT MORAL DEVELOPMENT IS
- **A.   What is Moral Development?**
  - 1.1   What is involved in moral development?
  - 1.2   What are the dimensions of moral development?

2.0   MORAL THOUGHT
- **A.   Piaget's Ideas on Cognitive Disequilibrium Theory**
  - 2.1   What is the difference between **Piaget's heteronomous morality** and his **autonomous morality**?
  - 2.2   What is the concept of **immanent justice**?
  - 2.3   What does the development of formal operational thought have to do with adolescent moral reasoning?
  - 2.4   What is **Hoffman's** proposed cognitive **disequlibrium theory** of moral development?
  - 2.5   What is **internalization**?
- **B.   Kohlberg's Ideas on Moral Development**
  - 2.6   What is **Kohlberg's** theory of moral development?
  - 2.7   What are the differences between **preconventional reasoning, conventional reasoning,** and **postconventional reasoning**?
  - 2.8   What stage of moral reasoning is characterized by **heteronomous morality**?
  - 2.9   What stage of moral reasoning is characterized by **individualism, instrumental purpose and exchange**?
  - 2.10   What state of moral reasoning is characterized by mutual interpersonal expectations, relationships, and interpersonal conformity?
  - 2.11   What is the meaning of the social contract or utility and individual rights?
  - 2.12   What are universal ethical principles?
  - 2.13   What are the justice perspective and care perspective?
  - 2.14   What is social conventional reasoning?
- **C.   Kohlberg's Critics**
  - 2.15   What are some major criticisms of **Kohlberg's** theories?
  - 2.16   What is the Defining Issues Test?
  - 2.17   According to **Richard Shweder**, there are three ethical orientations or world views, what are they?
  - 2.18   What was the basis for **Gilligan's** criticism of **Kohlberg**?
- **D.   Reasoning in Different Social Cognitive Domains**
  - 2.19   Why is it important to make distinctions regarding different domains when considering adolescent's sociocognitive reasoning?
  - 2.20   What three domains have been given the most attention?

3.0 DISCUSS MORAL BEHAVIOR

A. Basic Processes

3.1   How is moral behavior determined by the processes of reinforcement, punishment, and imitation?

3.2   What situational variations are involved in moral behavior?

3.3   What did **Hartshorne** and **May** find about situational variation in moral behavior?

B. Social Cognitive Theory of Moral Development

3.4   What is the nature of the **social cognitive theory of moral development**?

3.5   What is the difference between moral competence and moral behavior?

3.6   What are the social cognitive theorists' criticisms of Kohlberg's theory of moral development?

C. Altruism

3.7   What is the nature of **altruism**?

3.8   How are reciprocity and exchange involved in altruism?

3.9   What is the role of **forgiveness** in altruism?

3.10   Is there a developmental sequence for the development of altruism?

4.0 UNDERSTAND MORAL FEELINGS

A. Psychoanalytic Theory

4.1   According to **Freud**, what is the moral part of personality?

4.2   How does the process of identification affect moral development?

4.3   Why do children conform to moral standards, according to **Freud**?

4.4   What did **Freud** mean by the **ego ideal** and the **conscience**?

4.5   What were **Erikson's** views regarding three stages of moral development?

B. Child-Rearing Techniques

4.6   What do child-rearing techniques have to do with moral development?

4.7   How do love **withdrawal**, **power assertion**, and **induction** affect a child's moral development?

C. Empathy

4.8   What is **empathy** and how does it contribute to moral development?

D. The Contemporary Perspective

4.9   How are emotions interwoven with moral development?

5.0 DESCRIBE MORAL EDUCATION

A. The Hidden Curriculum

5.1   What is meant by the **hidden curriculum**?

5.2   Who was **John Dewey**?

B. Character Education

5.3   What is **character education**?

5.4   What is the nature of moral literacy?

C. Values Clarification

5.5   What is the nature of **values clarification**?

D. Cognitive Moral Education

5.6   What is cognitive moral education?

5.7   Whose theory of moral development is the basis for many **cognitive moral education** programs?

E. Service Learning

5.8   What is **service learning**?

6.0   EVALUATE VALUES IN ADOLESCENCE

A.   Values

6.1   How are **values** defined?

6.2   How are adolescent values changing?

7.0   DISCUSS RELIGION IN ADOLESCENCE

A.   Religion

7.1   What is the scope of religion interest in children and adolescents?

7.2   Is adolescence a special juncture in religious development?

7.3   What is Piaget's theory about the role of religion in development?

7.4   Are there links between religiousness and sexuality?

7.5   What is Fowler's life-span development view of the six stages of finding meaning in life?

8.0   KNOW ABOUT CULTS

A.   Cults

8.1   What is the nature of cults?

8.2   Why do people join cults?

8.3   What is a cult's potential for abuse?

Exercises

KEY TERMS
COMPLETION EXERCISE

Each key term is presented in the form of an incomplete sentence. Complete each sentence by either defining the term or giving an example. Compare your definitions with those given at the end of the study guide chapter.

1.   **Moral development** influences an adolescent's

   _____

   _____

2.   You can tell that Jack is in the stage of **heteronomous morality** because

   _____

   _____

3.   As Billy passes age 10, he enters the stage of **autonomous morality,** which means

   _____

   _____

4.   **Immanent justice** should be used when

   _____

   _____

5.   **Cognitive disequlibrium theory** suggests that

   _____

   _____

6.   **Internalization** refers to

   _____

   _____

7.   In **preconventional reasoning** children

   _____

   _____

8.   In **conventional reasoning** children began to

_____

_____

9.   During **postconventional reasoning** morality

_____

_____

10.   From the **justice perspective** individuals

_____

_____

11.   According to Carol Gilligan, **care perspective** is

_____

_____

12.   According to the **social cognitive theory of moral development**

_____

_____

13.   Characteristics of an act of **altruism** are

_____

_____

14.   **Forgiveness** is when

_____

_____

15.   Susan's behavior is consistent with her parent's **ego ideal** because

_____

_____

16.   You can tell Peggy has a **conscience** because

_____

_____

17.   Parents practicing **love withdrawal** are likely to

_____

_____

18.   **Power assertion** suggests a parenting style that uses

_____

_____

19.   According to Hoffman, **induction** is when parents

_____

_____

20.   A good example of **empathy** is

_____

_____

21.   **Hidden curriculum** in schools is

_____

_____

22.   Good **character education** begins with

_____

_____

23.   An example of **values clarification** is

_____

_____

24.   **Cognitive moral education** is based on the belief that

_____

_____

25.   **Service learning** is a form of education that

_____

_____

26. **Values** are

_____

_____

KEY PEOPLE
IN THE STUDY OF ADOLESCENCE

Match the person with the concept of adolescent moral development with which they are associated.

_____ 1. Jean Piaget

A. Associated with social-cognitive perspective of moral development

_____ 2. Martin Hoffman

B. Believes that parents play a role in moral development

_____ 3. Lawrence Kohlberg

C. Developed a six-stage model of moral development, with three levels of moral reasoning

_____ 4. James Rest

D. Believed that there were two types of morality, depending upon the age of the child

_____ 5. Robert Shweder

E. Believed that moral education was the schools' hidden curriculum

_____ 6. Carol Gilligan

F. Believed that adolescents develop an ideology as part of their identity

_____ 7. Hugh Hartshorne and Mark May

G. Developed the cognitive disequilibrium theory

_____ 8. Albert Bandura

H. Thought that resolution of the Oedipus complex was associated with moral development

_____ 9. Sigmund Freud

I. Developed the Defining Issues Test to measure morality

_____ 10. Erik Erikson

J. Believes that there are three types of ethical orientation

_____ 11. Nancy Eisenberg

K. Insists that girls' need for relationships is significant factor in their sense of morality

_____ 12. John Dewey

L. Involved in large study of situational morality

"DR. DETAIL'S"
STAGE MASTERY EXERCISE

Complete the table by listing the main characteristics of each of Kohlberg's stages of moral development.

Stage	Characteristic
Preconventional Reasoning	
Heteronomous morality	
Individualism, instrumental purpose, and exchange	
Conventional Reasoning	
Mutual interpersonal expectations, relationships, and interpersonal conformity	
Social systems morality	
Postconventional Reasoning	
Social contract or utility and individual rights	
Universal ethical principles	

WHAT MORAL DEVELOPMENT IS
SECTION REVIEW

1.　　What is moral development?

_____

_____

2.　　What are the dimensions of moral development?

_____

_____

MORAL THOUGHT
SECTION REVIEW

1. What is the difference between Piaget's heteronomous morality and his autonomous morality?

   _____

   _____

2. What is immanent justice?

   _____

   _____

3. What is Hoffman's proposed cognitive disequlibrium theory of moral development?

   _____

   _____

4. What is internalization?

   _____

   _____

5. What are the differences between preconventional reasoning, conventional reasoning, and postconventional reasoning?

   _____

   _____

6. What are the justice perspective and care perspective?

   _____

   _____

7. What are some major criticisms of Kohlberg's theories?

   _____

   _____

8. What is the Defining Issues Test?

   _____

   _____

9.   According to Shweder, there are three ethical orientations or world views, what are they?

_____

_____

MORAL BEHAVIOR
SECTION REVIEW

1.   What did Hartshorne and May find about situational variation in moral behavior?

_____

_____

2.   What is the nature of the social cognitive theory of moral development?

_____

_____

3.   What is the difference between moral competence and moral behavior?

_____

_____

4.   What is the nature of altruism?

_____

_____

5.   What is the role of forgiveness in altruism?

_____

_____

MORAL FEELINGS
SECTION REVIEW

1.   What is the best way for parents to help children develop moral maturity, other than setting a good behavioral example?

_____

_____

2. Why is an adolescent more likely to forgive someone if his friends encourage him to do so?

   _____

   _____

3. What did Freud mean by the ego ideal and the conscience?

   _____

   _____

4. What were Erikson's views regarding three stages of moral development?

   _____

   _____

MORAL EDUCATION
SECTION REVIEW

1. Name two books that promote character education.

   _____

   _____

2. What is meant by the hidden curriculum?

   _____

   _____

3. What is character education?

   _____

   _____

4. What is the nature of values clarification?

   _____

   _____

5. What is cognitive moral education?

   _____

   _____

6.   What is service learning?

_____

_____

VALUES IN ADOLESCENCE
SECTION REVIEW

1.   How are values defined?

_____

_____

2.   How are adolescent values changing?

_____

_____

RELIGION IN ADOLESCENCE
SECTION REVIEW

1.   Complete the table by filling in the name of Fowler's stage of religious development, the period of development in which it occurs, and brief descriptions of the characteristics of the stage.

Name of Stage	Developmental Period	Characteristics
1.		
2.		
3.		
4.		
5.		
6.		

2.   What is Piaget's theory about the role of religion in development?

_____

_____

CULTS
SECTION REVIEW

1. What is the nature of cults?

_____

_____

2. Why do people join cults?

_____

_____

COGNITIVE
CHALLENGE

1. A man who had been sentenced to serve 10 years for selling a small amount of marijuana walked away from a prison camp six months after he was there. Twenty-five years later he was caught. He is now in his 50s and has been a model citizen. Should he be sent back to prison? Why or why not? At what Kohlberg stage is your response? Would you feel differently if he were your sibling?

_____

_____

2. What are the five most important values to you? How did you get these values? Did they come from your parents, friends, teachers, or some event or experience? How carefully do you stick to societies ethical standards.

_____

_____

3. As you progressed through the first four stages of Fowler's stages of religious development, how were your experiences different from or similar to his characterizations? Are you resolved about your choice of religious practice, or do you have some doubts?

_____

_____

ADOLESCENCE
IN RESEARCH

Concerning Hartshorne and May's research (1928–1930), state the hypothesis, the research methods (if known), the research conclusions, and the implications and applications for adolescent development.

_____

_____

⊠ COMPREHENSIVE REVIEW

1. The three major aspects of moral development include
    a.   stimulus, response, and consequences.
    b.   thought, feeling, and behaving.
    c.   individual, family, and society.
    d.   id, ego, and superego.

2. Jean Piaget indicates that the heteronomous thinker
    a.   believes that rules can be changed because they are merely conventions.
    b.   recognizes that punishment for wrongdoing is not inevitable.
    c.   judges the goodness of behavior by focusing on the consequences of the behavior.
    d.   is usually a child between the ages of 10 and 12.

3. _____ is the idea that, if a rule is broken, punishment will be meted out immediately.
    a.   Autonomous morality
    b.   Immanent justice
    c.   Response cost
    d.   Love withdrawal

4. Six stages of moral development were proposed by _____
    a.   Martin Hoffman.
    b.   Jean Piaget.
    c.   Sigmund Freud.
    d.   Lawrence Kohlberg.

5. Which of the following was NOT a criticism of Kohlberg's theory of moral development?
    a.   Placed too little emphasis on moral behavior.
    b.   The research was of poor quality.
    c.   Placed too much emphasis on the development of the Superego.
    d.   Did not fully consider cultural or gender variables.

6. Martin Hoffman indicates that going to high school is associated with a dramatic change in moral reasoning because
    a.   there is more opportunity for sexual exploitation.
    b.   parental supervision is nullified.
    c.   peer pressure to violate community standards is high.
    d.   discussions reveal the variety of moral beliefs.

7. Which of the following is NOT a social cognitive domain noted in the chapter?
    a.   Moral domain
    b.   Human domain
    c.   Social-conventional domain
    d.   Personal domain

8. _____ an unselfish interest in helping another person.
    a. Forgiveness
    b. Conscience
    c. Induction
    d. altruism

9. Lawrence Kohlberg argues that the distinctions between the three levels of moral reasoning have to do with
    a. the degree of internalization.
    b. the immediacy of the consequences for moral actions.
    c. the severity of punishments experienced.
    d. the social pressure of peers.

10. An adolescent at Kohlberg's conventional level of moral reasoning
    a. obeys rules in order to meet his defined obligations.
    b. obeys rules in order to avoid punishment.
    c. will follow rules if they are in his immediate best interest.
    d. has developed a social contract involving self-chosen ethical principles.

11. Who is most likely to join a cult?
    a. Someone who is psychologically unstable
    b. A person just recently released from prison
    c. A normal, average person
    d. Someone with strong religious beliefs

12. James Rest developed the Defining Issues Test because
    a. there were no available measures of moral reasoning.
    b. he found Piaget's tests too hard for adolescents.
    c. Kohlberg's stories were too difficult to score.
    d. he didn't know that several other tests were available.

13. There is general agreement that Lawrence Kohlberg's theory
    a. is correct for adolescents, but not for adults.
    b. confused autonomy with autonomous morality.
    c. confused moral reasoning with moral behavior.
    d. underestimates the importance of culture.

14. Carol Gilligan has criticized Kohlberg's theory for
    a. overemphasizing people's connectedness and communication with other people.
    b. emphasizing moral behavior and ignoring moral reasoning.
    c. relying on a single method to assess individual's moral reasoning.
    d. understanding the importance of interpersonal relationships in moral development.

15. Adolescents' moral performance is influenced by
    a. skills.
    b. awareness of moral rules.
    c. cognitive-sensory processes.
    d. motivation.

16.   Which theory distinguishes between moral competence and moral performance?
    a.   Psychosocial
    b.   Moral development
    c.   Cognitive social learning
    d.   Behavioral moral reasoning

17.   Psychoanalytic theorists say that guilt develops when a child
    a.   turns her hostility inward following the withdrawal of parental love.
    b.   harnesses the drives of the superego and maintains the world as a safe place.
    c.   becomes disillusioned with the moral and religious beliefs she acquired during childhood.
    d.   participates in the feelings of an adult with whom she has identified.

18.   The part of the superego that enables us to feel proud when we do the right thing, even if no one else will know, is the
    a.   conscience.
    b.   ego ideal.
    c.   empathic aspect.
    d.   altruistic channel.

19.   Martin Hoffman believes that parents promote the moral development of their children and adolescents through
    a.   love withdrawal.
    b.   power assertion.
    c.   induction.
    d.   altruism.

20.   The failure to develop empathy, if not altruism, is associated with
    a.   excessive achievement orientation.
    b.   vulnerability to cults.
    c.   antisocial behaviors.
    d.   chronic depression.

21.   If a person can experience another's feelings and respond in a similar way, this is called
    a.   pity.
    b.   empathy.
    c.   sympathy.
    d.   understanding.

22.   Which of the following is an example of altruism?
    a.   Sharing possessions
    b.   Resisting temptation
    c.   Saying thank you
    d.   Not eating with your fingers

23.   Which term is used when a person "releases the injurer from possible behavioral retaliation"?
    a.   Altruism
    b.   Empathy
    c.   Sympathy
    d.   Forgiveness

24. Schools are one of the settings in which moral development occurs. The moral climate of the school is called the
    a. administrative morale.
    b. Damon Comprehensive Approach.
    c. hidden curriculum.
    d. classroom conscience.

25. According to a poll, _____ percent of the adolescents said that they prayed.
    a. 10
    b. 35
    c. 50
    d. 75

26. An adolescent refused to attend church, telling his parents that he would believe what he wants to believe, not what they tell him to believe. This adolescent demonstrates
    a. reflective faith.
    b. individuating-reflective faith.
    c. catastrophic conversion.
    d. moral fundamentalism.

ADOLESCENCE ON THE SCREEN

- *Clockwork Orange* An immoral and violent young man becomes the subject of an experiment to eradicate his violent tendencies.

- *Saving Private Ryan* Examines morality and the need for personal sacrifice in the context of war and military duty.

- *Stand by Me* Four 12-year-old boys trek into the wilderness to find the body of a missing boy.

- *Lost and Delirious* Tracks the moral development of a young girl at an "all-girls" boarding school, before and after young love goes sour.

ADOLESCENCE IN BOOKS

- *Meeting at the Crossroads*, by Lyn Mikel Brown and Carol Gilligan (Harvard University Press: MA, 1992), provides a vivid portrayal of how adolescent girls are often ignored and misunderstood.

- *The Lost Boys*, by James Garbarino (the Free Press: NY, 1999). Outstanding compilation of theories and facts related to why children "go bad" and what can be done to stop this.

- *She Said Yes: The Unlikely Martyrdom of Cassie Bernall,* by Misty Bernall (the Plough Publishing House: UK, 1999). A heart-wrenching and honest portrayal of a young, troubled girl who just after turning her life around, ends up being a victim in the Columbine massacre.

- *Postconventional Thinking*, by James Rest, Darcia Naraez, Muriel Bebeau, and Stephen Thoma (Erlbaum: NJ, 1999), presents a neo-Kolhbergian analysis of moral development.

Answer Key

KEY TERMS

1. **moral development** Thoughts, feelings, and behaviors regarding standards of right and wrong.

2. **heteronomous morality** The first stage of moral development in Piaget's theory, occurring at 4 to 7 years of age. Justice and rules are conceived of as unchangeable properties of the world, removed from the control of people.

3. **autonomous morality** The second stage of moral development in Piaget's theory, displayed by older children (about 10 years of age and older). The child becomes aware that rules and laws are created by people and that, in judging an action, one should consider the actor's intentions as well as the consequences.

4. **immanent justice** Piaget's concept that if a rule is broken, punishment will be meted out immediately.

5. **cognitive disequilibrium theory** Hoffman's theory that adolescence is an important period in moral development, in which, because of broader experiences associated with the move to high school or college, individuals recognize that their set of beliefs is but one of many and that there is considerable debate about what is right and wrong.

6. **internalization** The developmental change from behavior that is externally controlled to behavior that is controlled by internal standards and principles.

7. **preconventional reasoning** The lowest level in Kohlberg's theory of moral development. The individual shows no internalization of moral values—moral reasoning is controlled by external rewards and punishment.

8. **conventional reasoning** The second, or intermediate, level in Kohlberg's theory of moral development. Internalization is intermediate. Individuals abide by certain standards (internal), but they are the standards of others (external), such as parents or the laws of society.

9. **postconventional reasoning** The highest level in Kohlberg's theory of moral development. Morality is completely internalized.

10. **justice perspective** A moral perspective that focuses on the rights of the individual; individuals independently make moral decisions.

11. **care perspective** The moral perspective of Carol Gilligan, that views people in terms of their connectedness with others and emphasizes interpersonal communication, relationships with others, and concern for others.

12. **social cognitive theory of moral development** The theory that distinguishes between moral competence—the ability to produce moral behaviors—and moral performance—those behaviors in specific situations.

13. **altruism** Unselfish interest in helping another person.

14. **forgiveness** This is an aspect of altruism that occurs when an injured person releases the injured from possible behavioral retaliation.

15. **ego ideal** The component of the superego that involves ideal standards approved by parents.

16. **conscience** The component of the superego that involves behaviors disapproved of by parents.

17. **love withdrawal** Is a discipline technique in which a parent removes attention or love from the child.

18. **power assertion** A discipline technique in which a parent attempts to gain control over a child or a child's resources.

19. **induction** A discipline technique in which a parent uses reason and explanation of the consequences for others of a child's actions.

20. **empathy** Reacting to another's feelings with an emotional response that is similar to the other's response.

21. **hidden curriculum** The pervasive moral atmosphere that characterizes schools.

22. **character education** A direct moral education approach that involves teaching students a basic moral literacy to prevent them from engaging in immoral behavior or doing harm to themselves or others.

23. **values clarification** Helping people to clarify what their lives are for and what is worth working for. Students are encouraged to define their own values and understand others' values.

24. **cognitive moral education** Is based on the belief that students should learn to value things like democracy and justice as their moral reasoning develops; Kohlberg's theory has been the basis for many of the cognitive moral education approaches.

25. **service learning** A form of education that promotes social responsibility and service to the community.

26. **values** Beliefs and attitudes about the way people think things should be.

KEY PEOPLE
IN THE STUDY OF ADOLESCENCE

1.	D	2.	G	3.	C	4.	I	5.	J
6.	K	7.	L	8.	A	9.	H	10.	F
11.	B	12.	E						

"DR. DETAIL'S"
STAGE MASTERY EXERCISE

Stage	Characteristic
Preconventional Reasoning	Individual shows no internalization of moral values; moral reasoning is controlled by external rewards and punishment.
Heteronomous morality	Moral thinking is tied to punishment.
Individualism, instrumental purpose, and exchange	Individuals pursue their own interests but let others do the same.
Conventional Reasoning	Internalization is intermediate. Individuals abide by certain internal standards, but they are the standards of others, such as parents or the laws of society.
Mutual interpersonal expectations, relationships, and interpersonal conformity	Individuals value trust, caring, and loyalty to others as a basis of moral judgment.
Social systems morality	Moral judgments are based on understanding the social order, law, justice, and duty.
Postconventional Reasoning	Morality is completely internalized and is not based on others' standards. The individual recognizes alternative moral courses, explores the options, and then decides on a personal moral code.
Social contract or utility and individual rights	Individuals reason that values, rights, and principles underscore or transcend the law.
Universal ethical principles	The person has developed a moral standard based on universal human rights.

WHAT MORAL DEVELOPMENT IS
SECTION REVIEW

1. It involves thoughts, feelings, and behaviors regarding standards of right and wrong.

2. (a) How do adolescents think about rules for ethical conduct? (b) How do adolescents actually behave in moral circumstances? (c) How do adolescents feel about moral matters?

MORAL THOUGHT
SECTION REVIEW

1. Heteronomous morality is the first stage of moral development. Justice and rules are conceived of as unchangeable properties of the world, removed from the control of people. Autonomous morality is the second stage. Here the child becomes aware that rules and laws are created by people and that in judging an action one should consider the actor's intentions as well as the consequences.

2. Piaget's concept that if a rule is broken, punishment will be meted out immediately.

3. This states that adolescence is an important period in moral development, especially as individuals move from the relatively homogeneous grade school to the more heterogeneous high school and college environments, where they are faced with contradictions between the moral concepts they have accepted and experiences outside their family and neighborhood.

4. The developmental change from behavior that is externally controlled to behavior that is controlled by internal standards and principles.

5. Preconventional—moral reasoning is controlled by external rewards and punishments. Conventional reasoning—individuals abide by others standards, such as the laws of society. Postconventional reasoning—morality is completely internalized and is not based on other's standards. The individual recognizes alternative moral courses, explores options, and then decides on a personal moral code.

6. Justice perspective is a moral perspective that focuses on the rights of the individual; individuals who stand alone and independently make moral decisions. The care perspective is a moral perspective that views people in terms of their connectedness with others and emphasizes interpersonal communication, relationships with others, and concern for others.

7. Some of the major criticisms of Kohlberg's theories are that they are culturally and gender biased.

8. The DIT attempts to determine which moral issues individuals feel are more critical in a given situation by presenting them with a series of dilemmas.

9. (a) an ethic of autonomy, (b) an ethic of community, and (c) an ethic of diversity.

MORAL BEHAVIOR
SECTION REVIEW

1. Adolescents were more likely to cheat when their friends pressured them to do so and when the chances of being caught were slim.

2. The theory distinguishes between moral competence and moral performance.

3. Moral competence—the ability to produce moral behaviors. Moral performance—those behaviors in specific situations.

4. Altruism is an unselfish interest in helping another person.

5. Forgiveness is an aspect of altruism that occurs when the injured person releases the injurer from possible behavioral retaliation.

MORAL FEELINGS
SECTION REVIEW

1. Trying to probe and elicit their child's opinions, instead of giving too much information that may come across as preaching or lecturing.

2. It is often difficult for the victim of harm to try to take steps towards forgiveness. His friends can encourage him to consider why that might be the better response.

3. Ego ideal is the component of the superego that involves ideal standards approved by parents, whereas conscience is the component of the superego that involves behaviors not approved of by parents.

4. Specific moral learning in childhood, ideological concerns in adolescence, and ethical consolidation in adulthood.

MORAL EDUCATION
SECTION REVIEW

1. William Bennett's *Book of Virtues* (1993) and William Damon's *Greater Expectations* (1995).

2. Hidden curriculum is conveyed by the moral atmosphere that is a part of every school.

3. Character education is a direct approach that involves teaching students a basic moral literacy to prevent them from engaging in immoral behavior and doing harm to themselves or others.

4. It is an educational approach that is intended to help people clarify what their lives are for and what is worth working for.

5. It is an educational approach based on the belief that students should learn to value things like democracy and justice.

6. Service learning is a form of education that promotes social responsibility and service to the community.

VALUES IN ADOLESCENCE
SECTION REVIEW

1. Values are beliefs and attitudes about the way things should be.

2. Over the past two decades, adolescents have shown increased concern for personal well-being and less concern for the well-being of others.

RELIGION IN ADOLESCENCE
SECTION REVIEW

1.

	Name of Stage	Developmental Period	Characteristics
1.	Intuitive-Projective Faith	Early Childhood	Intuitive images of good and evil; fantasy and reality are the same.
2.	Mythical-Literal Faith	Middle/Late Childhood	More logical, concrete thought; literal interpretation of religious stories.
3.	Synthetic-Conventional Faith	Early Adolescence	More abstract thought; conformity to religious beliefs of others.
4.	Individuative-Reflective Faith	Late Adolescence, Early Adulthood	Capable of taking full responsibility for religious beliefs; In-depth exploration of one's own values and beliefs.
5.	Conjunctive Faith	Middle Adulthood	More open to opposing viewpoints; awareness of one's finiteness and limitations.
6.	Universalizing Faith	Middle and Late Adulthood	Transcending belief systems to achieve a sense of oneness with all.

2. Piaget felt that they progressed through three stages: preoperational intuitive religious thought; concrete operational religious thought; and formal operational religious thought.

CULTS
SECTION REVIEW

1. They are usually controlled by a charismatic leader and their energies and focus are turned inward, as opposed to outward. The more isolated the cult is, the greater likelihood of abuse or dangerous practices.

2. They are usually normal, regular people who are in a transitional phase of life. Only about 5 percent are disturbed.

COGNITIVE
CHALLENGE

1. Individual activity. No answers provided.

2. Individual activity. No answers provided.

3. Individual activity. No answers provided.

ADOLESCENCE
IN RESEARCH

The hypothesis was that moral behavior is situationally dependent. The researchers observed the moral responses of 11,000 children and adolescents who were given the opportunity to lie, cheat, and steal in a variety of circumstances—at home, school, social events, and in athletics. Situation-specific moral behavior was the rule. Adolescents were more likely to cheat when their friends pressured them to do so and when the chances of getting caught were slim.

⊠ COMPREHENSIVE REVIEW

1.	b	2.	c	3.	b	4.	d	5.	c
6.	d	7.	b	8.	d	9.	a	10.	a
11.	c	12.	c	13.	d	14.	d	15.	d
16.	c	17.	a	18.	b	19.	c	20.	c
21.	b	22.	a	23.	d	24.	c	25.	d
26.	b								

Chapter 13   Achievement, Careers, and Work

Learning Goals with Key Terms and Key People in Boldface

1.0   WHY ADOLESCENCE IS A CRITICAL JUNCTURE IN ACHIEVEMENT
    A.   **The Importance of Adolescence in Achievement**
        1.1   What is the importance of adolescence in achievement?
        1.2   What determines how well adolescents adapt to social and academic pressures?

2.0   DISCUSS ACHIEVEMENT PROCESSES
    A.   **Extrinsic and Intrinsic Motivation**
        2.1   What is **extrinsic motivation**?
        2.2   What is **intrinsic motivation**?
    B.   **Self-Determination and Personal Choice**
        2.3   What are the self-determining characteristics of **intrinsic motivation**?
        2.4   What can be done to increase students' internal motivation?
    C.   **Optimal Experiences and Flow**
        2.5   What is **flow**?
        2.6   When is **flow** most likely to occur?
    D.   **Attribution**
        2.7   What is **attribution theory**?
        2.8   What, according to **Weiner**, are the three dimensions of causal attributions?
        2.9   What are locus, stability, and controllability?
        2.10   How do these dimensions produce different explanations of failures?
    E.   **Mastery Motivation**
        2.11   What is **mastery orientation**?
        2.12   What is meant by **helpless orientation**?
        2.13   What is **performance orientation**?
    F.   **Self-Efficacy**
        2.14   What is **self-efficacy**?
        2.15   What is **Bandura's** view of **self-efficacy**?
        2.16   What is **Schunk's** view of **self-efficacy**?
        2.17   What are some educational applications for **self-efficacy**?
    G.   **Goal-Setting, Planning, and Self-Monitoring**
        2.18   How does goal-setting benefit students' self-efficacy and achievement?
        2.19   How do **Dweck** and **Nicholls** define goals?
        2.20   What are the characteristics of a good planner?
    H.   **Anxiety**
        2.21   What is the nature of **anxiety**?
        2.22   Where does high anxiety come from?
        2.23   What can be done to help students cope with anxiety?

3.0 DESCRIBE THE ROLES OF ETHNICITY AND CULTURE IN ACHIEVEMENT

A. Ethnicity and Culture

3.1   What are the respective roles of ethnicity and culture in achievement?

3.2   Why is it important to consider diversity of achievement within an ethnic group?

3.3   How do American adolescents size up against their Asian counterparts in terms of achievement?

4.0 HOW TO MOTIVATE HARD-TO-REACH, LOW-ACHIEVING STUDENTS

4.1   What are the characteristics of the discouraged student?

4.2   According to **Brophy**, what does it take to reach a discouraged student?

4.3   What is **failure syndrome**, and where does it come from?

4.4   What strategies benefit adolescents who are motivated to protect self-worth and avoid failure?

4.5   What are **self-handicapping strategies**?

4.6   According to **Covington**, what strategies can teachers use to protect student self-worth and avoid failure?

5.0 KNOW ABOUT CAREER DEVELOPMENT

A. Theories of Career Development

5.1   What are the three theories of career development?

5.2   What are the characteristics of **Ginzberg's developmental career choice theory**?

5.3   What are the characteristics of **Super's** vocational **career self-concept theory**?

5.4   What is the nature of **Holland's personality type theory** of career development?

B. Cognitive Factors

5.5   What are the cognitive dimensions of career development?

5.6   What are the roles of exploration, decision making, and planning in adolescent career development?

5.7   According to Grotevant and Durrett (1980), what two aspects of careers do students lack information on?

C. Social Contexts

5.8   What are the most important social contexts that influence career development?

5.9   What roles do socioeconomic status, parents and peers, schools, gender, and ethnicity play in career development?

6.0 THE ROLE OF WORK IN ADOLESCENCE

A. Sociohistorical Context of Adolescent Work

6.1   How likely are adolescents to hold full-time jobs today?

6.2   How many adolescents work part-time?

6.3   What kind of jobs are adolescents working today?

6.4   Do male and female adolescents take the same types of jobs, and are they paid equally?

B. Advantages and Disadvantages of Part-Time Work in Adolescence

6.5   Does the increase in work have benefits for adolescents?

6.6   What are the advantages of part-time work for adolescents?

6.7   What are the disadvantages of part-time work for adolescents?

C. The Transition from School to Work

6.8   What are the rates of adolescent unemployment?

6.9   What can be done to bridge the gap between school and work?

D.   Work/Career-Based Learning

6.10   What is career-based learning?

6.11   What three types of high schools exemplify a college-and-career approach?

6.12   What are single-theme schools?

6.13   What are schools-within-schools?

6.14   What are majors, clusters, or pathways in the school curriculum?

Exercises

KEY TERMS
COMPLETION EXERCISE

Each key term is presented in the form of an incomplete sentence. Complete each sentence by either defining the term or giving an example. Compare your definition with those given at the end of the study guide chapter.

1.   **Extrinsic motivation** causes

_____

_____

2.   **Intrinsic motivation** is noted when

_____

_____

3.   **Flow** describes

_____

_____

4.   **Attribution theory** suggests that individuals are

_____

_____

5.   **Mastery orientation** is a very good approach to

_____

_____

6.   A **helpless orientation** can lead to

_____

_____

7.   When people have a **performance orientation** then

_____

_____

8.   **Self-efficacy** is a belief

_____

_____

9.   Symptoms of **anxiety** are

_____

_____

10.   Simon suffers from the **failure syndrome** because

_____

_____

11.   **Self-handicapping strategies** are used when

_____

_____

12.   **developmental career choice theory** is Ginzberg's theory that

_____

_____

13.   **Career self-concept theory** is Super's theory that

_____

_____

14.   **Personality type theory** is Holland's belief that

_____

_____

KEY PEOPLE
IN THE STUDY OF ADOLESCENCE

Match the person with the concept of adolescent development with which they are associated.

_____	1. Mihalyi Csikszentmihalyi	A. Believes that today's parents are pressuring adolescents to achieve too much
_____	2. Bernard Weiner	B. Proponent of the career self-concept theory
_____	3. Carol Dweck	C. Examined the work experience of California students
_____	4. Albert Bandura	D. Credited with the development of the personality type theory of career development
_____	5. Dale Schunk	E. Conceptualized the developmental career choice theory
_____	6. Sandra Graham	F. Studies cross-cultural comparisons of school performance
_____	7. Harold Stevenson	G. Believes that self-efficacy influences a student's choice of tasks
_____	8. Martin Covington	H. Believes that self-efficacy is a critical factor in student development
_____	9. Eli Ginzberg	I. Studies ethnic differences in achievement
_____	10. Donald Super	J. Proposed strategies that teachers can use to help adolescents protect self-worth and avoid failure
_____	11. John Holland	K. Believes that parent-child relationships play an important role in occupation selection
_____	12. David Elkind	L. Developed strategies for improving motivation of hard-to-teach and low-achieving adolescents
_____	13. Anna Roe	M. Theorized about the three dimensions of causal attribution
_____	14. Ellen Greenberger and Laurence Steinberg	N. Uses the term "flow" to refer to optimal experiences in life

"DR. DETAIL'S"
THEORY MASTERY EXERCISE

Complete the table by listing the career areas that match each of Holland's personality type.

Personality Type	Career
Realistic	
Intellectual	
Social	
Conventional	
Enterprising	
Artistic	

Complete the table by listing the career areas that match each of Ginzberg's career choice stages.

Career Choice Stage	Careers
Fantasy	
Tentative	
Realistic	

Complete the table by listing the developmental information that match each of Super's career choice phases.

Phase	Developmental Information
crystalization	
specification	
implementation	
stabilization	
consolidation	

ADOLESCENCE AS A CRITICAL JUNCTURE IN ACHIEVEMENT
SECTION REVIEW

1. What determines how well adolescents adapt to social and academic pressures?

_____

_____

DISCUSS ACHIEVEMENT PROCESS
SECTION REVIEW

1. Complete the table by filling in the outcomes for each of the combinations of students' perceived level of skill and challenge.

Students' Perceived Level of Skill

Perceived Level of Challenge	Low	High
Low		
High		

2. Complete the table by listing students' reasons for failure that correspond with the given combination of Weiner's three main categories of attributions: locus (internal-external), stability (stable-unstable), and controllability (controllable-uncontrollable).

Combination of Causal Attributes	Reason Students Give for Failure
Internal-Stable-Uncontrollable	
Internal-Stable-Controllable	
Internal-Unstable-Uncontrollable	
Internal-Unstable-Controllable	
External-Stable-Uncontrollable	
External-Stable-Controllable	
External-Unstable-Uncontrollable	
External-Unstable-Controllable	

3.   What are the self-determining characteristics of intrinsic motivation?

_____

_____

4.   What is flow?

_____

_____

5.   When is flow most likely to occur?

_____

_____

6.   What is attribution theory?

_____

_____

7.   What, according to Weiner, are the three dimensions of causal attributions?

_____

_____

8.   What are locus, stability, and controllability?

_____

_____

9.   What is mastery orientation?

_____

_____

10.   What is helpless orientation?

_____

_____

11.   What is performance orientation?

_____

_____

12.   What is self-efficacy?

_____

_____

13.   Contrast Bandura's and Schunk's view of self-efficacy.

_____

_____

14.   How do Dweck and Nicholls define goals?

_____

_____

THE ROLES OF ETHNICITY AND CULTURE IN ACHIEVEMENT
SECTION REVIEW

1.   What are the respective roles of ethnicity and culture in achievement?

_____

_____

2.   How do American adolescents size up against their Asian counterparts in terms of achievement?

_____

_____

HOW TO MOTIVATE HARD-TO-REACH, LOW-ACHIEVING STUDENTS
SECTION REVIEW

1.   According to Brophy, what does it take to reach a discouraged student?

_____

_____

2.   What is failure syndrome and where does it come from?

_____

_____

3.   What are self-handicapping strategies?

        _____

        _____

4.   According to Covington, what strategies can teachers use to protect student self-worth and avoid failure?

        _____

        _____

KNOW ABOUT CAREER DEVELOPMENT
SECTION REVIEW

1.   What are the three theories of career development?

        _____

        _____

2.   According to Grotevant and Durrett, what are two aspects of careers in which students lack information?

        _____

        _____

3.   What are the most important social contexts that influence career development?

        _____

        _____

THE ROLE OF WORK IN ADOLESCENCE
SECTION REVIEW

1.   How many adolescents work part-time?

        _____

        _____

2.   Do male and female adolescents take the same types of jobs, and are they paid equally?

        _____

        _____

3.   What are the advantages of part-time work for adolescents?

_____

_____

4.   What can be done to bridge the gap between school and work?

_____

_____

5.   What are single-theme schools?

_____

_____

COGNITIVE CHALLENGE

1.   What are your career dreams? With your dreams in mind, write down your specific work, job and career goals for the next 20 years, 10 years, and 5 years. Begin with the long-term goals first so that you can envision how to plan now to reach that "dream" career goal.

_____

_____

2.   What achievement-related challenges did you encounter in middle school and high school? How did you resolve them? Looking back, how might you have coped with these challenges in a more effective way?

_____

_____

3.   How long have you had your current career goals? Since kindergarten? Since elementary school? Since secondary school? Or has it only been recently that you have started to focus on your career?

_____

_____

ADOLESCENCE
IN RESEARCH

Concerning the research of Mihal Csikszentmihalyi and Barbara Schneider (2000), state the hypothesis, the research methods (if known), the research conclusions, and the implications and applications for adolescent development.

_____

_____

_____

_____

_____

_____

⊠ COMPREHENSIVE REVIEW

1. The motive with the greatest impact on the quality of adult life is
    a. sexuality.
    b. fear.
    c. affiliation.
    d. achievement.

2. Aaron studies very hard. He concentrates on the sciences because he wants to become an environmental biologist. Aaron could be described as
    a. motivated.
    b. intelligent.
    c. unrealistic.
    d. a hurried adolescent.

3. Attribution theory indicates that individuals attribute people's behavior to two causes:
    a. direct and indirect.
    b. inferred and observed.
    c. internal and external.
    d. scientific and psychological.

4. A parent of an adolescent decides to join the community band. His daughter asks why he joined, since he won't make any money and few people attend the concerts. He responds, "I just like playing with the band." He is _____ motivated.
    a. achievement
    b. intrinsically
    c. extrinsically
    d. mastery

5. One key feature of the helpless orientation is
   a. attributing failure to internal causes.
   b. overestimating the role of effort.
   c. underestimating the importance of external incentives.
   d. fear of failure.

6. It is very difficult and dangerous to make sweeping generalizations about achievement motivation in ethnic minority adolescents because
   a. it has never been studied systematically.
   b. there is more variability within groups than among groups.
   c. all American groups score lower than Asian groups.
   d. social class is a more powerful predictor.

7. Japanese children often outperform American children in math and science areas, perhaps because all of the following are true except that
   a. Japanese parents have higher expectations.
   b. Japanese children spend more time in school each week.
   c. Japanese teachers are better trained in math and science.
   d. the Japanese school year is longer.

8. According to your text, the major reason for the "super achiever" image of Asian American adolescents (whose parents immigrated to the United States in the late 1960s to mid-1970s) is that
   a. their families have had more time to adjust to the culture.
   b. they are more intelligent.
   c. the males are encouraged to excel more than the females.
   d. they come from better-educated families.

9. According to Eli Ginzberg, youngsters between the ages of 11 and 17 years progressively evaluate three aspects of career choice. The order of occurrence is:
   a. values, capacities, and interests.
   b. interests, capacities, and values.
   c. interests, values, and capacities.
   d. capacities, values, and interests.

10. When individuals complete their education or training and enter the work force, Donald Super refers to this as the _____ stage.
    a. crystallization
    b. implementation
    c. stabilization
    d. specification

11. Your son always had a way with words and got along well with peers and adults. According to John Holland, he would prefer the job of
    a. social worker.
    b. bank teller.
    c. construction worker.
    d. sales manager.

12. The most important contribution made by John Holland's personality type theory to the career field was its
    a. consideration of the role of motivation on job performance.
    b. introduction of the conventional personality type.
    c. focus on psychological testing as a way of insuring job suitability.
    d. emphasis on linking individuals' personalities to the characteristics of given jobs.

13. In order to benefit from career guidance courses and to show more systematic career planning, students need
    a. accurate knowledge concerning the educational requirements of careers.
    b. self-directed opportunities to engage in career exploration.
    c. courses that are taught by trained guidance counselors.
    d. to be in the implementation stage of vocational choice.

14. When both parents work and seem to enjoy it,
    a. the parents try to live vicariously through their children's occupational choices.
    b. boys and girls learn work values from both parents.
    c. boys and girls aspire to higher status occupations.
    d. schools don't need to motivate students to get a good education.

15. Which kind of job employs the most adolescents in part-time work?
    a. Unskilled laborers
    b. Clerical assistants
    c. Restaurant work
    d. Retail

16. An adolescent female (16 years of age) who takes a part-time job can expect to
    a. make more money than males.
    b. work shorter hours than males.
    c. easily find a job as a newspaper carrier.
    d. easily find a job as a gardener.

17. Which of the following represents an advantage of working during adolescence?
    a. Extensive on-the-job training
    b. Improved ability to manage money
    c. Improved school grades
    d. Greater enjoyment of school

18. A number of adolescent problem behaviors are associated with part-time work, such as insufficient sleep and exercise. At what level of work does this begin to be apparent?
    a. 1 to 5 hours per week
    b. 6 to 10 hours per week
    c. 15 to 20 hours per week
    d. More than 20 hours per week

19. Which foundation in the United States has been very active in developing programs for unemployed youth?
    a. John S. Sage
    b. William T. Grant
    c. Richard B. Williams
    d. John F. Kennedy Education

20. Jaime Ecsalante was a(n) _____ teacher at Garfield High School, in East Los Angeles, California.
    a. English
    b. geography
    c. math
    d. physical education

ADOLESCENCE IN MOVIES

- *Cider House Rules* depicts an orphan who rejects the medical profession his foster father planned for him—until he chooses it for himself.

- *October Sky* is the true story of Homer Hickman, a West Virginia coal miner's son, who went from setting off rockets in his back yard to joining the NASA space program.

- *Stand and Deliver* is the story of Jaime Escalante's math classrooms in a largely Latino California high school.

ADOLESCENCE IN BOOKS

- *All Grown Up & No Place to Go: Teenagers in Crisis*, by David Elkind (Addison-Wesley: MA, 1984), argues that teenagers are expected to confront adult challenges too early in their development.

- *Mentors*, by Thomas Evans (Peterson's Guides: NJ, 1992), describes the experiences of motivated individuals, from corporate executives to parents.

- *What Color Is Your Parachute?* by Richard Bolles (Ten Speed Press: CA, 2000), is a popular book on career choice that is updated annually.

Answer Key

KEY TERMS

1. **extrinsic motivation** Response to external incentives such as rewards and punishments.

2. **intrinsic motivation** Internal motivational factors such as self-determination, curiosity, challenge, and effort.

3. **flow** Csikszentmihalyi's concept that describes optimal life experiences, which he believes occur most often when people develop a sense of mastery and are absorbed in a state of concentration when they are engaged in a activity.

4. **attribution theory** The concept that individuals are motivated to discover the underlying causes of their own behavior or performance in their effort to make sense of it.

5. **mastery orientation** An outlook in which individuals focus on the task rather than on their ability, have positive affect, and generate solution-oriented strategies that improve performance.

6. **helpless orientation** An outlook in which individuals focus on their personal inadequacies often attribute their difficulty to a lack of ability, and display negative affect (including boredom and anxiety). This orientation undermines performance.

7. **performance orientation** An outlook in which individuals are concerned with performance outcome rather than performance process. For performance-oriented students, winning is what matters.

8. **self-efficacy** The belief that one can master a situation and produce positive outcomes.

9. **anxiety** A vague, highly unpleasant feeling of fear and apprehension.

10. **failure syndrome** Having low expectations for success and giving up at the first sign of difficulty.

11. **self-handicapping strategies** Some adolescents deliberately do not try in school, put off studying until the last minute, and use other self-handicapping strategies so that if their subsequent performance is at a low level, these circumstances, rather than lack of ability, will be seen as the cause.

12. **developmental career choice theory** Ginzberg's theory that children and adolescents go through three career-choice stages: fantasy, tentative, and realistic.

13. **career self-concept theory** Super's theory that individuals' self-concepts play a central role in their career choices and that in adolescence individuals first construct their career self-concept.

14. **personality type theory** Holland's belief that an effort should be made to match an individual's career choice with his or her personality.

KEY PEOPLE
IN THE STUDY OF ADOLESCENCE

1.	N	**2.**	M	**3.**	L	**4.**	H	**5.**	G
6.	I	**7.**	F	**8.**	J	**9.**	E	**10.**	B
11.	D	**12.**	A	**13.**	K	**14.**	C		

"DR. DETAIL'S"
THEORY MASTERY EXERCISE

Holland's personality type:

Personality Type	Career
Realistic	labor, farming, truck driving, construction
Intellectual	math and science careers
Social	teaching, social work, counseling
Conventional	bank tellers, secretaries, file clerks
Enterprising	sales, politics, management

Ginzberg's career choice stages:

Career Choice Stage	Careers
Fantasy	Doctor, superhero, teacher, movie star, etc.
Tentative	Big plans of youth are changed to fit skills and abilities.
Realistic	Explore careers and settle upon one within reach that fits their goals and personality

Super's career choice phases:

Phase	Developmental Information
crystallization	Age 14 to 18, develop ideas that mesh with existing self-concept
specification	Age 18 to 22, narrow career choices and take steps toward career
implementation	Age 21 to 24, compete education and training
stabilization	Age 25 to 35, enter their career of choice
consolidation	After 35, seek to reach higher status positions

ADOLESCENCE AS A CRITICAL JUNCTURE IN ACHIEVEMENT
SECTION REVIEW

1.   Psychological, motivational, and contextual factors.

DISCUSS ACHIEVEMENT PROCESS
SECTION REVIEW

1. **Students' Perceived Level of Skill**

Perceived Level of Challenge	Low	High
Low	Apathy	Boredom
High	Anxiety	Flow

2.

Combination of Causal Attributes	Reason Students Give for Failure
Internal-Stable-Uncontrollable	Low aptitude
Internal-Stable-Controllable	Never study
Internal-Unstable-Uncontrollable	Sick the day of the test
Internal-Unstable-Controllable	Did not study for this particular test
External-Stable-Uncontrollable	School has tough requirements
External-Stable-Controllable	The instructor is biased
External-Unstable-Uncontrollable	Bad luck
External-Unstable-Controllable	Friends failed to help

3. Adolescents want to believe that they are doing something because of their own will.

4. The concept of optimal life experiences, which occur most often when people develop a sense of mastery.

5. More likely to occur when materials are mastered.

6. This states that in their effort to make sense out of their own behavior or performance, individuals are motivated to discover its underlying causes.

7. Locus, stability, and controllability.

8. Locus—whether the cause is internal or external; stability—the extent to which the cause remains the same or changes; controllability—the extent to which the individual can control the cause.

9. Focusing on the task rather than on ability and generating solution-oriented strategies to completion.

10. Focusing too much on personal inadequacies and displaying negative affect.

11. Involves being concerned with outcome rather than process.

12. The belief that one can master a situation and produce favorable outcomes.

13. Bandura—believes that self-efficacy is a crucial factor in whether or not adolescents achieve. Schunk—believes that self-efficacy influences a student's choice of activities; therefore it has an important indirect role.

14. They define goals in terms of immediate achievement-related focus and definition of success.

THE ROLES OF ETHNICITY AND CULTURE IN ACHIEVEMENT
SECTION REVIEW

1. Ethnicity and culture play and important role in achievement. The orientation of the parents in particular is important. SES is more associated with poor achievement than is ethnicity or culture.

2. There are differences in school, parent attitudes and the likelihood of students doing homework. Taken together, Asian students often out-perform American students.

HOW TO MOTIVATE HARD-TO-REACH, LOW-ACHIEVING STUDENTS
SECTION REVIEW

1. Convince them that effort and work pays off.

2. Having low expectations for success. It comes from falling behind and struggling with academics with mostly failure as a result.

3. Some adolescents deliberately do not try in school, this way they have an excuse if they fail.

4. (a) Give these adolescents assignments that are interesting and stimulate curiosity. (b) Establish a reward system. (c) Help adolescents set challenging but realistic goals. (d) Strengthen the association between effort and self-worth. (e) Encourage students to have positive beliefs about their abilities. (f) Improve teacher-student relations.

KNOW ABOUT CAREER DEVELOPMENT
SECTION REVIEW

1. Ginzberg's development theory, Super's self-concept theory, and Holland's personality type theory.

2. Educational requirements of careers they desire, and the vocational interests predominantly associated with their career choices.

3. SES, parents and peers, schools, gender, culture and ethnicity.

THE ROLE OF WORK IN ADOLESCENCE
SECTION REVIEW

1. Three out of every four high school students works at least part-time.

2. Males work more labor-intensive jobs, work longer hours, and get paid more than females.

3. Better time management skills, and spending money.

4.   (a) monitored work experiences, (b) community youth-guided services, (c) vocational education should be redirected, (d) incentives need to be introduced, (e) career information and counseling need to be improved, and (f) more school volunteers should be used.

5.   The curriculum is organized around a single theme, such as agriculture.

COGNITIVE CHALLENGE

1.   Individual activity. No answers provided.

2.   Individual activity. No answers provided.

3.   Individual activity. No answers provided.

ADOLESCENCE IN RESEARCH

Csikszentmihalyi and Schneider studied how U.S. adolescents develop attitudes and acquire skills to achieve their career goals and expectations. They assessed (using questionnaires) the progress of more than 1000 students from 13 school districts across the United State (cross-sectional). Among the findings: (a) girls anticipated the same lifestyles as boys in terms of education and income; (b) lower-income minority students were more positive about school than more affluent students; (c) students who got the most out of school were those who perceived school as more playlike than worklike; and (d) clear vocational goals and good work experiences did not guarantee a smooth transition to adult work.

⊠ COMPREHENSIVE REVIEW

1.	d	2.	a	3.	c	4.	b	5.	a
6.	d	7.	c	8.	d	9.	b	10.	b
11.	a	12.	d	13.	a	14.	b	15.	d
16.	b	17.	b	18.	a	19.	b	20.	c

SECTION V
ADOLESCENT PROBLEMS, STRESS, HEALTH, AND COPING

Chapter 14   Adolescent Problems

Learning Goals with Key Terms and Key People in Boldface

1.0   **KNOW ABOUT THE NATURE OF ADOLESCENT PROBLEMS**

A.   **Exploring Adolescent Problems**

1.1   What are the three factors that might be the basis for adolescent problem behavior?

1.2   What are two sociocultural factors that influence the development of adolescent problems?

B.   **The Biopsychosocial Approach**

1.3   What roles do the three factors play in the development of problem behavior?

C.   **The Developmental Approach**

1.4   What is the focus of **developmental psychopathology**?

1.5   Compare and contrast **internalizing** and **externalizing problems**.

1.6   According to **Sroufe**, anxiety problems in adolescence are linked with what?

D.   **Characteristics of Adolescent Problems**

1.7   What correlation did **Achenbach** find between SES and behavior problems?

E.   **Resilience**

1.8   Why might the study of resilience be important in understanding problem behavior?

2.0   **DISCUSS DRUGS AND ALCOHOL**

A.   **Drugs and Alcohol**

2.1   Why do people use drugs?

2.2   What is **tolerance**?

2.3   What is **physical dependence**?

2.4   What is the nature of addiction?

2.5   What are the characteristics of **psychological dependence**?

B.   **Trends in Overall Drug Use**

2.6   What was the nature of drug use in the 1960s and 1970s?

2.7   What has been the trend of drug use in the 1980s and 1990s?

2.8   How does adolescent drug use in the United States compare to that in other industrialized countries?

C.   **Alcohol**

2.9   What type of drug is alcohol?

2.10   How much is alcohol used by American adolescents?

2.11   What are some potential negative outcomes of alcohol abuse?

2.12   What are the risk factors for adolescent alcohol use?

2.13   Is there a genetic predisposition to alcoholism?
2.14   Is there a personality profile for someone who is likely to develop an alcohol problem?
2.15   What are some possible preventative strategies for alcoholism?

D.   Hallucinogens
2.16   What drugs other than alcohol are harmful to adolescents?
2.17   What are the nature and characteristics of **hallucinogens**, LSD, and marijuana?

E.   Stimulants
2.18   What are the most widely used **stimulants?**
2.19   How does cigarette smoking play a role in the drug problems of youth?
2.20   Have school health programs had success in deterring youth from smoking?
2.21   What is the history of cocaine use?
2.22   How many adolescents use cocaine?
2.23   How prevalent is the use of amphetamines among adolescents?
2.24   What is Ecstasy, and what are some special concerns associated with it?

F.   Depressants
2.25   What are **depressants**?
2.26   How has the use of depressants changed over the past 25 years?

G.   Anabolic Steroids
2.27   What are the risks of using **anabolic steroids**?

H.   Factors in Adolescent Drug Use
2.28   What role does early drug use play in adolescent development?
2.29   How can parents and peers help prevent adolescent drug abuse?
2.30   What school-based intervention programs can help reduce adolescent drug use?

3.0   EVALUATE JUVENILE DELINQUENCY

A.   Juvenile Delinquency
3.1   What is the nature of **juvenile delinquency**?
3.2   What is the difference between **index offenses** and **status offenses**?
3.3   Is it appropriate to try juveniles as adults in court?
3.4   What is **conduct disorder**?
3.5   What percentage of adolescents engage in delinquent behaviors?
3.6   In the Pittsburgh Youth Study, what were noted as the three developmental pathways to delinquency?

B.   Antecedents of Juvenile Delinquency
3.7   What are the predictors of delinquency?
3.8   What is Erikson's beliefs regarding youth and delinquency?
3.9   Can siblings influence delinquency?

C.   Violence and Youth
3.10   Why is the high rate of youth violence an increasing concern?
3.11   What percent of public schools experience one or more serious violent incidents each year?
3.12   What factors are often present in at-risk youths and seem to propel them towards violence?
3.13   What strategies have been proposed for reducing youth violence?
3.14   What is the **cadre approach** to reducing violence?
3.15   What is meant by the **total student body approach** to reducing school-related violence?
3.16   What are the steps students learn in mediation?

4.0 DESCRIBE DEPRESSION AND SUICIDE

A. Depression and Suicide

4.1   What is the rate of depression in females as opposed to males?

4.2   How serious a problem is depression in adolescence?

4.3   What is a **major depressive disorder**?

4.4   Will a depressed adolescent be more likely to suffer from depression as an adult?

4.5   What are the treatments for depression?

4.6   What is the rate of adolescent suicide and how has it changed since the 1950s?

4.7   Why do adolescents attempt suicide?

4.8   What proximal and distal factors are involved in suicide?

4.9   What is the psychological profile of the suicidal adolescents like?

5.0 UNDERSTANDING EATING DISORDERS

A. Obesity

5.1   What percent of adolescents are obese?

5.2   What hereditary and environmental factors are involved in obesity?

B. Anorexia Nervosa

5.3   What are the characteristics of **anorexia nervosa**?

5.4   Are certain adolescents more prone to anorexia than others?

5.5   What societal, psychological, and physiological causes of **anorexia nervosa** have been proposed?

C. Bulimia Nervosa

5.6   What is the nature of **bulimia nervosa**?

6.0 DISCUSS THE INTERRELATION OF PROBLEMS AND PREVENTION/ INTERVENTION

6.1   Are adolescent problem behaviors interrelated?

6.2   What are the common components of successful prevention/intervention programs for adolescent problem behaviors?

Exercises

KEY TERMS
COMPLETION EXERCISE

Each key term is presented in the form of an incomplete sentence. Complete each sentence by either defining the term or giving an example of it. Compare your definitions with those given at the end of the study guide chapter.

1.   **Developmental psychopathology** focuses on

   _____

   _____

2.   **Internalizing problems** appear as

   _____

   _____

3.   Examples of **externalizing problems** are

   _____

   _____

4.   **Tolerance** of a drug means

   _____

   _____

5.   **Physical dependence** on a drug means

   _____

   _____

6.   **Psychological dependence** on a substance suggests

   _____

   _____

7.   **Hallucinogens** are a grouping of drugs that

   _____

   _____

8.   Overuse of **stimulants** can lead to

_____

_____

9.   The use of **depressants** in recent years has

_____

_____

10.   **Anabolic steroids** are used to

_____

_____

11.   Involvement in **juvenile delinquency** leads to

_____

_____

12.   **Index offenses** are crimes which

_____

_____

13.   **Status offenses** are crimes that

_____

_____

14.   Example of a **conduct disorder** is

_____

_____

15.   A **major depressive disorder** is

_____

_____

16.   **Anorexia nervosa** is defined as

_____

_____

17.   **Bulimia nervosa** differs from anorexia in that

_____

_____

KEY PEOPLE
IN THE STUDY OF ADOLESCENCE

Match the person with the concept of adolescent development with which they are associated.

_____   1. Thomas Achenbach and   A. Believes that resilient children triumph over life's adversities
            Craig Edelbrock

_____   2. Lloyd Johnston,   B. Found that adolescents from lower-SES background were more
            Patrick O'Malley, and   likely to have problems than those from a middle-SES
            Gerald Bachman   background

_____   3. Norman Garmezy   C. Monitor the drug use of America's high school students through
                                            a project at the University of Michigan

_____   4. Joy Dryfoos   D. Interviewed young men who were murderers

_____   5. James Garbarino   E. Interested in the interrelationship between adolescent problem
                                            behaviors

_____   6. David and Roger Johnson   F. Believe in teaching conflict resolution skills in schools

"DR. DETAIL'S"
MATCHING EXERCISE

Match the following contributors to the study of adolescence to their area of contribution.

_____   1. Alan Sroufe   A. Experimented with therapeutic uses of cocaine
_____   2. Ann Masten   B. Proposed a developmental model of adolescent drug abuse
_____   3. Sigmund Freud   C. Studied traits associated with alcoholism
_____   4. Lloyd Johnson,   D. Believes that adolescents, whose development has restricted
            Patrick O'Malley, and   them from acceptable social roles, might choose a negative
            Gerald Bachman   identity

_____   5. Robert Cloninger   E. Found that anxiety problems in adolescence are linked with
                                            anxious/resistant attachment in infancy

_____   6. Cheryl Perry   F. Found that good intellectual functioning and parenting served
                                            protective roles in keeping adolescent from antisocial behaviors

_____   7. Judith Brooks   G. Developed the Midwestern Prevention Program
_____   8. Mary Ann Dentz   H. Taught conflict resolution training in schools
_____   9. Erik Erikson   I. Have monitored the drug use of American Seniors in public and
                                            private schools

_____ 10. David and Roger Johnson   J. Developed an approach to stop smoking by adolescents

THE NATURE OF ADOLESCENT PROBLEMS
SECTION REVIEW

1. What are the three factors that might be the basis for adolescent problem behavior?

    _____

    _____

2. What are two sociocultural factors that influence the development of adolescent problems?

    _____

    _____

3. What is focus of developmental psychopathology?

    _____

    _____

4. Compare and contrast internalizing and externalizing problems?

    _____

    _____

5. According to Sroufe, anxiety problems in adolescence are linked with what?

    _____

    _____

6. What correlations did Achenbach find between SES and behavior problems.

    _____

    _____

7. Why might the study of resilience be important in understanding problem behavior?

    _____

    _____

DRUGS AND ALCOHOL
SECTION REVIEW

1. Identify the class of drugs by placing a "D" for depressants, "S" for stimulants, and "H" for hallucinogens.

    _____ 1.   Marijuana
    _____ 2.   Alcohol
    _____ 3.   Barbiturates
    _____ 4.   Amphetamines
    _____ 5.   Tranquilizers
    _____ 6.   Cocaine
    _____ 7.   Narcotics
    _____ 8.   LSD

2. What is tolerance?

    _____

    _____

3. What is physical dependence?

    _____

    _____

4. What type of drug is alcohol?

    _____

    _____

5. What are the risk factors for adolescent alcohol use?

    _____

    _____

6. What are some possible preventative strategies for alcoholism?

    _____

    _____

7. Have school health programs had success in deterring youth from smoking?

    _____

    _____

8. How many adolescents use cocaine?

    _____

    _____

9.   What are depressants?

   _____

   _____

10.   How has the use of depressants changed over the past 25 years?

   _____

   _____

11.   What seven criteria have been generally accepted as necessary for effective school-based drug abuse prevention programs?

   a.   _____

   _____

   b.   _____

   _____

   c.   _____

   _____

   d.   _____

   _____

   e.   _____

   _____

   f.   _____

   _____

   g.   _____

   _____

EVALUATE JUVENILE DELINQUENCY
SECTION REVIEW

1. Complete the table for listing the association with delinquency that matches each antecedent of delinquency.

Antecedent	Association with Delinquency
Identity	
Self-control	
Age	
Sex	
Expectations for education and school grades	
Parental influences	
Peer influences	
Socioeconomic status	
Neighborhood quality	

2. What is the nature of juvenile delinquency?

_____

_____

3. In the Pittsburgh Youth Study, what were noted as the three developmental pathways to delinquency?

_____

_____

4. What is Eriksson's beliefs regarding youth and delinquency?

_____

_____

5.   What are the four factors often present in at-risk youth that seem to propel them toward acts of violence?

      a. _____

      b. _____

      c. _____

      d. _____

6.   What four recommendations for reducing youth violence were suggested by The Oregon Social Learning Center?

      a. _____

      b. _____

      c. _____

      d. _____

7.   What is the cadre approach to reducing violence?

_____

_____

DEPRESSION AND SUICIDE
SECTION REVIEW

1.   What is a major depressive disorder?

_____

_____

2.   What proximal and distal factors are involved in suicide?

_____

_____

EATING DISORDERS
SECTION REVIEW

1. What hereditary and environmental factors are involved in obesity?

   _____

   _____

2. What are the characteristics of anorexia nervosa?

   _____

   _____

3. What is the nature of bulimia nervosa?

   _____

   _____

PROBLEMS AND PREVENTION/INTERVENTION
SECTION REVIEW

1. Are adolescent problem behaviors interrelated?

   _____

   _____

2. What are the common components of successful prevention/intervention programs for adolescent problem behaviors?

   _____

   _____

COGNITIVE
CHALLENGE

1. Imagine that you have just been appointed the head of the President's Commission on Adolescent Drug Abuse. What would be the first program you would try to put into place? What would be its main components? Would it be school-focused? What role, if any, would the media play in promoting the program?

   _____

   _____

2.　Why are the consequences of risky behavior more serious today than they have ever been?

_____

_____

3.　What role might David Elkind's conceptualizations of the Personal Fable and Imaginary Audience have played in the atrocities at Columbine and Thurston High Schools?

_____

_____

ADOLESCENCE IN RESEARCH

Concerning Ann Masten's research concerning resilience, state the hypothesis, the research methods (if known), the research conclusions, and the implications and applications for adolescent development.

_____

_____

 COMPREHENSIVE REVIEW

1.　The condition where a greater amount of a drug is needed to produce the same effect is referred to as
　　a.　tolerance.
　　b.　physical dependence.
　　c.　psychological dependence.
　　d.　emotional dependence.

2.　Physical need for a drug that is accompanied by unpleasant withdrawal symptoms when the drug is withdrawn is referred to as
　　a.　tolerance.
　　b.　physical dependence.
　　c.　psychological dependence.
　　d.　emotional dependence.

3.　Strong desire and craving to repeat the use of a drug for various emotional reasons is referred to as
　　a.　tolerance.
　　b.　physical dependence.
　　c.　psychological dependence.
　　d.　emotional dependence.

4. Which therapist experimented with therapeutic uses of cocaine?
    a. Jean Piaget
    b. Erik Erikson
    c. Sigmund Freud
    d. Lawrence Kohlberg

5. Most developmentalists accept an interactionist approach to the study of abnormal behavior because
    a. the evidence shows that all disorders have both psychological and sociocultural causes.
    b. neither the biological nor psychological and sociocultural viewpoints can account for the complexity of problems.
    c. it's the only way to keep peace in the profession.
    d. adolescents tell us that the interactionist approach is best.

6. Which nation has the highest rate of adolescent drug use?
    a. Thailand
    b. Germany
    c. United States
    d. France

7. Which of the following is NOT a risk factor for abuse of alcohol?
    a. Heredity
    b. Peer relations
    c. Alcohol tolerance
    d. Family influences

8. Which two behavioral problems are the most common causes for referring adolescents to mental health clinics?
    a. Conflict with parents and substance abuse
    b. Poor school work and depression
    c. Suicide attempt and depression
    d. Substance abuse and poor schoolwork

9. Your textbook indicates that adolescents use drugs
    a. because Sigmund Freud used cocaine.
    b. as adaptations to changing environments.
    c. as aids to sexual gratification.
    d. because their parents use drugs at home.

10. Drugs that modify an individual's perceptual experiences and produce hallucinations are known as
    a. stimulants.
    b. depressants.
    c. hallucinogens.
    d. anabolic steroids.

11. An adolescent has been drinking white wine for about three years. He has noticed that over this period, it takes more and more wine to get "looped." This indicates
    a. the wine producers have decreased the alcoholic content.
    b. tolerance.
    c. the disorganized thinking associated with ingesting alcohol at a young age.
    d. his psychological dependence.

12. The most widely used illicit drug is
    a.   marijuana.
    b.   cocaine.
    c.   barbiturates.
    d.   alcohol.

13. Which of the following is NOT a risk factor for alcohol abuse?
    a.   Secure attachment to parents
    b.   Having friends who abuse alcohol
    c.   Coming from an unhappy home
    d.   Susceptibility to peer pressure

14. The parents of an 11-year-old boy have been advised by a psychologist to provide more structure in the home, more caring support, and a more stimulating environment. According to Robert Cloninger, what are they trying to prevent in their youngsters?
    a.   Eventually acquiring a sexually transmitted disease
    b.   Attempting suicide
    c.   Alcoholism as an adult
    d.   The youngster from eventually abusing his parents

15. Nembutal and Seconal are
    a.   stimulants.
    b.   hallucinogens.
    c.   opiates.
    d.   depressants.

16. Which of the new school-based drug prevention programs appears to be the most promising?
    a.   Counselor-led programs
    b.   The use of testimonials from ex-drug users
    c.   Social skills training
    d.   Attendance at juvenile court when drug cases are heard

17. In the United States, theft, rape, and assault are _____ offenses.
    a.   status
    b.   index
    c.   matrix
    d.   conduct

18. Between February and September, Harry, a 14-year-old, ran away from home and got involved in a series of break-and-enter offenses. The parents say he is "out of control." According to your text, the court psychiatrist will likely diagnose him as
    a.   being a delinquent.
    b.   having a conduct disorder.
    c.   a problem child.
    d.   having poor parents.

19.   Which of the following individuals would say that delinquency is a manifestation of the search for "Who am I?"
    a.   Gilbert Botvin
    b.   Peter Blos
    c.   John Bowlby
    d.   Erik Erikson

20.   Which of the following is NOT associated with juvenile delinquency?
    a.   negative identity
    b.   learned helplessness
    c.   failed self-control
    d.   lower-class culture

21.   A recent review of all the approaches to prevention of delinquency has revealed that _____ seems to be effective.
    a.   a multiple components approach
    b.   work experience
    c.   preventative casework
    d.   security guards in school

22.   Which is NOT a recommendation for dealing with a suicidal adolescent?
    a.   Find out if the person has a plan for killing himself.
    b.   Pay attention to warning signs and take them seriously.
    c.   Assure the person that everything is under control.
    d.   Help the person find appropriate counseling.

23.   All but one of the following is a characteristic of successful programs for reducing adolescent problems.
    a.   Remove adolescents from the situation that seems to be causing their problems.
    b.   Make sure that each adolescent gets personal attention from a responsible adult.
    c.   Coordinate the activities of different agencies and institutions.
    d.   Begin intervention programs early in adolescent's lives.

24.   _____ helps provide a buffer to stress for children and adolescents.
    a.   Resilience
    b.   Acculturation
    c.   Cheerful optimism
    d.   Self-efficacy

ADOLESCENCE
ON THE SCREEN

■   *Ordinary People* A young man struggles with depression and thoughts of suicide as a result of surviving an accident that took his younger brother's life.

■   *Trainspotting* Portrays the grim reality of lives ruined by heroin addiction.

■   *The Killer at Thurston High* (Frontline) Portrays the events that lead up to Kip Kinkel's assault on his parents and the school at Thurston. The content is shocking, but gives much insight.

■ *The River's Edge* A group of high school friends must come to terms with the fact that one of them killed another.

ADOLESCENCE
IN BOOKS

■ *Developmental Psychopathology*, edited by Suniya Luthar, Jacob Burack, Dante Cicchetti, and John Weisz (Cambridge University Press: MA, 1999), explores the many aspects of developmental psychopathology.

■ *Lost Boys*, by James Garbarino (The Free Press: NY, 1999), examines why young men grow up to be murderers.

Answer Key

KEY
TERMS

1.   **developmental psychopathology** Focuses on describing and exploring the developmental pathways of problems and disorders.

2.   **internalizing problems** Occur when individuals turn problems inward. Anxiety and depression.

3.   **externalizing problems** Occur when individuals turn problems outward. Such as juvenile delinquency.

4.   **tolerance** A greater amount of a drug is needed to produce the same effect.

5.   **physical dependence** The physical need for a drug that is accompanied by unpleasant withdrawal symptoms when the drug is discontinued.

6.   **psychological dependence** The strong desire and craving to repeat the use of a drug for various emotional reasons, such as a feeling of well-being and reduction of distress.

7.   **hallucinogens** Drugs that alter an individual's perceptual experiences and produce hallucinations—also called psychedelic or mind-altering drugs.

8.   **stimulants** Drugs that increase the activity of the central nervous system.

9.   **depressants** Drugs that slow the central nervous system, bodily functions, and behavior.

10.   **anabolic steroids** Drugs derived from the male sex hormone, testosterone. They promote muscle growth and lean body mass.

11.   **juvenile delinquency** A broad range of child and adolescent behaviors, including socially unacceptable behavior, status offenses, and criminal acts.

12.   **index offenses** Whether they are committed by juveniles or adults, these are criminal acts, such as robbery, rape, and homicide.

13.   **status offenses** Performed by youths under a specified age, these are juvenile offenses that are not as serious as index offenses. These offenses may include such acts as drinking under age, truancy, and sexual promiscuity.

14.   **conduct disorder** The psychiatric diagnostic category for the occurrence of multiple delinquent activities over a 6-month period. These behaviors include truancy, running away, fire setting, and cruelty to animals, breaking and entering, and excessive fighting.

15. **major depressive disorder** The diagnosis when an individual experiences a major depressive episode and depressed characteristics, such as lethargy and depression, for two weeks or longer and daily functioning becomes impaired.

16. **anorexia nervosa** An eating disorder that involves the relentless pursuit of thinness through starvation.

17. **bulimia nervosa** In this eating disorder, the individual consistently follows a binge-and-purge eating pattern.

KEY PEOPLE
IN THE STUDY OF ADOLESCENCE

1. B   2. C   3. A   4. E   5. D
6. F

"DR. DETAIL'S"
MATCHING EXERCISE

1. E   2. F   3. A   4. I   5. C
6. J   7. B   8. G   9. D   10. H

THE NATURE OF ADOLESCENT PROBLEMS
SECTION REVIEW

1. Psychological, Sociocultural, and Biopsychosocial.

2. Socioeconomic status and neighborhood quality.

3. Focuses on describing and exploring the developmental pathways of problems.

4. Internalizing problems occur when individuals turn their problems inward. Externalizing problems occur when problems are turned outward.

5. They are linked with anxious/resistant attachment in infancy.

6. Adolescents from a lower SES background were more likely to have problems than those from a higher SES background.

7. It may give important insight into why some children, against all odds, succeed.

DRUGS AND ALCOHOL
SECTION REVIEW

1. 1. H   2. D   3. D   4. S   5. D
    6. S   7. D   8. H

2. A greater amount of a drug is needed to produce the same effect.

3. Physical need for a drug that is accompanied by unpleasant withdrawal symptoms when the drug is discontinued.

4. It is a widely used and powerful drug.

5. Heredity, family influences, peer relations, personality characteristics, and the college transition.

6. A strong family support system is a very important preventative strategy.

7. No. While informative, their impact has been minimal.

8. In 1999 it had dropped to 2.6 percent.

9. Drugs that slow down the central nervous system, bodily functions, and behavior.

10. The use of depressants has dropped dramatically over the past 25 years.

11. a. Early intervention in schools is believed to be more effective than later intervention.
    b. School-based drug-abuse prevention requires a kindergarten through grade 12 approach.
    c. Teacher training is important.
    d. Social skills training is a most-promising new approach to prevention.
    e. Peer-led programs are often more effective than those led by teachers or counselors.
    f. More programs aimed at high-risk kids are needed.
    g. The most effective programs are often part of community-wide programs.

EVALUATE JUVENILE DELINQUENCY
SECTION REVIEW

1.

Antecedent	Association with Delinquency
Identity	Negative identity
Self-control	Low degree
Age	Early initiation
Sex	Males
Expectations for education and school grades	Low expectations and low grades
Parental influences	Low monitoring, low support, ineffective discipline
Peer influences	Heavy influence, low resistance
Socioeconomic status	Low
Neighborhood quality	Urban, high crime, high mobility

2.   It refers to a broad range of behaviors, from socially unacceptable, to status offenses to criminal acts.

3.   (a) authority conflict, (b) covert conflict, and (c) overt conflict.

4.   He believes that adolescents whose development has restricted them from acceptable social roles might choose a negative identity.

5.   a.   Early involvement with drugs and alcohol.
        b.   Easy access to weapons.
        c.   Association with a deviant peer group.
        d.   Pervasive exposure to violence in the media.

6.   a.   Recommit to raising children safely and effectively.
        b.   Make prevention a reality.
        c.   Give more support to schools.
        d.   Forge effective partnerships among families.

7.   In the cadre approach, a small number of students are trained to serve as peer mediators for the entire school.

DEPRESSION AND SUICIDE
SECTION REVIEW

1.   An individual experiences a major depressive episode and depressed characteristics, such as lethargy and hopelessness, for at least two weeks or longer and daily functioning becomes impaired.

2.   Drugs may present a proximal risk for suicide. Distal risks tend to be things that grow out of the family history or environment.

EATING DISORDER
SECTION REVIEW

1.   Some inherit a tendency to be overweight. Only 10% of those children not having obese parents become obese. Strong evidence supporting the role of the environment is the doubling of the rate of obesity since 1900.

2.   It is an eating disorder that involves the relentless pursuit of thinness through starvation. Weighing less than 85% of the recommended weight is a key indicator.

3.   Bulimia is an eating disorder in which the individual consistently follows a binge-and-purge eating pattern.

PROBLEMS AND PREVENTION/INTERVENTION
SECTION REVIEW

1.   Adolescents tend to have more than one problem. And researchers tend to suggest that these are interrelated.

2.   (a) Intensive individualized attention, (b) Community-wide multiagency collaborative approaches, and (c) Early identification and intervention.

COGNITIVE
CHALLENGE

1.   Individual activity. No answer provided.

2.   Individual activity. No answer provided.

3.   Individual activity. No answer provided.

ADOLESCENCE
IN RESEARCH

The research method was meta-analysis, a review of the research on resilience. The review concluded that a number of individual, family, and extrafamilial factors characterize resilient children.

⊠ COMPREHENSIVE REVIEW

1. a	2. b	3. c	4. c	5. b
6. c	7. c	8. b	9. b	10. c
11. b	12. d	13. a	14. c	15. d
16. b	17. b	18. d	19. b	20. a
21. c	22. c	23. a	24. a	

Notes

Notes

Notes

Notes

Notes

Notes

Notes

Notes

Notes

Notes

Notes

Notes

Notes

Notes